The Complete Book of
Sight Words

220 Words Your Child Needs to Know to Become a Successful Reader

Written by **Shannon Keeley**

Illustrations by **Janee Trasler, Christy Schneider, Mark Stephens, and Remy Simard**

FlashKids

New York

New York

An Imprint of Sterling Publishing Co., Inc.
1166 Avenue of the Americas
New York, NY 10036

ISBN 978-1-4114-4958-9

Distributed in Canada by Sterling Publishing Co., Inc.
c/o Canadian Manda Group, 664 Annette Street
Toronto, Ontario M6S 2C8, Canada
Distributed in the United Kingdom by GMC Distribution Services
Castle Place, 166 High Street, Lewes, East Sussex BN7 1XU, England
Distributed in Australia by NewSouth Books
University of New South Wales, Sydney, NSW 2052, Australia

For information about custom editions, special sales, and premium and corporate purchases, please contact Sterling Special Sales at 800-805-5489 or specialsales@sterlingpublishing.com.

Manufactured in Malaysia

Lot #:
18 20 19 17
11/19

sterlingpublishing.com

Dear Parent,

Every time your child reads a text, 50 to 75 percent of the words he or she encounters are from the Dolch Sight Word List. The Dolch Sight Word List is a core group of 220 common words that are represented frequently in reading material. Children need extra practice learning these words, many of which can't be represented by simple pictures. Often, these sight words do not follow regular spelling rules and cannot be "sounded out." Learning to immediately recognize these words "at sight" is a critical skill for fluent reading.

The Complete Book of Sight Words introduces all 220 Dolch sight words, divided into four levels of increasing difficulty. The book presents and then reinforces each word in a way that promotes understanding and retention. Children ages five through eight will find memorizing these words both simple and fun. The book's entertaining activities offer lots of practice with tracing and writing, while word puzzles and games provide an extra challenge. Your child can color the pictures, laugh at the funny characters, and enjoy learning about sight words.

a	come	has	must	seven	upon
about	could	have	my	shall	us
after	cut	he	myself	she	use
again	did	help	never	show	very
all	do	her	new	sing	walk
always	does	here	no	sit	want
am	done	him	not	six	warm
an	don't	his	now	sleep	was
and	down	hold	of	small	wash
any	draw	hot	off	so	we
are	drink	how	old	some	well
around	eat	hurt	on	soon	went
as	eight	I	once	start	were
ask	every	if	one	stop	what
at	fall	in	only	take	when
ate	far	into	open	tell	where
away	fast	is	or	ten	which
be	find	it	our	that	white
because	first	its	out	thank	who
been	five	jump	over	the	why
before	fly	just	own	their	will
best	for	keep	pick	them	wish
better	found	kind	play	then	with
big	four	know	please	there	work
black	from	laugh	pretty	these	would
blue	full	let	pull	they	write
both	funny	light	put	think	yellow
bring	gave	like	ran	this	yes
brown	get	little	read	those	you
but	give	live	red	three	your
buy	go	long	ride	to	
by	goes	look	right	today	
call	going	made	round	together	
can	good	make	run	too	
came	got	many	said	try	
carry	grow	may	saw	two	
clean	green	me	say	under	
cold	had	much	see	up	

Level A

The sight words included in this section are:

a	did	in	on	three
all	down	is	one	to
am	find	it	play	two
and	for	like	ran	up
away	funny	little	red	was
be	go	look	run	we
big	good	make	said	what
blue	he	me	see	where
but	help	my	so	yellow
can	here	no	that	yes
come	I	not	the	you

a

Say the word **a**
aloud as you trace it.

Now practice writing the word once on each line.

I see _____ bird.

Careful Crossing

Show how the bunny crosses the stream. Cross out each rock that does not have the word **a** inside.

 **say the word go aloud as you trace it.**

go

Now practice writing the word once on each line.

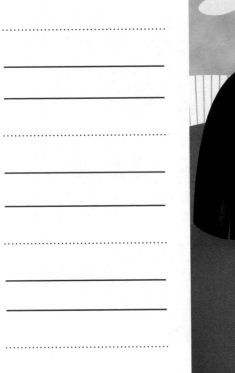

Let's _____ in the house.

Stay on Track

The word **go** is hidden two times on each track. Find the words and circle them.

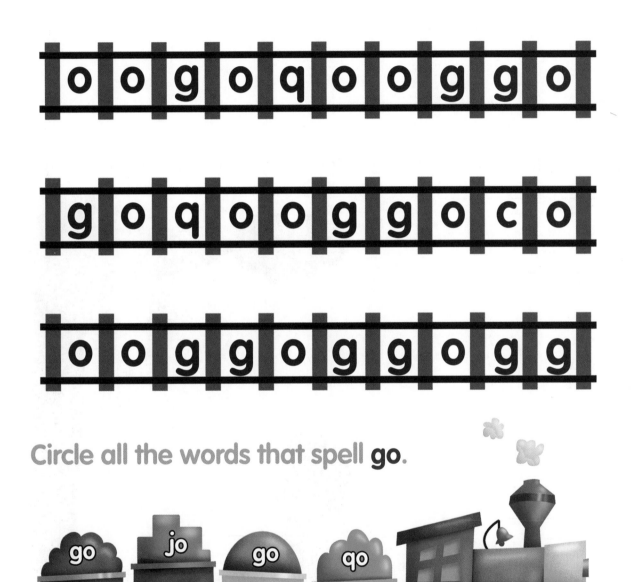

o o g o q o o g g o

g o q o o g g o c o

o o g g o g g o g g

Circle all the words that spell **go**.

go jo go qo

goo go gow go

up

say the word up
aloud as you trace it.

Now practice writing the word once on each line.

My cat is _____ in the tree!

Lucky Letters

Write **up** on the line under each lucky clover that makes the word up.

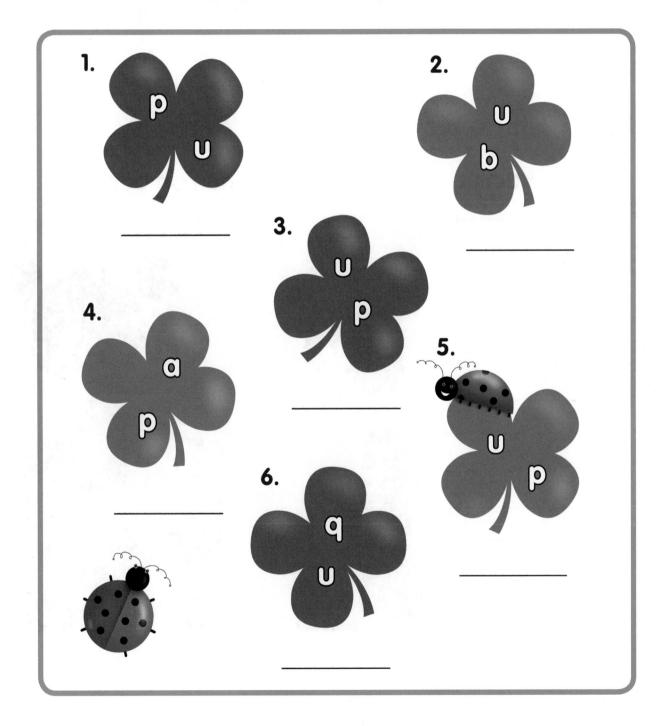

1. _____

2. _____

3. _____

4. _____

5. _____

6. _____

 **you** say the word **you** aloud as you trace it.

you

Now practice writing the word once on each line.

Do _____ like ice cream?

12

Dot-to-Dot

Draw lines to connect the letters **y-o-u** and complete the picture.

 **for**

Say the word for aloud as you trace it.

Now practice writing the word once on each line.

This is _____ you.

Hide and Seek

Some of the words in the treetop have **for** hidden inside. Find the words and write them on the lines below. Circle the letters **f-o-r** in each word.

fork
frog   four   foot
from
form
fort
forget

Review: Word Search

Find each word in the word search.

| a | go | up | you | for |

p	y	o	o	f
o	o	u	p	y
b	u	y	o	r
a	f	p	o	f
g	o	f	y	u

Color the box that has all five review words spelled correctly.

1.	2.	3.	4.	5.
a	a	a	a	e
goe	go	go	go	go
up	up	op	up	ub
you	you	you	yuo	you
far	for	for	fur	for

Review: Wormy Words

Read each sentence. Every time you see one of the review words, circle it. Then count how many circled words are in each sentence.

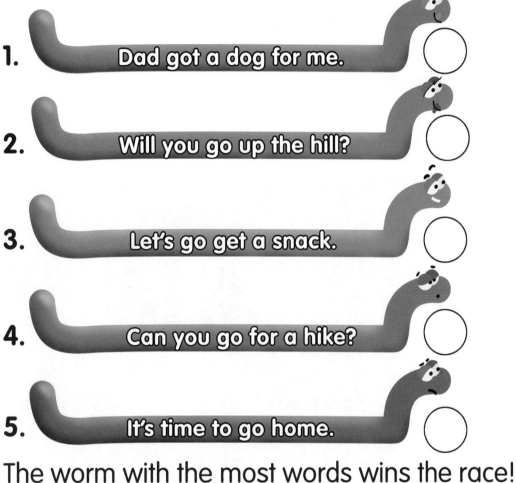

1. Dad got a dog for me. ◯

2. Will you go up the hill? ◯

3. Let's go get a snack. ◯

4. Can you go for a hike? ◯

5. It's time to go home. ◯

The worm with the most words wins the race! Which worm is the winner? _____

Write your own sentence. Use as many of the review words as you can.

_____

the

say the word **the**
aloud as you trace it.

the

Now practice writing the word once on each line.

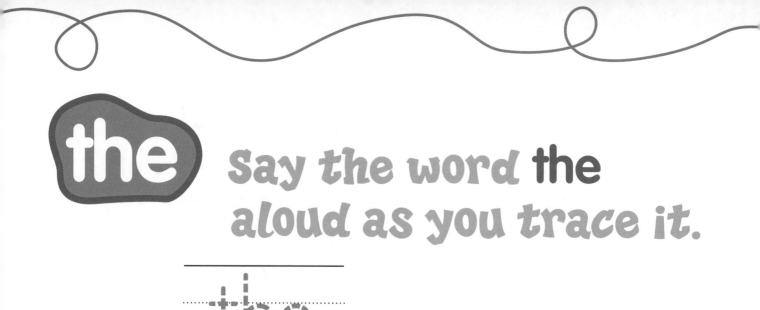

bat
cat
sat

Open _____ book.

Tic-Tac-Toe

Circle the row that spells the word **the**.

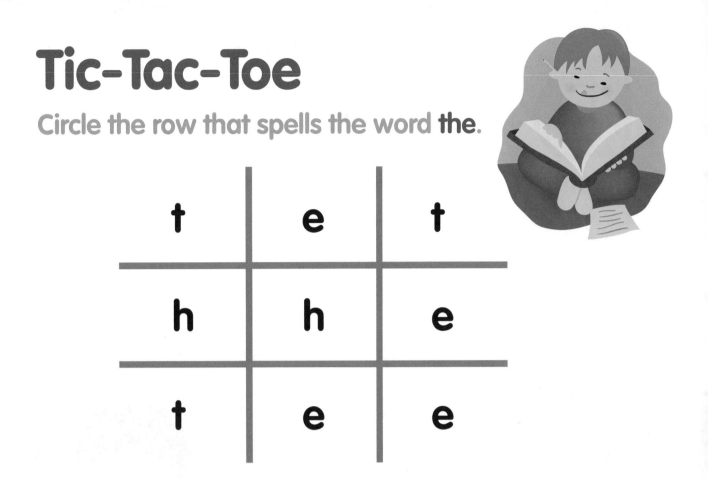

t	e	t
h	h	e
t	e	e

Circle the row that has the word **the** three times.

the	tbe	the
hte	teh	the
thh	the	the

 **is**

say the word is aloud as you trace it.

Now practice writing the word once on each line.

This _____ my dog.

Lost and Found

The word **is** is hidden once in each line. Find the word and circle the letters.

s	j	i	z	i	s
1	2	3	4	5	6

j	s	i	s	i	z
1	2	3	4	5	6

i	s	s	i	z	j
1	2	3	4	5	6

To complete the message, look at the number below each circled letter. Find the matching number in the message below and write the letter on the line.

H___ ___   hat   ___ ___   ___n
  1 2   3 4   5

the ___ ink.
      6

away

say the word **away** aloud as you trace it.

_____

Now practice writing the word once on each line.

_____
....
_____
_____
....
_____
....
_____
_____
....
_____

Let's put _____ the toys.

Linking Letters

Draw a line to link the letters that make the word **away**.

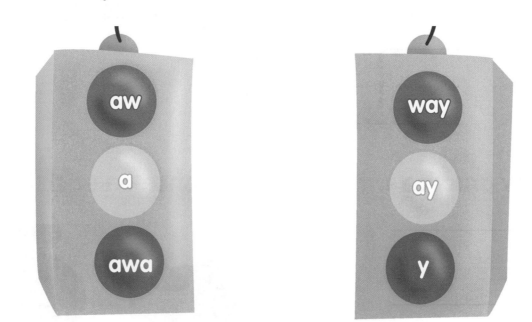

Write the missing letters to make the word **away**.

a____ a____

____ ____ay

a____ ____y

____w____y

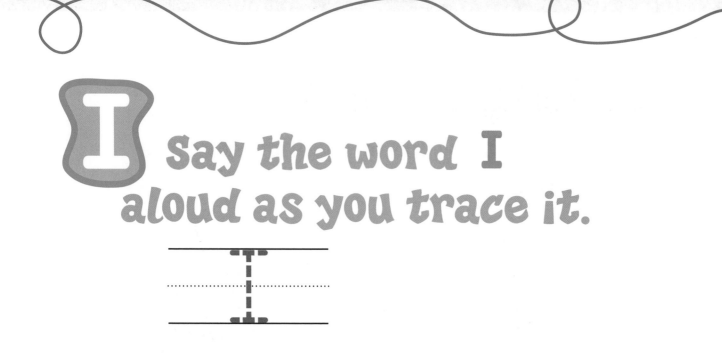

I say the word **I** aloud as you trace it.

I

Now practice writing the word once on each line.

_____ am at the top.

Follow the Line

Circle the word I in each sentence. Then draw a line to connect the circled words, and see which letters you pass through. Write the letters below to answer the riddle.

1. I like ice cream.

a　o　c　b　n

2. Dad and I went to get ice cream.

w　e　g　n　r

3. "It's a big scoop," I said.

c　a　b　q　m

4. It was much more than I could eat.

d　a　p　e　o

5. So I shared it with my dad.

What did the cone say to the ice cream?

Dessert is ____ ____ ____ ____ !

**and**

say the word **and** aloud as you trace it.

Now practice writing the word once on each line.

I put on my socks _____ shoes.

Rhyme Time

Circle the pictures that rhyme with **and**. Underline the letters **a-n-d** in each word.

sand

hang

stand

sad

pan

hand

land

ant

Review: Word Search

Find each word in the word search.

the	is	I	away	and

```
h  s  t  i  h
t  w  a  n  d
h  y  w  d  e
e  t  a  s  I
i  s  y  a  y
```

Color the box that has all five review words spelled correctly.

1.	2.	3.	4.	5.
the	thu	the	the	the
iz	is	is	is	si
away	away	awhy	away	awye
I	I	i	I	I
anb	ahd	and	and	and

Review: Story Surprise

Write the correct word from the word box to complete each sentence in the story.

the   I   is   away   and

My dog's name ___ ___ Roofus.
            1

I took him to ___ ___ ___ beach.

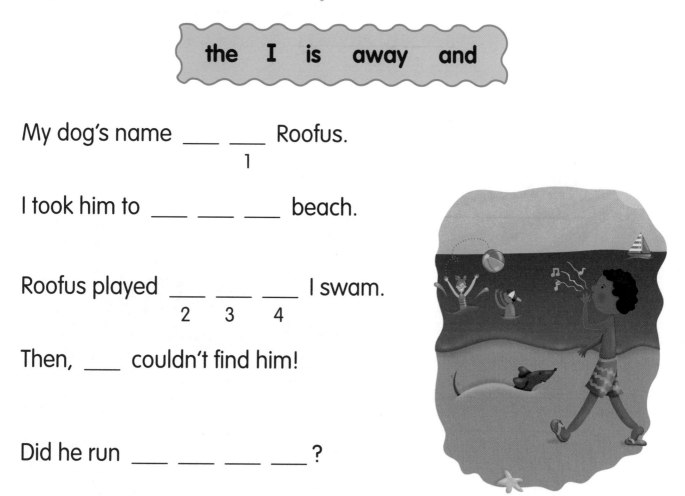

Roofus played ___ ___ ___ I swam.
              2   3   4

Then, ___ couldn't find him!

Did he run ___ ___ ___ ___ ?

For each number in the story sentences, find the matching number below. Write the letter on the line to find out what happened!

Where was Roofus?
Roofus was under the ___ ___ ___ ___ .
                      1   2   3   4

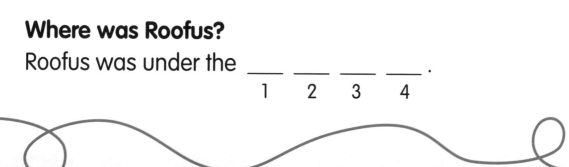

29

 **big**

say the word **big** aloud as you trace it.

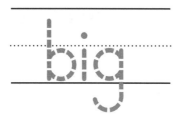

Now practice writing the word once on each line.

This hat is _____.

Careful Crossing

Show how the frog crosses the pond. Cross out each lily pad that does not have the word **big** inside.

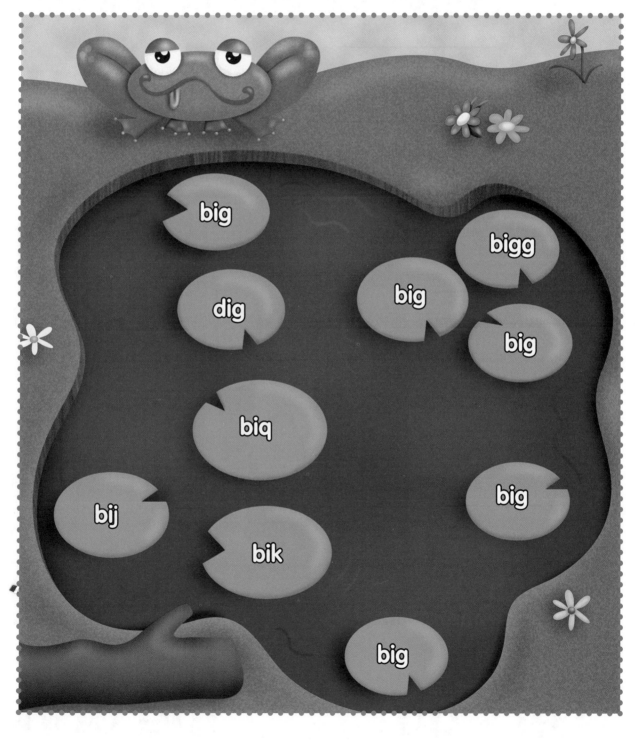

 **say the word to aloud as you trace it.**

—————

‎‑‑‑‑ t o

Now practice writing the word once on each line.

Let's go _____ the park.

Stay on Track

The word **to** is hidden two times on each track. Find the words and circle them.

| t | t | f | t | o | o | f | o | t | o |

| o | t | o | o | o | t | t | o | t | t |

| t | o | t | a | t | o | t | f | o | o |

Circle all the words that spell **to**.

too

ot

to

tto

to

to

ttoo

to

look

say the word look aloud as you trace it.

Now practice writing the word once on each line.

Hey, _____ at me go!

Lucky Letters

Write **look** on the line under each lucky clover that makes the word **look**.

 **say the word run aloud as you trace it.**

run

Now practice writing the word once on each line.

I can _____ up the hill.

Dot-to-Dot

Draw lines to connect the letters **r-u-n** and complete the picture.

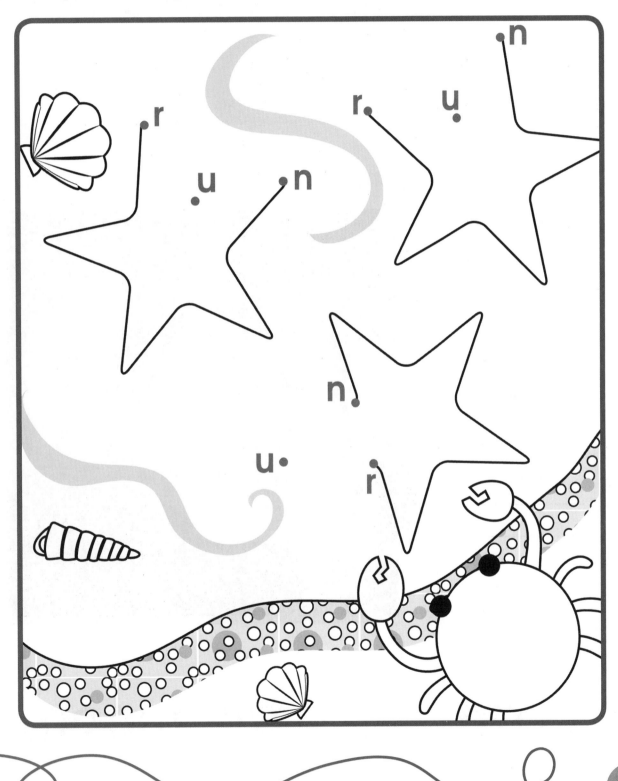

 **say the word see aloud as you trace it.**

Now practice writing the word once on each line.

I can _____ the moon.

Hide and Seek

Some of the words in the treetop have **see** hidden inside. Find the words and write them on the lines below. Circle the letters **s-e-e** in each word.

sea

seesaw

seal   seek

sleep

seem

bees

seed

Review: Word Search

Find each word in the word search.

| big | to | look | run | see |

```
g  u  r  u  n
o  l  u  t  k
s  b  o  o  s
e  s  i  o  e
e  g  l  g  k
```

Color the box that has all five review words spelled correctly.

1.	2.	3.	4.	5.
big	big	bip	big	big
look	look	look	loock	look
to	ta	to	to	ot
run	ron	ruh	run	run
see	see	see	se	see

Review: Wormy Words

Read each sentence. Every time you see one of the review words, circle it. Then count how many circled words are in each sentence.

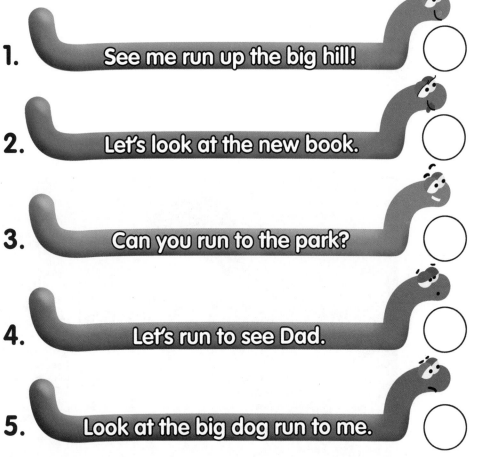

1. See me run up the big hill! ⃝

2. Let's look at the new book. ⃝

3. Can you run to the park? ⃝

4. Let's run to see Dad. ⃝

5. Look at the big dog run to me. ⃝

The worm with the most words wins the race! Which worm is the winner? _____

Write your own sentence. Use as many of the review words as you can.

_____

**not**

Say the word **not** aloud as you trace it.

not

Now practice writing the word once on each line.

This does _____ fit.

Tic-Tac-Toe

Circle the row that spells the word **not**.

o	n	o
n	o	t
t	n	t

Circle the row that has the word **not** three times.

not	nat	not
not	nof	not
hot	not	not

 **me** **say the word me aloud as you trace it.**

Now practice writing the word once on each line.

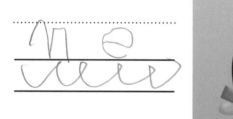

This one is for ___.

Lost and Found

The word **me** is hidden once in each line. Find the word and circle the letters.

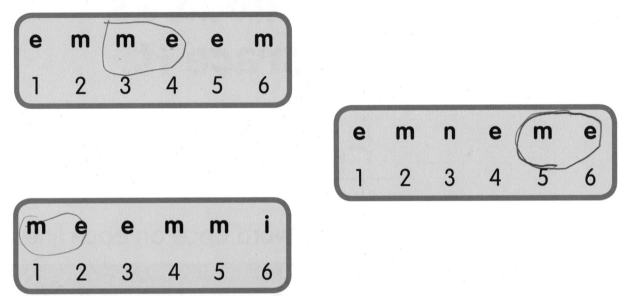

e m m e e m
1 2 3 4 5 6

e m n e m e
1 2 3 4 5 6

m e e m m i
1 2 3 4 5 6

To complete the message, look at the number below each circled letter. Find the matching number in the message below and write the letter on the line.

Sa_m_'s n_e_w _M_ _e_dal is under
   1   2   3   4

the _m_ _e_s s.
    5   6

 **here**

say the word here aloud as you trace it.

Now practice writing the word once on each line.

Please put it _____.

46

Linking Letters

Draw a line to link the letters that make the word **here**.

Write the missing letters to make the word **here**.

 **can**

Say the word can aloud as you trace it.

can

Now practice writing the word once on each line.

I _____ go fast.

Follow the Line

Circle the word **can** in each sentence. Then draw a line to connect the circled words, and see which letters you pass through. Write the letters below to answer the riddle.

1. I can help at home.

m p r w a

2. Folding clothes is one thing I can do.

o s d b a

3. I can get it done quickly.

s n z k t

4. Can you help me at home too?

d h p b c

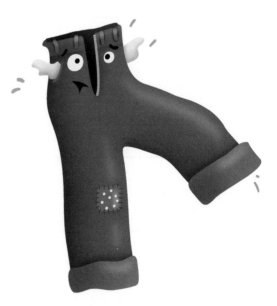

5. I think I can!

What did the old jeans say?

I'm all _____ _____ _____ _____ed up!

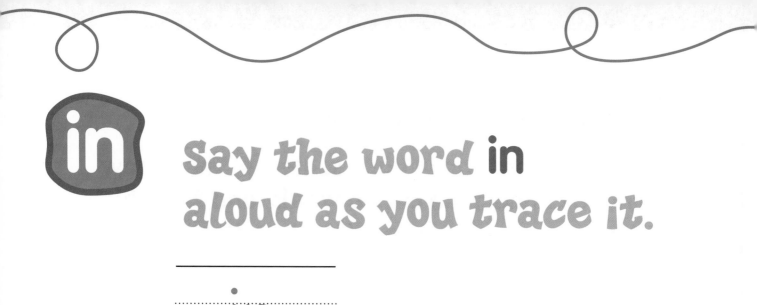

say the word in aloud as you trace it.

in

Now practice writing the word once on each line.

My lunch is ____ the bag.

Rhyme Time

Circle the pictures that rhyme with **in**. Underline the letters **i-n** in each word.

chin

STOP!

sign

him

fan

pin

lion

win

fin

Review: Word Search

Find each word in the word search.

| not | me | here | can | in |

```
h   r   e   h   c
n   e   t   e   a
m   i   n   r   h
e   a   o   e   c
c   n   t   i   t
```

Color the box that has all five review words spelled correctly.

1.	2.	3.	4.	5.
nat	not	not	not	not
me	mee	me	me	me
nere	here	here	heer	here
can	can	cah	can	can
in	in	in	in	in

Review: Story Surprise

Write the correct word from the word box to complete each sentence in the story.

not   me   here   in   can

My brother plays hide and seek with ___ ___.

I can hide ___ ___ the kitchen.
         3

"Ready or ___ ___ ___ , here I come!" he says.
        4   6

He'll never find me in ___ ___ ___ ___.
                  5

___ ___ ___ you find me?
1   2

For each number in the story sentences, find the matching number below. Write the letter on the line to find out what happened!

Where is he?
He's hiding in the ___ ___ b ___ ___ ___ ___.
           1   2   3   4   5   6

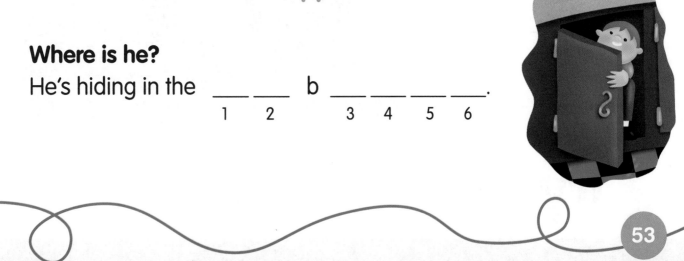

53

find

say the word find aloud as you trace it.

Now practice writing the word once on each line.

Try to _____ me.

Careful Crossing

Show how the explorer goes across the hot lava. Cross out each rock that does not have the word **find** inside.

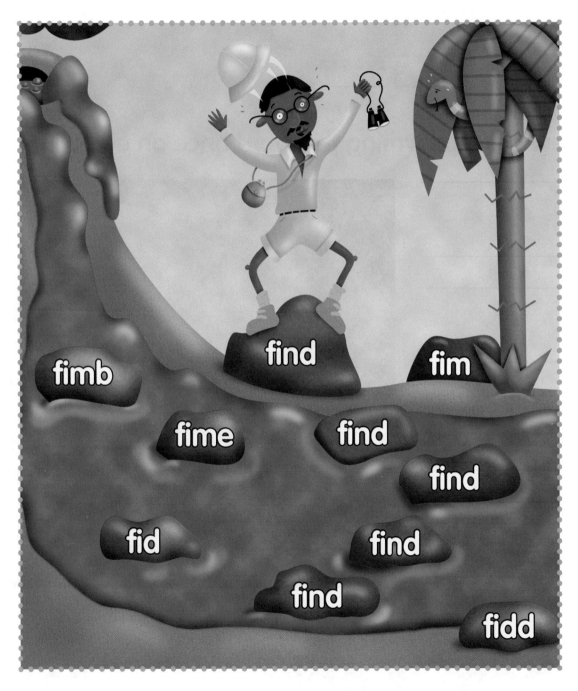

one

say the word one aloud as you trace it.

one

Now practice writing the word once on each line.

There is only _____ more.

Stay on Track

The word **one** is hidden two times on each track.
Find the words and circle them.

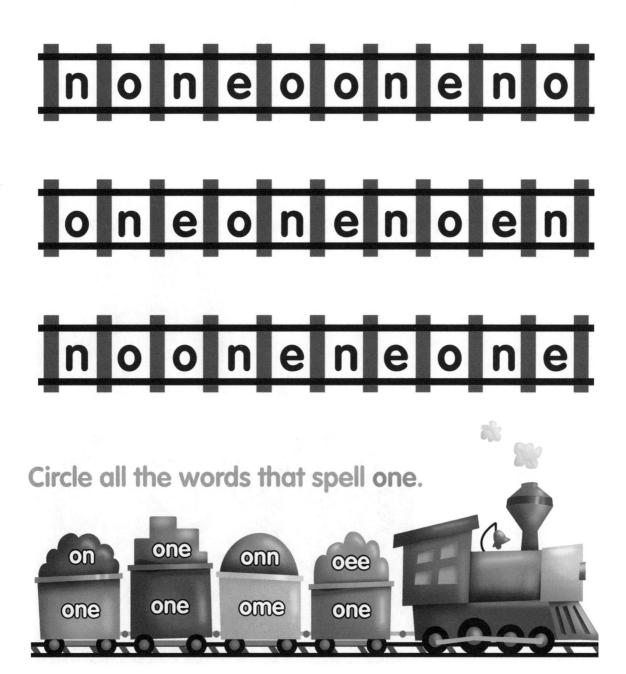

n o n e o o n e n o

o n e o n e n o e n

n o o n e n e o n e

Circle all the words that spell **one**.

on
one
one
one
onn
ome
oee
one

said

say the word **said** *aloud as you trace it.*

Now practice writing the word once on each line.

Dad _____ to be careful.

Lucky Letters

Write **said** on the line under each lucky clover that makes the word **said**.

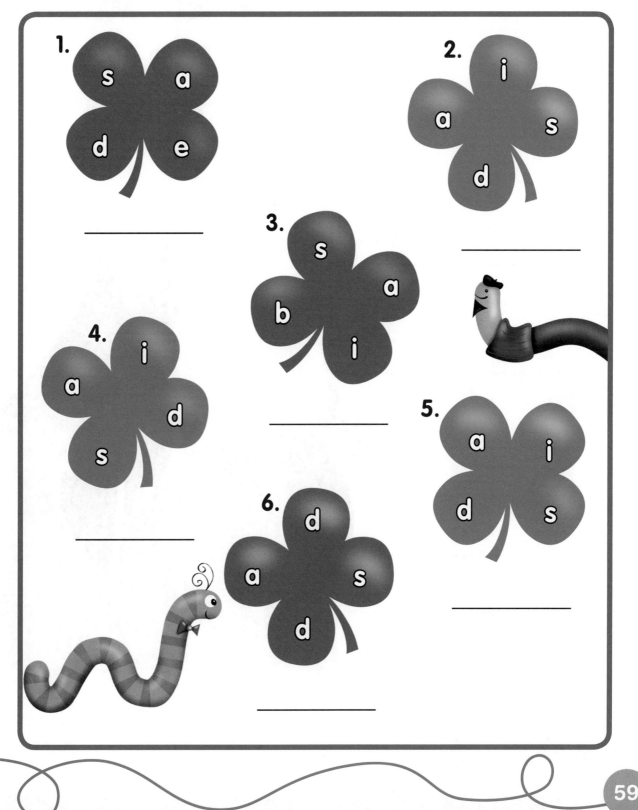

1. s a d e _____

2. i a s d _____

3. s a b i _____

4. a i d s _____

5. a i d s _____

6. d a s d _____

where

say the word where aloud as you trace it.

Now practice writing the word once on each line.

This is _____ I live.

Dot-to-Dot

Draw lines to connect the letters w-h-e-r-e and complete the picture.

ran say the word **ran** aloud as you trace it.

ran

Now practice writing the word once on each line.

I _____ very fast!

Hide and Seek

Some of the words in the treetop have **ran** hidden inside. Find the words and write them on the lines below. Circle the letters **r-a-n** in each word.

ramp

rant   grand   rain

tram

run

ranch

bran

_____ _____

_____ _____

Review: Word Search

Find each word in the word search.

find   one   said   where   ran

f	s	r	a	f
n	i	a	o	i
o	d	n	i	n
h	n	e	n	d
w	h	e	r	e

Color the box that has all five review words spelled correctly.

1.	2.	3.	4.	5.
fid	find	find	find	find
one	onn	one	one	oen
said	said	said	saib	said
where	whre	where	where	where
nan	ran	ran	ran	ran

Review: Wormy Words

Read each sentence. Every time you see one of the review words, circle it. Then count how many circled words are in each sentence.

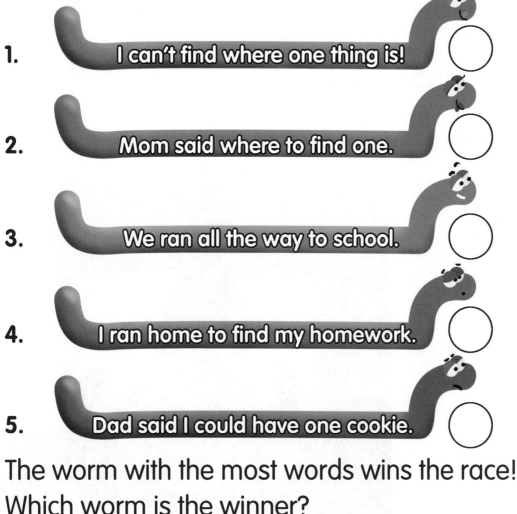

1. I can't find where one thing is!

2. Mom said where to find one.

3. We ran all the way to school.

4. I ran home to find my homework.

5. Dad said I could have one cookie.

The worm with the most words wins the race! Which worm is the winner? _____

Write your own sentence. Use as many of the review words as you can.

_____

red

Say the word **red** aloud as you trace it.

red

Now practice writing the word once on each line.

The fire truck is _____.

Tic-Tac-Toe

Circle the row that spells the word **red**.

d	r	d
r	e	r
r	r	d

Circle the row that has the word **red** three times.

red	red	ned
wed	red	red
rde	red	rod

 **say the word down aloud as you trace it.**

down

Now practice writing the word once on each line.

I can go _____ the slide.

Lost and Found

The word **down** is hidden once in each line. Find the word and circle the letters.

d	w	d	o	d	o	w	n
1	2	3	4	5	6	7	8

d	o	w	n	d	o	w	d
1	2	3	4	5	6	7	8

To complete the message, look at the number below each circled letter. Find the matching number in the message below and write the letter on the line.

Sam's ___ ___ g is ___ear the ___ i ___ ___ ___ ___.
    1 2   4   3   8   5 6 7

play say the word play aloud as you trace it.

play

Now practice writing the word once on each line.

Let's _____ ball!

Linking Letters

Draw a line to link the letters that make the word **play**.

Write the missing letters to make the word **play**.

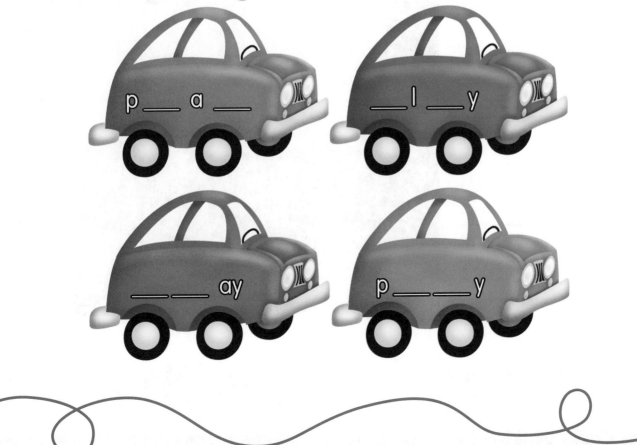

come say the word **come** aloud as you trace it.

come

Now practice writing the word once on each line.

You can _____ with me.

Follow the Line

Circle the word **come** in each sentence. Then draw a line to connect the circled words, and see which letters you pass through. Write the letters below to answer the riddle.

1. Everywhere I go, my dog will come along.

   n   l   b   r   w

2. "Come here," I shout.

   m   h   a   o   t

3. He will always come running.

   c   o   u   k   t

4. He barks when he wants to come with me.

   u   s   v   i   c

5. He can't come with me to school!

What type of dog always knows what time it is?

A ___ ___ ___ ___ h   dog!

73

 **Say the word am aloud as you trace it.**

am

Now practice writing the word once on each line.

I _____ very tall.

Rhyme Time

Circle the pictures that rhyme with am. Underline the letters a-m in each word.

man

clam

slam

jam

ham

van

arm

palm

Review: Word Search

Find each word in the word search.

red   down   play   come   am

```
r  e  p  d  r
d  p  l  a  y
c  o  m  e  r
e  n  w  w  e
a  m  t  n  d
```

Color the box that has all five review words spelled correctly.

1.	2.	3.	4.	5.
red	red	reb	red	red
dovn	down	down	down	down
play	blay	play	play	plya
com	come	cume	come	come
an	ann	an	am	an

Review: Story Surprise

Write the correct word from the word box to complete each sentence in the story.

red	down	play	come	am

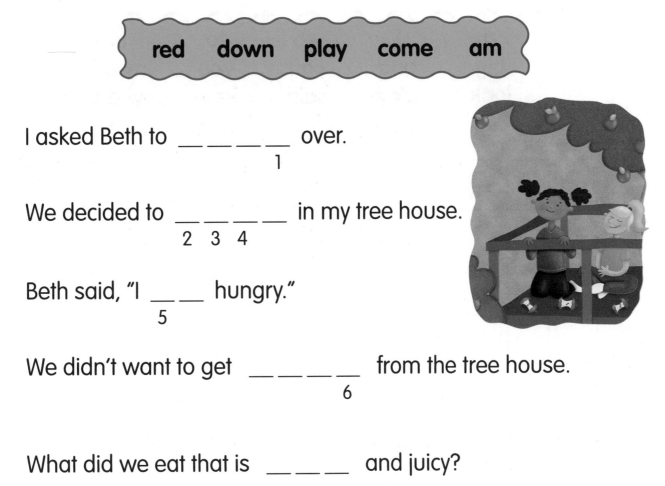

I asked Beth to __ __ __ __ over.
                    1

We decided to __ __ __ __ in my tree house.
               2 3 4

Beth said, "I __ __ hungry."
              5

We didn't want to get __ __ __ __ from the tree house.
                        6

What did we eat that is __ __ __ and juicy?

For each number in the story sentences, find the matching number below. Write the letter on the line to find out what happened!

What did we eat?

We ate ___ ___ ___ ___p___ ___ from the tree.
        5   6   4   2   3   1

Review: Puzzle

Look at each set of boxes. Find the word whose letters fit in the boxes.

a	I	up	to	is
big	and	can	you	away
look	play	said	here	where

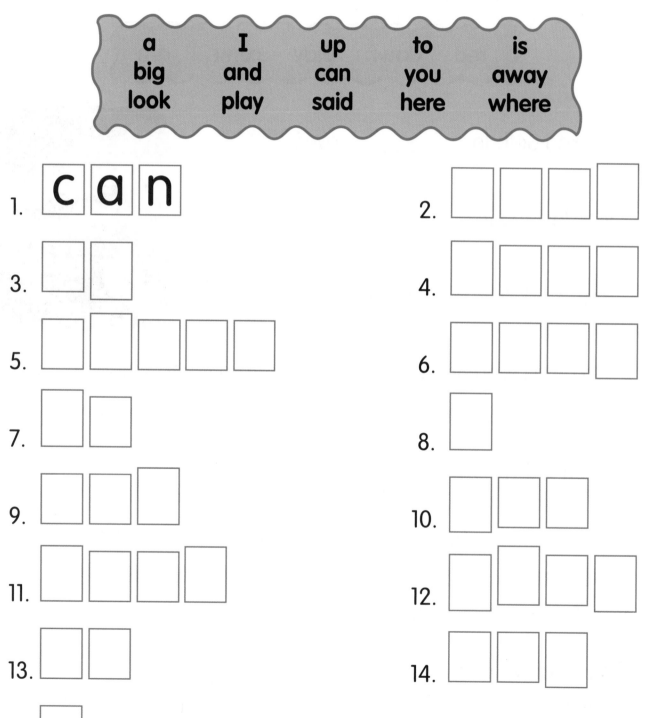

1. c a n

2. ☐☐☐☐

3. ☐☐

4. ☐☐☐☐

5. ☐☐☐☐☐

6. ☐☐☐☐

7. ☐☐

8. ☐

9. ☐☐☐

10. ☐☐☐

11. ☐☐☐☐

12. ☐☐☐☐

13. ☐☐

14. ☐☐☐

15. ☐

Review: Riddle

Use the code to fill in the missing letters and solve the riddle.

go: s   **for:** r   **run:** A   **see:** p   **not:** l

me: p   **in:** s   **find:** a   **one:** r   **am:** o

here: e   **ran:** i   **red:** f   **down:** p   **come:** i

What do you call two banana peels?

run	see	find	ran	for		am	red

in	not	come	me	down	here	one	go

 **my**

Say the word **my** aloud as you trace it.

 my

Now practice writing the word once on each line.

This is _____ lunch.

Careful Crossing

Show how the lizard crosses the swamp. Cross out each log that does not have the word **my** inside.

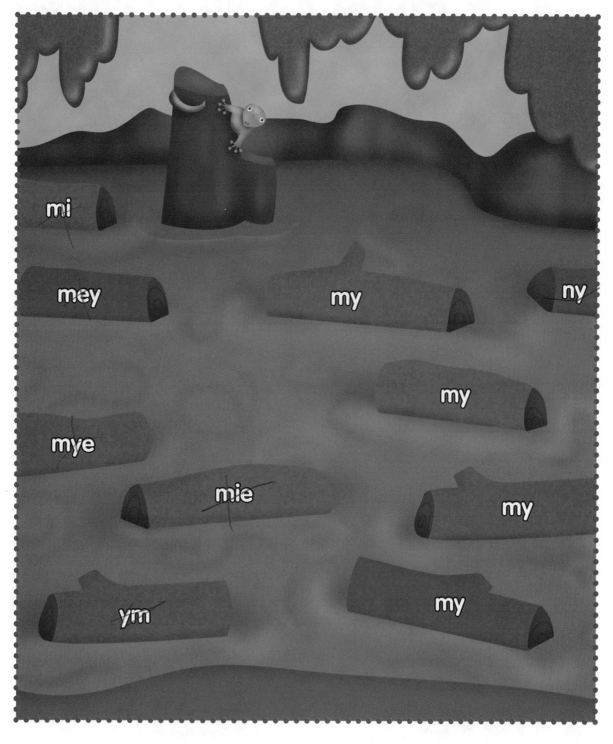

two *say the word two aloud as you trace it.*

two

Now practice writing the word once on each line.

I have _____ feet.

Stay on Track

The word **two** is hidden two times on each track.
Find the words and circle them.

| t | w | o | t | o | o | w | t | w | o |

| w | o | t | o | t | w | o | t | w | o |

| t | w | o | t | o | t | w | o | w | t |

Circle all the words that spell **two**.

two
two
tow
wot
two
two
twoo
tuo

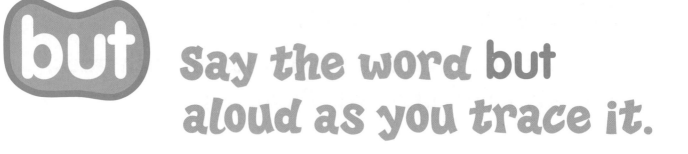

but say the word **but**
aloud as you trace it.

but

Now practice writing the word once on each line.

My brother likes gum,
I don't.

Lucky Letters

Write **but** on the line under each lucky clover that makes the word **but**.

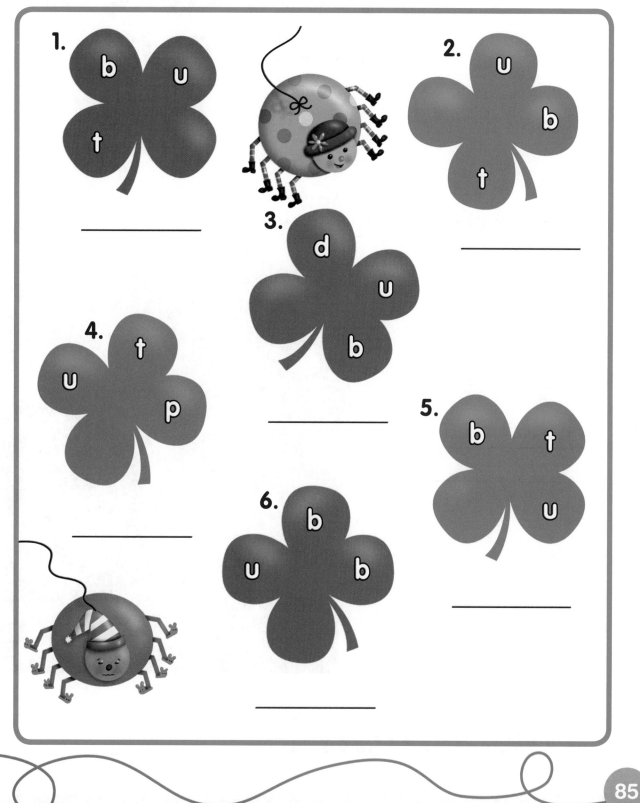

1. _____

2. _____

3. _____

4. _____

5. _____

6. _____

yellow

say the word yellow aloud as you trace it.

yellow

Now practice writing the word once on each line.

The lemon is _____.

Dot-to-Dot

Draw lines to connect the letters **y-e-l-l-o-w** and complete the picture.

good say the word good aloud as you trace it.

good

Now practice writing the word once on each line.

My lunch was _____.

Hide and Seek

Some of the words in the treetop have good hidden inside. Find the words and write them on the lines below. Circle the letters g-o-o-d in each word.

goodnight

golfer   goodbye

goat

goodness

goodly

gooseberry

goldfish

_____   _____

_____   _____

Review: Word Search

Find each word in the word search.

| my | two | but | yellow | good |

```
g  o  s  t  w  o
t  o  t  u  l  b
o  d  o  t  l  u
m  u  e  d  d  t
y  e  l  l  o  w
```

Color the box that has all five review words spelled correctly.

	1.	2.	3.	4.	5.
	my	my	ny	my	my
	two	twu	two	two	two
	but	but	but	bot	but
	yellow	yellow	yellaw	yelow	yellow
	good	gode	good	good	goud

Review: Story Surprise

Write the correct word from the word box to complete each sentence in the story.

| my | two | but | yellow | good |

There is a tree in ___ ___ backyard.
1

The ___ ___ ___ ___ ___ ___ lemons are ready to eat.
2   3

We had ___ ___ ___ yellow lemons today.
4

I went to pick them, ___ ___ ___ they were gone.

My mom used them to make something ___ ___ ___ ___ !
5   6

For each number in the story sentences, find the matching number below. Write the letter on the line to find out what happened!

What did she make?

A ___lass of ___ ___ ___ ___ na ___ e.
5   3 2 1 4   6

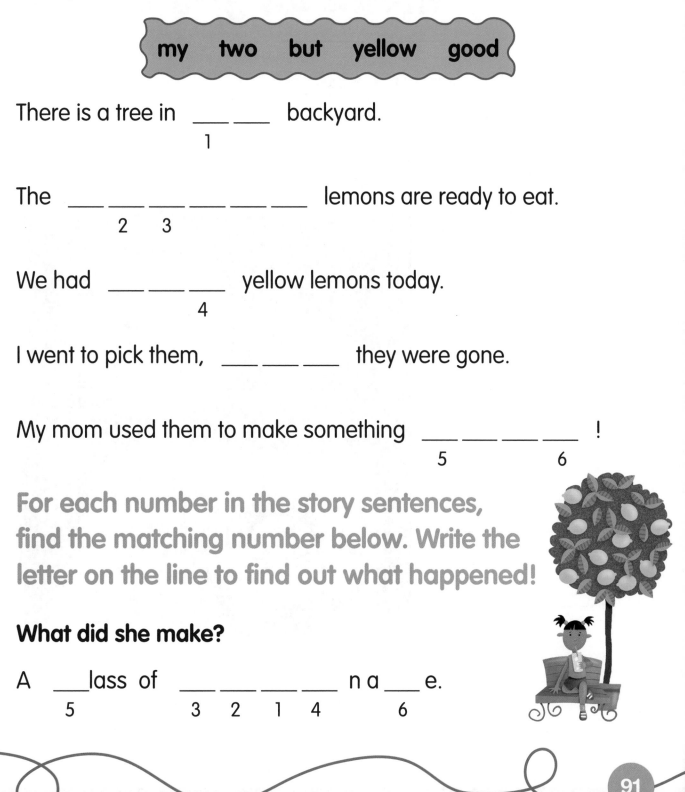

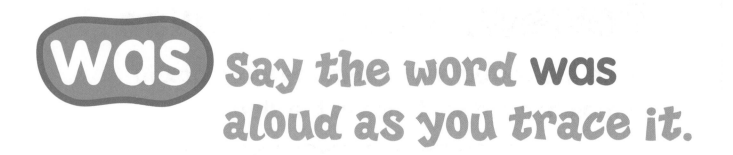

was

say the word **was** aloud as you trace it.

_____

was

Now practice writing the word once on each line.

I _____ a cat for Halloween.

Tic-Tac-Toe

Circle the row that spells the word **was**.

a	w	s
w	a	w
s	s	s

Circle the row that has the word **was** three times.

was	was	saw
mas	wsa	was
was	was	was

say the word three aloud as you trace it.

three

Now practice writing the word once on each line.

I have _____ boxes.

Lost and Found

The word **three** is hidden once in each line. Find the word and circle the letters.

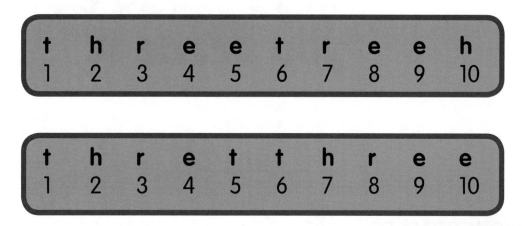

t	h	r	e	e	t	r	e	e	h
1	2	3	4	5	6	7	8	9	10

t	h	r	e	t	t	h	r	e	e
1	2	3	4	5	6	7	8	9	10

To complete the message, look at the number below each circled letter. Find the matching number in the message below and write the letter on the line.

Sam's s___ o___s a___ ___ in ___ ___e ___ ___ ___ ___.
     2   4   3 5   6 7   1 8 9 10

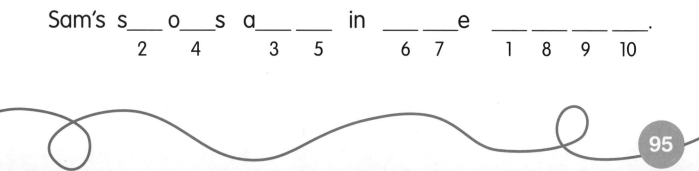

**little**

Say the word little aloud as you trace it.

little

Now practice writing the word once on each line.

The baby is _____.

Linking Letters

Draw a line to link the letters that make the word **little**.

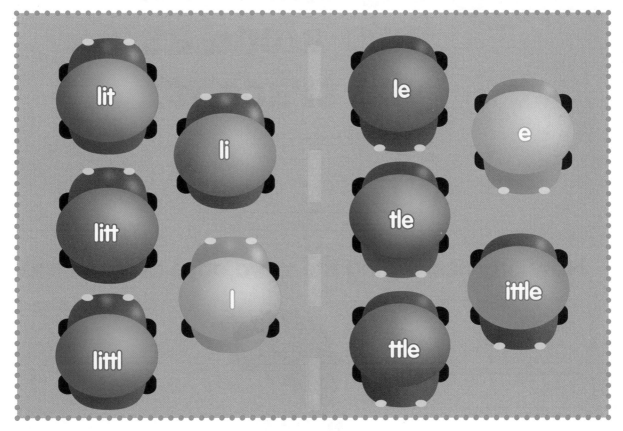

Write the missing letters to make the word **little**.

help say the word help aloud as you trace it.

help

Now practice writing the word once on each line.

I can _____ you.

Follow the Line

Circle the word **help** in each sentence. Then draw a line to connect the circled words, and see which letters you pass through. Write the letters below to answer the riddle.

1. I always help my mom.

    d   g   n   u   b

2. Sometimes she asks me to help make dinner.

    v   s   i   y   a

3. I like to help her in the kitchen.

    t   i   l   q   m

4. I can help my mom cook the food.

    u   o   h   x   a

5. When dinner is ready, I can help eat it all up!

Why did the kids eat dinner on a seesaw?

To have a well- ___ ___ ___ ___ nced meal!

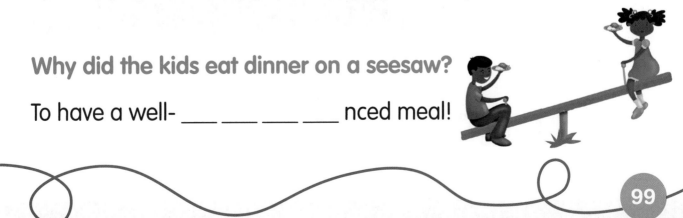

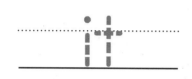

Say the word it aloud as you trace it.

it

Now practice writing the word once on each line.

I made _____ for you.

Rhyme Time

Circle the pictures that rhyme with **it**. Underline the letters **i-t** in each word.

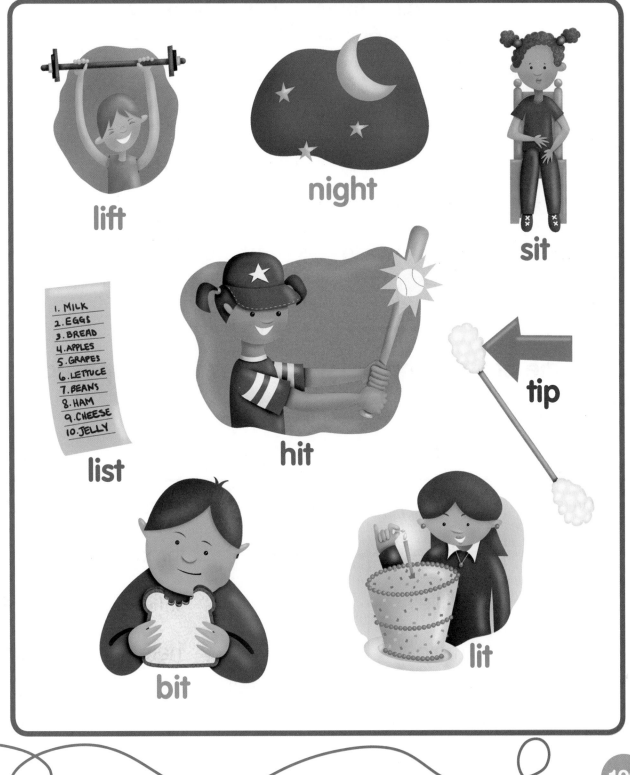

lift

night

sit

1. MILK
2. EGGS
3. BREAD
4. APPLES
5. GRAPES
6. LETTUCE
7. BEANS
8. HAM
9. CHEESE
10. JELLY

list

hit

tip

bit

lit

Review: Word Search

Find each word in the word search.

| was | three | little | help | it |

```
l  t  w  s  i  t
t  p  h  e  l  p
c  h  e  r  l  e
w  a  s  w  e  e
l  i  t  t  l  e
```

Color the box that has all five review words spelled correctly.

1.	2.	3.	4.	5.
was	wos	waz	was	was
thre	three	three	threa	three
little	litlle	liltle	little	little
hlep	help	help	help	help
it	it	it	itt	it

Review: Wormy Words

Read each sentence. Every time you see one of the review words, circle it. Then count how many circled words are in each sentence.

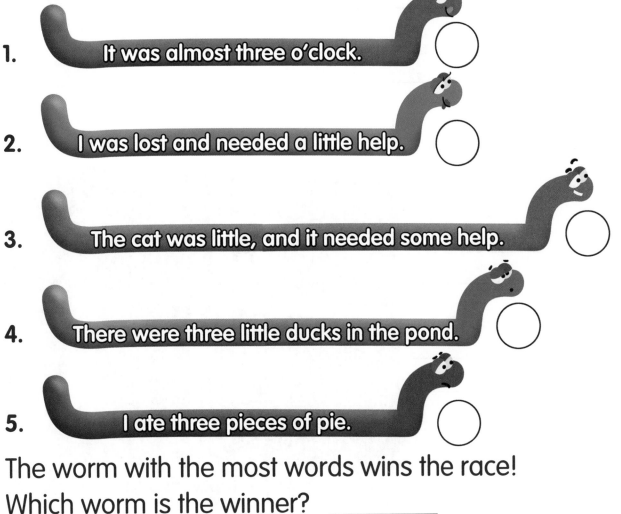

1. It was almost three o'clock.

2. I was lost and needed a little help.

3. The cat was little, and it needed some help.

4. There were three little ducks in the pond.

5. I ate three pieces of pie.

The worm with the most words wins the race! Which worm is the winner? _____

Write your own sentence. Use as many of the review words as you can.

_____

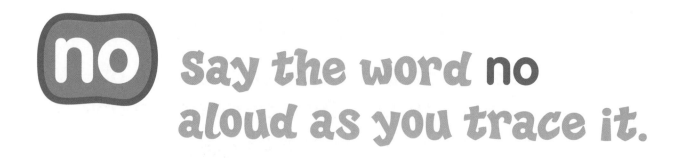

no

Say the word no aloud as you trace it.

_____

no

Now practice writing the word once on each line.

There are _____ pets allowed.

Careful Crossing

Show how the grasshopper crosses the puddle. Cross out each leaf that does not have the word **no** inside.

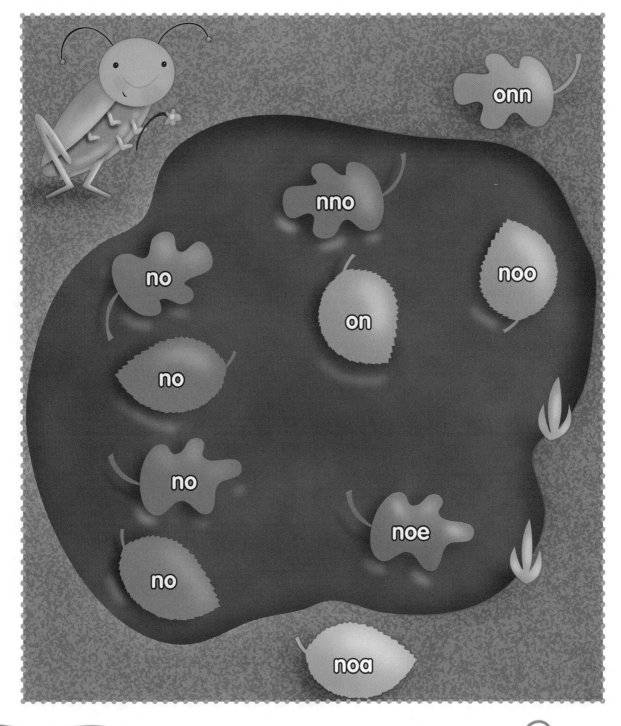

 **say the word we aloud as you trace it.**

we

Now practice writing the word once on each line.

Can _____ have ice cream?

Stay on Track

The word **we** is hidden two times on each track. Find the words and circle them.

w e e m e w w e e w

e e w w e w w e w w

w w e e w w e m e w

Circle all the words that spell **we**.

we
we
wi
we
wee
wy
we
ew

like say the word **like** aloud as you trace it.

like

Now practice writing the word once on each line.

like

like

like

like

I __like__ candy.

Lucky Letters

Write **like** on the line under each lucky clover that makes the word **like**.

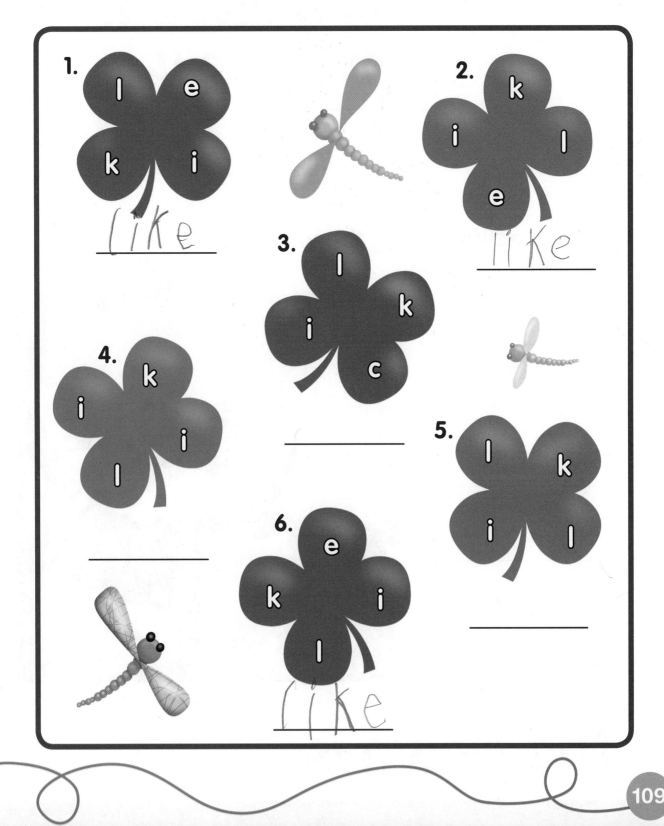

1. l e k i — _like_

2. k i l e — _like_

3. l i k c — _____

4. k i i l — _____

5. l k i l — _____

6. e k i l — _like_

funny

say the word funny aloud as you trace it.

funny

Now practice writing the word once on each line.

The clown is _____!

Dot-to-Dot

Draw lines to connect the letters f-u-n-n-y and complete the picture.

say the word be aloud as you trace it.

be

Now practice writing the word once on each line.

I want to _____ a fireman!

Hide and Seek

Some of the words in the treetop have **be** hidden inside. Find the words and write them on the lines below. Circle the letters **b-e** in each word.

ballet

because

bicycle

become

believe

begin

bread

_____ _____

_____ _____

Review: Word Search

Find each word in the word search.

| no | we | like | funny | be |

```
w  l  i  k  y
f  e  s  n  i
u  y  n  a  z
n  u  o  y  b
f  l  i  k  e
```

Color the box that has all five review words spelled correctly.

1.	2.	3.	4.	5.
ro	no	mo	no	no
we	we	we	ve	we
like	like	like	licke	like
funy	funny	funni	funny	fuuny
be	be	be	be	be

Review: Wormy Words

Read each sentence. Every time you see one of the review words, circle it. Then count how many circled words are in each sentence.

1. We like to be funny! ◯

2. Can you be funny, like a clown? ◯

3. No, thank you, I don't like carrots. ◯

4. We don't like rainy days. ◯

5. We have no homework today. ◯

The worm with the most words wins the race! Which worm is the winner? _____

Write your own sentence. Use as many of the review words as you can.

_____

 **Say the word yes aloud as you trace it.**

Now practice writing the word once on each line.

_____, I'd like more.

Tic-Tac-Toe

Circle the row that spells the word yes.

y	s	y
y	e	s
e	s	e

Circle the row that has the word yes three times.

yes	yss	yes
yee	yes	yes
yes	yes	yec

SO say the word so aloud as you trace it.

SO

Now practice writing the word once on each line.

It is _____ hot.

Lost and Found

The word **so** is hidden once in each line. Find the word and circle the letters.

s	o	o	s	s	s
1	2	3	4	5	6

o	s	s	o	o	s
1	2	3	4	5	6

o	o	s	s	s	o
1	2	3	4	5	6

To complete the message, look at the number below each circled letter. Find the matching number in the message below and write the letter on the line.

Sam's ___ ___ck___   are ___n the ___t___ve.
　　　 1　2　　3　　　　　4　　　　 5　　6

 **say the word what aloud as you trace it.**

what

Now practice writing the word once on each line.

What

what

what

what

I wonder what is inside!

Linking Letters

Draw a line to link the letters that make the word **what**.

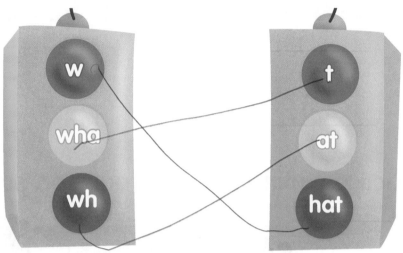

Write the missing letters to make the word **what**.

 **on** say the word **on** aloud as you trace it.

_____

 on _____

Now practice writing the word once on each line.

_____
_____
_____
_____
_____
_____
_____
_____

My books are _____ the desk.

Follow the Line

Circle the word **on** in each sentence. Then draw a line to connect the circled words, and see which letters you pass through. Write the letters below to answer the riddle.

1. It was time to put on my coat.

    l   g   i   n   t

2. It wasn't hanging on the coat rack.

    p   e   s   a   o

3. I looked on my bed, but no coat.

    d   b   y   r   b

4. Oops! I didn't turn the lights on!

    c   i   w   v   l

5. It was on the table all along.

What has four legs but can't walk?

A ___ ___ ___ ___ e!

all

say the word all
aloud as you trace it.

all

Now practice writing the word once on each line.

I used _____ the puzzle pieces.

Rhyme Time

Circle the pictures that rhyme with **all**. Underline the letters **a-l-l** in each word.

pail

call

fall

tall

salt

ball

bell

wall

Review: Word Search

Find each word in the word search.

| yes | so | what | on | all |

```
y  e  s  w  n
e  w  o  n  l
a  t  l  l  y
w  h  a  t  a
l  l  s  y  e
```

Color the box that has all five review words spelled correctly.

1.	2.	3.	4.	5.
yes	yas	yes	yes	yes
soo	so	so	so	so
what	what	what	what	what
on	on	onn	on	on
all	all	all	all	ali

Review: Story Surprise

Write the correct word from the word box to complete each sentence in the story.

> yes   so   what   on   all

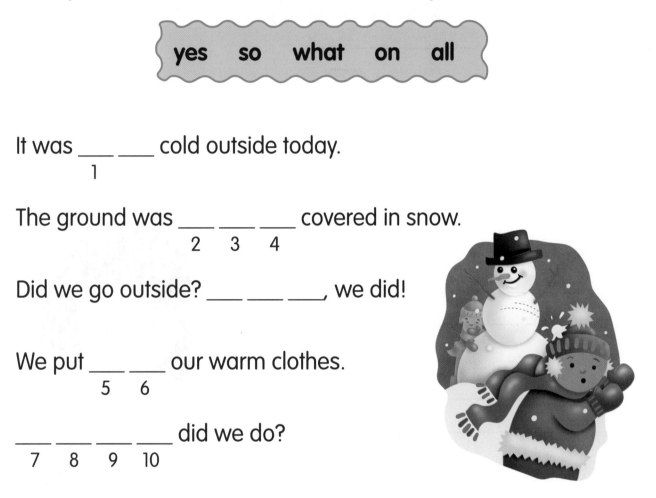

It was ___ ___ cold outside today.
  1

The ground was ___ ___ ___ covered in snow.
  2   3   4

Did we go outside? ___ ___ ___, we did!

We put ___ ___ our warm clothes.
  5   6

___ ___ ___ ___ did we do?
 7   8   9   10

For each number in the story sentences, find the matching number below. Write the letter on the line to find out what happened!

What did we do outside?

We h___d a ___ ___ ___ ___ b___ ___ ___ fig___ ___ !
   2   1   6   5   7   9   3   4   8   10

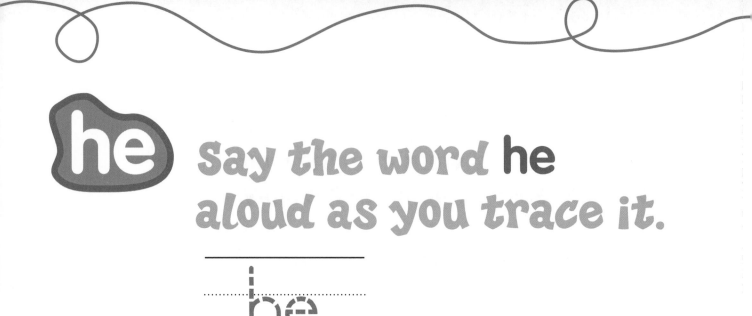

he say the word **he** aloud as you trace it.

he

Now practice writing the word once on each line.

_____ is my brother.

Stay on Track

The word **he** is hidden two times on each track. Find the words and circle them.

h h e e e h e e h h

e e h i e h e e h e

h e e h h e n e e h

Circle all the words that spell **he**.

 **make**

Say the word make **aloud as you trace it.**

make

Now practice writing the word once on each line.

I can _____ my lunch.

Lucky Letters

Write make on the line under each lucky clover that makes the word make.

did

say the word **did** aloud as you trace it.

Now practice writing the word once on each line.

The dog _____ it.

Tic-Tac-Toe

Circle the row that spells the word **did**.

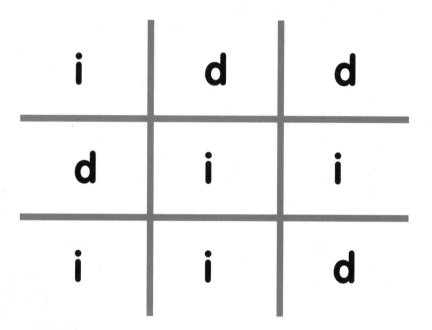

i	d	d
d	i	i
i	i	d

Circle the row that has the word **did** three times.

did	did	bid
did	did	idd
did	dib	dad

blue say the word **blue** aloud as you trace it.

blue

Now practice writing the word once on each line.

My jeans are _____.

Lost and Found

The word **blue** is hidden once in each line. Find the word and circle the letters.

b	l	u	e	b	l	e	u
1	2	3	4	5	6	7	8

b	u	b	l	b	l	u	e
1	2	3	4	5	6	7	8

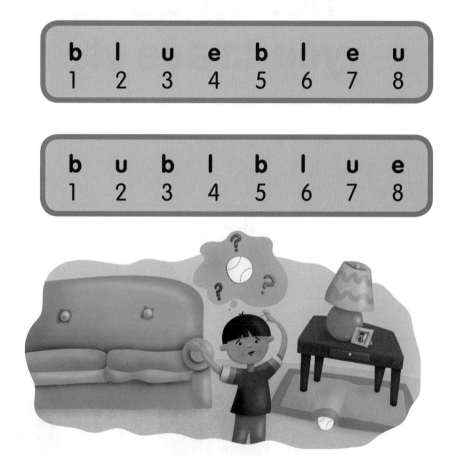

To complete the message, look at the number below each circled letter. Find the matching number in the message below and write the letter on the line.

Sam's ___as___ ___a___ ___ is ___nd___r the r___g.
     1   4   5   2 6   3   8   7

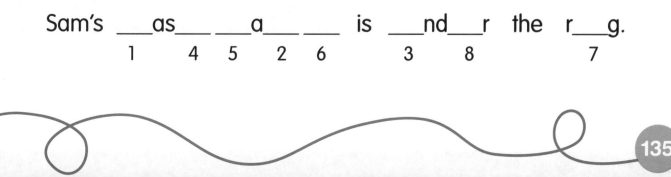

135

that say the word **that** aloud as you trace it.

that

Now practice writing the word once on each line.

I want _____ one.

Linking Letters

Draw a line to link the letters that make the word **that**.

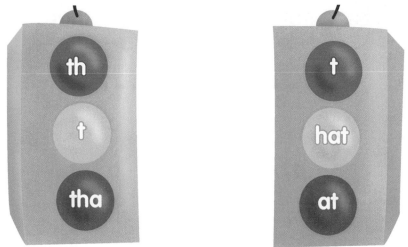

Write the missing letters to make the word **that**.

137

Review: Word Search

Find each word in the word search.

| he | make | did | blue | that |

```
i  t  d  i  d
d  h  t  d  b
m  a  k  e  l
k  t  b  l  u
e  m  h  e  e
```

Color the box that has all five review words spelled correctly.

1.	2.	3.	4.	5.
he	ne	he	he	he
did	did	did	dib	did
maxe	make	make	make	make
blue	blue	blue	bloe	blue
that	that	thaf	that	that

Review: Wormy Words

Read each sentence. Every time you see one of the review words, circle it. Then count how many circled words are in each sentence.

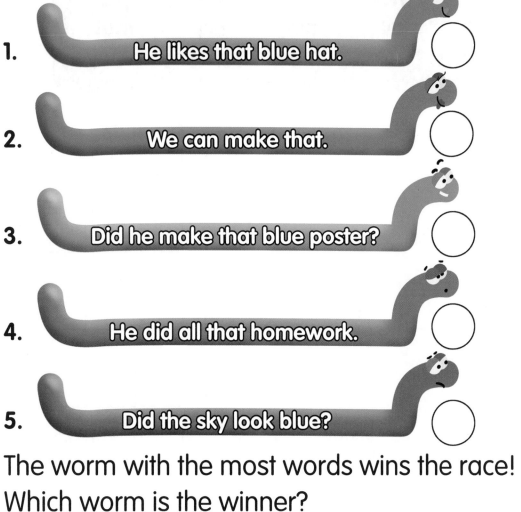

1.   He likes that blue hat.

2.   We can make that.

3.   Did he make that blue poster?

4.   He did all that homework.

5.   Did the sky look blue?

The worm with the most words wins the race! Which worm is the winner? _____

Write your own sentence. Use as many of the review words as you can.

_____

Review: Puzzle

Look at each set of boxes. Find the word whose letters fit in the boxes.

my	no	it	he	yes
say	all	did	help	that
blue	like	three	yellow	funny

1. h e

2.

3.

4.

5.

6.

7.

8.

9.

10.

11.

12.

13.

14.

15.

Review: Riddle

Use the code to fill in the missing letters and solve the riddle.

good: b   **make:** r   **little:** A   **help:** m   **we:** u

be: n   **what:** e   **on:** l   **was:** l   **but:** a

What goes up when the rain is falling down?

___ ___ ___ ___ ___ ___ ___ ___ ___ ___

little   be   we   help   good   make   what   was   on   but

Level B

The sight words included in this section are:

after	could	her	please	they
again	do	him	pretty	this
any	eat	how	ride	too
are	every	into	round	under
as	four	let	saw	want
at	from	must	say	well
ate	get	new	she	went
black	give	now	some	white
brown	going	of	soon	who
by	had	our	thank	will
came	have	out	there	with

came Say the word **came** aloud as you trace it.

came

Now practice writing the word once on each line.

I _____ home late.

Stay on Track

Find the word **came** on each track and circle it.

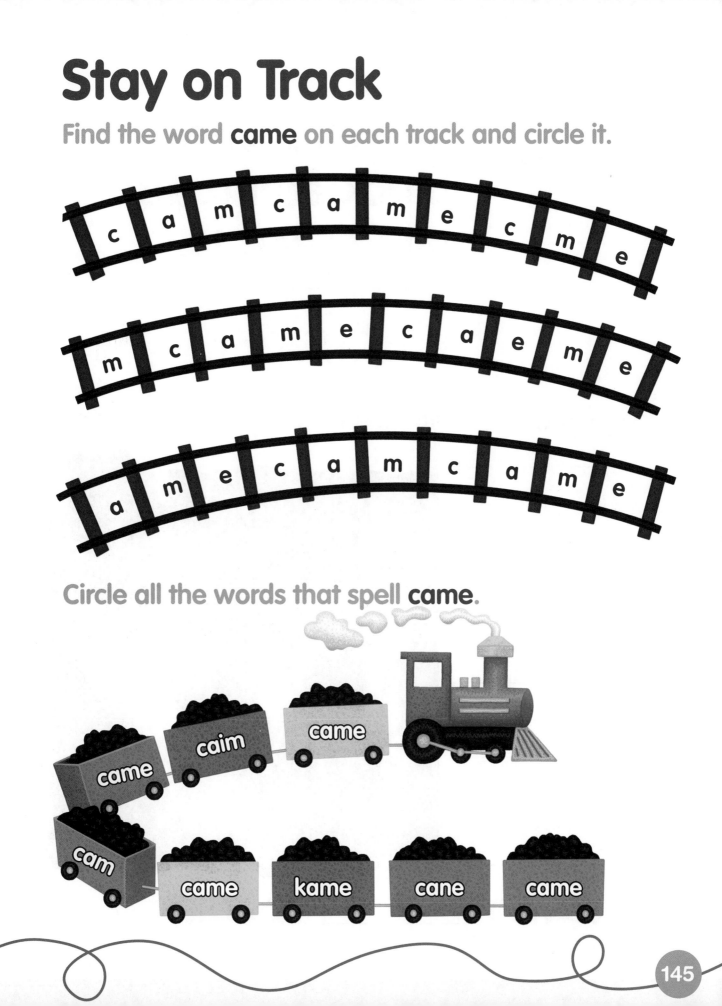

| c | a | m | c | a | m | e | c | m | e |

| m | c | a | m | e | c | a | e | m | e |

| a | m | e | c | a | m | c | a | m | e |

Circle all the words that spell **came**.

came

caim

came

cam

came

kame

cane

came

 **black**

say the word black aloud as you trace it.

black

Now practice writing the word once on each line.

I saw a _____ bear.

Maze Craze

Help the bee find its way through the maze.
Connect the letters **b-l-a-c-k** to make the word
black.

**four**

say the word four aloud as you trace it.

four

Now practice writing the word once on each line.

I am _____ years old.

Out of Order

The letters for the word **four** are out of order! If the letters can be unscrambled to make the word **four**, write the word on the line. If not, leave it blank.

_____

_____

_____

_____

_____

_____

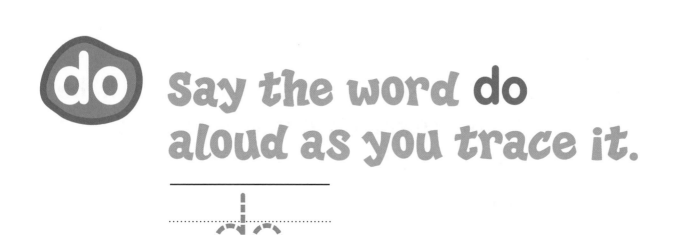

do **say the word do aloud as you trace it.**

do

Now practice writing the word once on each line.

What _____ you want to eat?

Three Cheers

Circle the word **do** every time it appears. Count the number of circled words in each cheer and write it in the box.

Do we want to win?
Yes, we do!
We'll do all we can.
How about you?

We'll do just great!
We'll do our best.
How do we do it?
We'll do better than the rest!

Team A

Team B

Which team's cheer has the higher number? _____

too **say the word too aloud as you trace it.**

Now practice writing the word once on each line.

It's _____ hot.

152

Hide and Seek

Some of the words in the treetop have too hidden inside. Find the words and write them on the lines below. Circle the letters t-o-o in each word.

stop   tool   toe

town   tooth

                          toot

             cartoon

                              toad

      stoop

                   stool

too

_____

_____

_____

_____

_____

_____

Review: Word Search

Find each word in the word search.

came   black   four   do   too

b	t	o	o	f
l	l	c	m	o
a	o	a	k	u
c	f	m	c	r
d	o	e	d	k

Color the column that has all five words spelled correctly.

1.	2.	3.	4.	5.
back	tou	came	bak	four
due	four	do	came	too
came	do	four	do	cawe
foar	came	too	too	do
too	back	black	four	back

Review: Black Out!

Read each sentence, then find the missing word in the boxes. Put an X through all the boxes that show the missing word.

A.

black	too
do	four

B.

came	do
black	too

1. It was _____ muddy to play outside.

2. So we _____ inside.

3. Later, Mom saw _____ mud on the floor.

4. I didn't _____ it!

5. My dog had left _____ muddy footprints.

Which square has all its boxes marked off first? _____

 **say the word into aloud as you trace it.**

into

Now practice writing the word once on each line.

I fell _____ the hole.

Crack the Code

The word **into** is hidden once in each line. Find the word and circle the letters. Then use the code to complete the riddle below.

i	n	t	o	n	t	o	t
#	=	<	@	X	+	*	&

i	n	t	n	i	n	t	o
<	@	#	=	*	X	+	&

Why is the moon always so tired?

Because ___t stays ___u___ all ___ ___ gh___ l___ ___ g!
　　　　　　# 　　　　　@　 < 　　　　X　 *　　 + 　　 &　 =

 **say the word are aloud as you trace it.**

are

Now practice writing the word once on each line.

are

are

are

are

We _are_ dancers.

Tic-Tac-Toe

Circle the row that spells the word **are**.

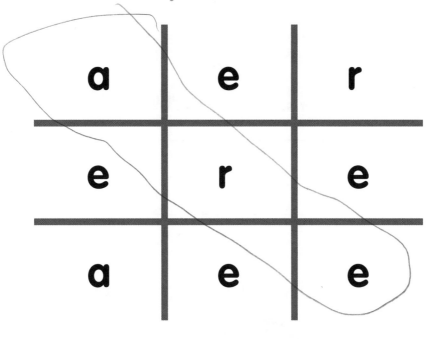

a	e	r
e	r	e
a	e	e

Circle the row that has the word **are** three times.

are	are	aer
art	are	are
are	are	arr

**going** say the word going aloud as you trace it.

Now practice writing the word once on each line.

I am _____ to school.

The Finish Line

Draw a line to the flag with the letters that finish the word **going**.

go

g

goin

goi

oing

g

ing

ng

Do the letters in the flags make the word **going**?
Circle Yes or No.

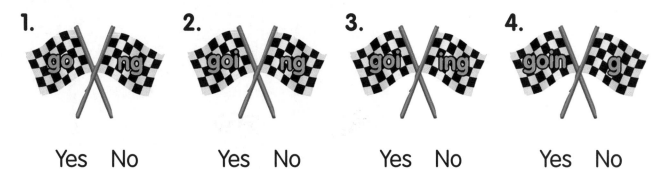

1. go ng

2. goi ng

3. goi ing

4. goin g

Yes   No   Yes   No   Yes   No   Yes   No

have

say the word
have aloud as
you trace it.

have

Now practice writing the word once on each line.

I _____ a new doll.

162

Word Hunt

The word **have** is in the story five times. Hunt for the word and circle it each time it appears.

Have you seen my hat? I have been looking for half the day. I need some help to find it. I usually hang it in the hall. I have a special hook for my hat. But it's not there!

I have to find it soon. My head needs a hat. It's the only hat I have!

Circle the hats with the word have inside.

1. have
2. hvae
3. have
4. have
5. hava
6. haev

at Say the word **at** aloud as you trace it.

----

at

Now practice writing the word once on each line.

I am _____ the park.

Rhyme Time

Circle the pictures that rhyme with **at**. Underline the letters **a-t** in each word.

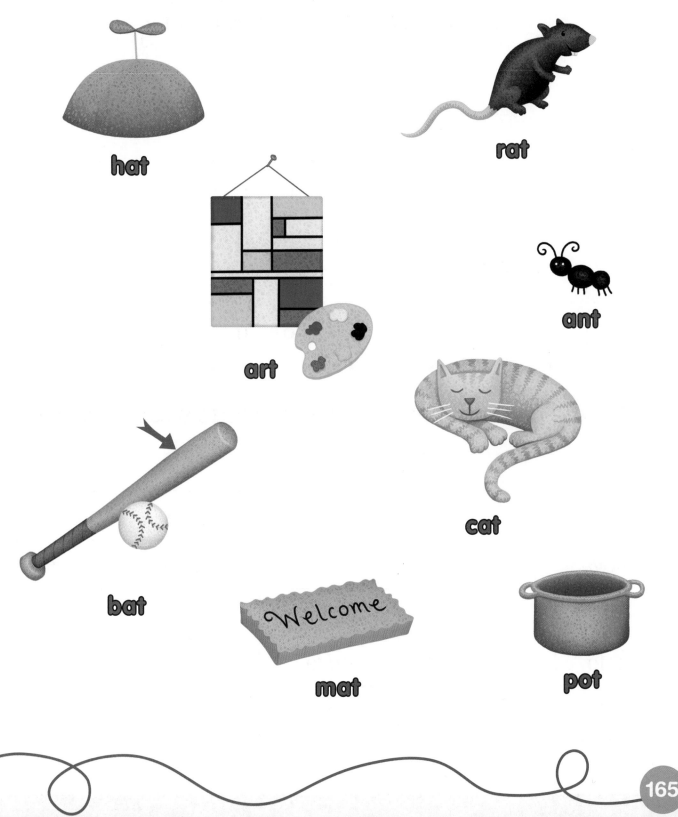

hat

rat

art

ant

cat

bat

mat

pot

Review: Word Search

Find each word in the word search.

into   are   going   have   at

```
h  a  v  e  i
a  v  n  i  o
g  o  i  n  g
a  r  e  t  o
t  g  h  o  n
```

Color the column that has all five words spelled correctly.

1.	2.	3.	4.	5.
gonig	are	into	have	at
have	at	are	intoo	hane
are	imto	going	going	going
into	going	have	at	ane
att	hawe	at	are	into

Review: Story Code

Look for the review words as you read the story. Follow the code each time you see a review word.

(into) circle it

[going] make a box

✓at put a check

are underline

have wavy line

I always have my birthday party at home. This year, I wanted to have it someplace new.

"We are going somewhere different," my family said. "You are going to have a great time."

We all got into the car.

"Where are we going?" I asked.

"It's a surprise," they said. "You have to close your eyes."

"Are we there yet?" I asked.

"You have to be patient!" they said.

After a long drive, the car stopped.

"We're at the beach!" I said.

We all jumped into the water.

must say the word **must** aloud as you trace it.

----

must

Now practice writing the word once on each line.

You _____ go to bed.

Stay on Track

Find the word **must** on each track and circle it.

| u | m | u | s | t | u | s | t | m | u |

| m | s | t | u | m | t | m | u | s | t |

| m | u | t | m | u | s | t | m | u | s |

Circle all the words that spell **must**.

mist

mast

must

must

musd

must

muse

must

brown

say the word **brown** aloud as you trace it.

brown

Now practice writing the word once on each line.

The peanuts are _____.

Maze Craze

Help the monkey find its way through the maze. Connect the letters **b-r-o-w-n** to make the word brown.

d

b

x

o

b

r

i

h

w

e

p

n

soon

Say the word soon aloud as you trace it.

_____

soon

Now practice writing the word once on each line.

The pie will be done _____.

Out of Order

The letters for the word **soon** are out of order! If the letters can be unscrambled to make the word **soon**, write the word on the line. If not, leave it blank.

_____

....

_____

_____

....

_____

_____

....

_____

_____

....

_____

_____

....

_____

 **Say the word say aloud as you trace it.**

Now practice writing the word once on each line.

You _____ it first.

Three Cheers

Circle the word **say** every time it appears. Count the number of circled words in each cheer and write it in the box.

When I say "go" you say "fight." Go! Go! Fight! Fight! When I say "win" you say "tonight." Win! Win! Tonight! Tonight!

You say you're so great. You say you're the best. But we're here to say we're better than the rest.

Team A

Team B

Which team's cheer has the higher number? _____

under *say the word under aloud as you trace it.*

under

Now practice writing the word once on each line.

My shoes are _____ the bed.

Hide and Seek

Some of the words in the treetop have **under** hidden inside. Find the words and write them on the lines below. Circle the letters **u-n-d-e-r** in each word.

blender

thunder

kinder

underneath

wander

wonderful

underground

underwear

understand

under

_____

_____

_____

_____

_____

Review: Word Search

Find each word in the word search.

| must | brown | soon | say | under |

```
m  u  s  a  y
u  n  o  u  m
s  d  o  n  u
t  e  n  a  s
b  r  o  w  n
```

Color the column that has all five words spelled correctly.

	1.	**2.**	**3.**	**4.**	**5.**
	ander	soon	broun	must	under
	must	muzt	under	brown	say
	soo	brown	must	soon	must
	brown	under	soon	say	browm
	soon	say	say	under	soom

Review: Black Out!

Read each sentence, then find the missing word in the boxes. Put an X through all the boxes that show the missing word.

A.

say	must
brown	under

B.

brown	soon
say	must

1. My parents _____ it's getting late.

2. It will be time for bed _____.

3. First you _____ brush your teeth.

4. Don't forget your _____ teddy bear.

5. Get _____ the covers and fall asleep.

Which square has all its boxes marked off first? _____

 **ride**

say the word ride aloud as you trace it.

ride

Now practice writing the word once on each line.

I can _____ my bike.

Crack the Code

The word ride is hidden once in each line. Find the word and circle the letters. Then use the code to complete the riddle below.

d	r	i	d	e	r	i	d
*	#	+	@	X	<	=	&

i	r	d	r	i	d	e	r
X	@	X	=	*	<	&	+

Why did the girl put her umbrella in her piggy bank?

She want___ ___ to sav___ ___t fo___ a ___a___ny
       X @   & *   =   # +

___ay.
 <

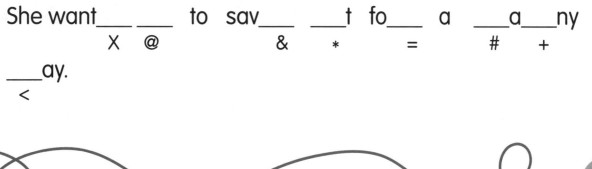

 **say the word get aloud as you trace it.**

get

Now practice writing the word once on each line.

Can I _____ a candy bar?

Tic-Tac-Toe

Circle the row that spells the word **get**.

e	t	g
g	e	t
g	t	e

Circle the row that has the word **get** three times.

got	pet	get
get	get	gte
get	get	gel

 **after** say the word **after** aloud as you trace it.

Now practice writing the word once on each line.

You can have dessert _____ dinner.

The Finish Line

Draw a line to the flag with the letters that finish the word **after**.

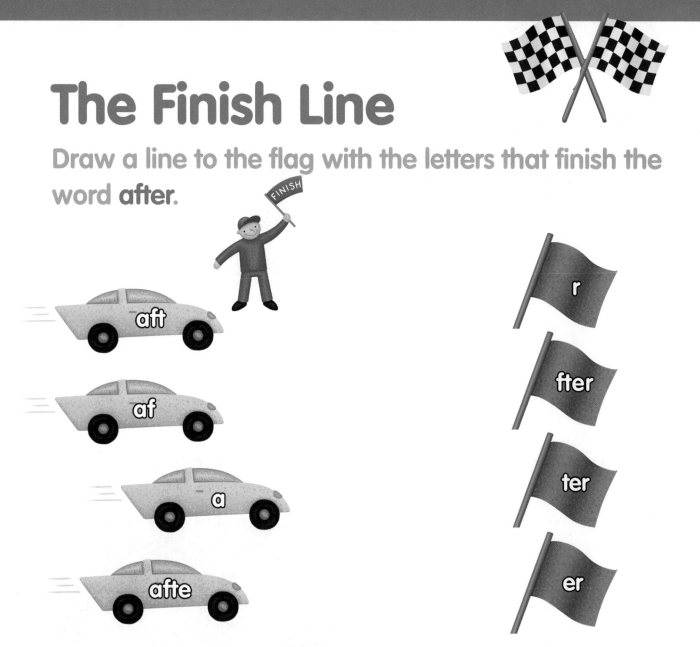

Do the letters in the flags make the word **after**?
Circle Yes or No.

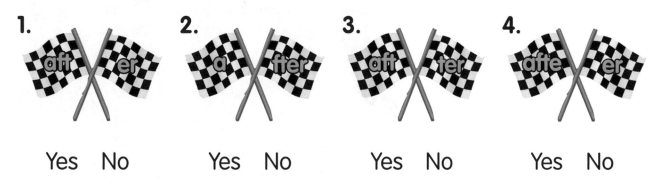

1. Yes   No

2. Yes   No

3. Yes   No

4. Yes   No

they say the word **they** aloud as you trace it.

they

Now practice writing the word once on each line.

they
they
they
they
They

are my parents.

Word Hunt

The word **they** is in the story five times. Hunt for the word and circle it each time it appears.

I have twin brothers, Tim and Jim. (They) look exactly the same. (They) have brown hair and blue eyes. Today (they) have on matching clothes. Both of them are wearing white shirts and jeans. Hey, I can't tell them apart! I hope (they) tell me who is who. If not, then (they) will be in big trouble!

Circle the shirts with the word **they** inside.

1. thay

2. they

3. they

4. they

5. thy

6. then

 **say the word ate aloud as you trace it.**

────────

ate

Now practice writing the word once on each line.

I _____ all the cake.

Rhyme Time

Circle the pictures that rhyme with **ate**. Underline the letters **a-t-e** in each word.

eat

date

bath

gate

boat

late

tape

plate

Review: Word Search

Find each word in the word search.

> ride   get   after   they   ate

```
t  a  f  e  r
h  t  h  e  i
e  a  t  g  d
y  f  e  e  e
a  t  e  t  r
```

Color the column that has all five words spelled correctly.

1.	2.	3.	4.	5.
gat	after	they	ate	ride
after	thye	ate	ride	get
atte	get	ribe	after	they
they	ride	get	gete	after
ride	ate	after	they	ate

Review: Story Code

Look for the review words as you read the story.
Follow the code each time you see a review word.

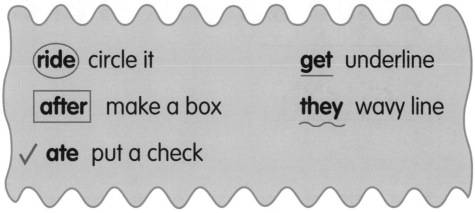

(ride) circle it

after make a box

✓ ate put a check

get underline

they wavy line

Amy and Ella went to the fair. First they saw the animals. A pony ate a carrot out of Ella's hand. After that, Ella wanted to go on a ride.

"Let's ride the Ferris wheel," Ella said.

"We need to get some tickets first," Amy said.

After they got tickets, they went on the ride. Then they decided to get hot dogs.

After they ate, they went home. They decided to come to the fair every year!

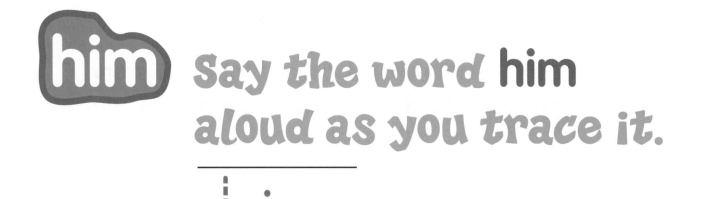

him

say the word him aloud as you trace it.

him

Now practice writing the word once on each line.

I sit next to _____ .

Stay on Track

Find the word **him** on each track and circle it.

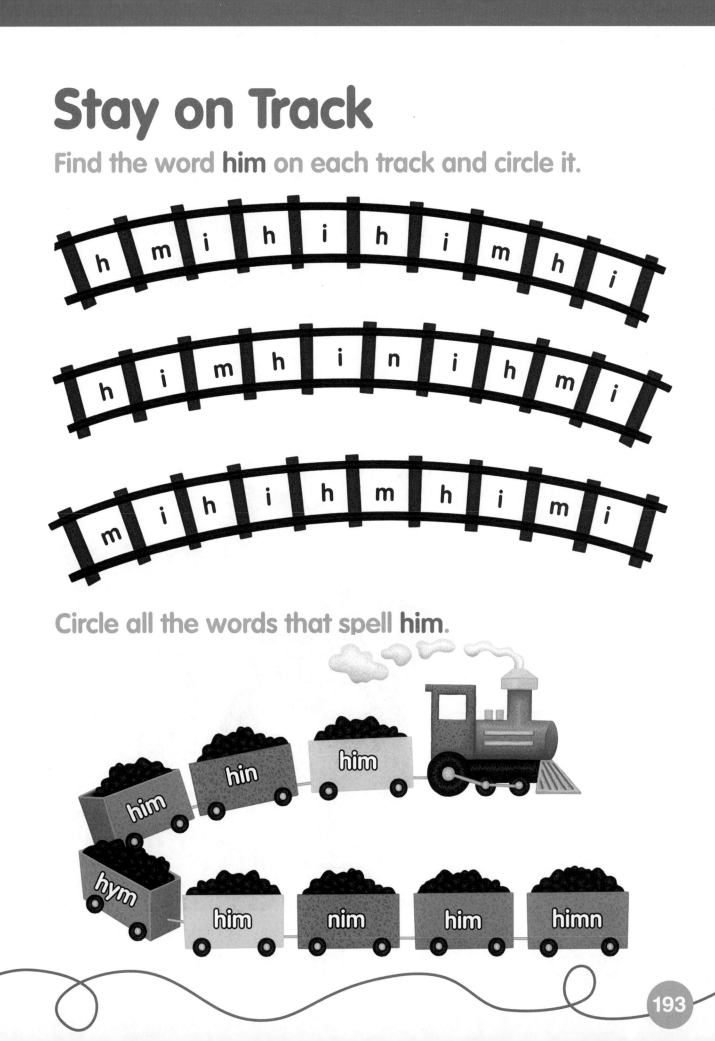

Track 1: h m i i h i h i m h i

Track 2: h i m h i n i h m i

Track 3: m i h i h m h i m i

Circle all the words that spell **him**.

him hin him

hym him nim him himn

 **please** **Say the word please aloud as you trace it.**

please

Now practice writing the word once on each line.

May I _____ have some more?

Maze Craze

Help the fish find its way through the maze.
Connect the letters p-l-e-a-s-e to make the word
please.

 **say the word let aloud as you trace it.**

let

Now practice writing the word once on each line.

Please _____ me in.

Out of Order

The letters for the word **let** are out of order! If the letters can be unscrambled to make the word **let**, write the word on the line. If not, leave it blank.

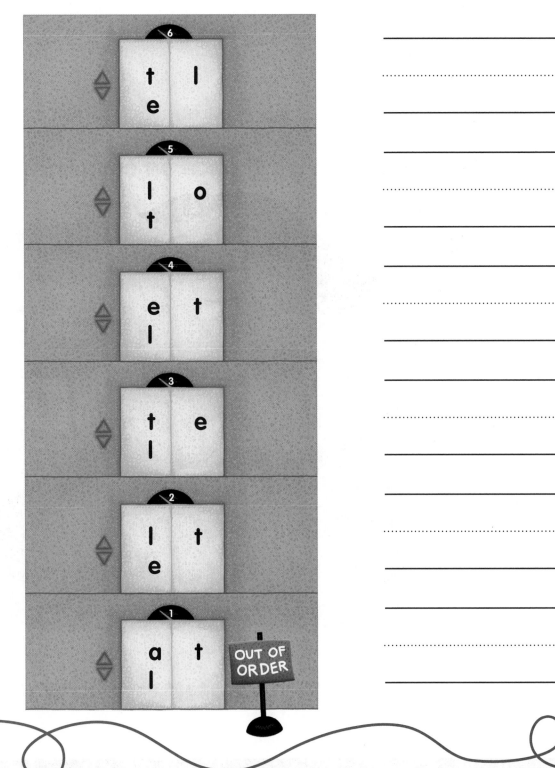

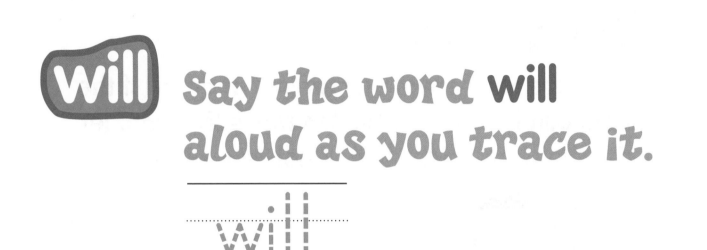

will say the word **will** aloud as you trace it.

will

Now practice writing the word once on each line.

We _____ have lunch soon.

Three Cheers

Circle the word **will** every time it appears. Count the number of circled words in each cheer and write it in the box.

Who will clap their hands?
Who will give a cheer?
Who will shout "Go Team"?
So everyone will hear!

Our team will play
Our team will score
And when they win
The crowd will roar

Team A

Team B

Which team's cheer has the higher number? _____

 **any**

Say the word **any** aloud as you trace it.

 any

Now practice writing the word once on each line.

Do you have _____ gum?

Hide and Seek

Some of the words in the treetop have **any** hidden inside. Find the words and write them on the lines below. Circle the letters **a-n-y** in each word.

animal   anyway   nanny

anyone

annoy   wonderful   answer

anywhere

anybody   many

anything

any

Review: Word Search!

Find each word in the word search.

| him | please | let | will | any |

```
t   w   h   p   w
h   i   m   l   i
l   l   l   e   t
p   l   y   a   s
a   n   w   s   n
a   p   e   e   h
```

Color the column that has all five words spelled correctly.

1.	2.	3.	4.	5.
lef	him	will	let	please
will	please	amy	him	will
please	let	please	wiil	anv
hin	will	let	any	hlm
any	any	hin	please	let

Review: Black Out!

Read each sentence, then find the missing word in the boxes. Put an X through all the boxes that show the missing word.

A.

let	please
will	him

B.

any	him
will	let

1. Could you _____ open the door?

2. The dog needs to be _____ out.

3. You should take _____ outside.

4. _____ you take him on a walk?

5. Don't let him bark at _____ kids.

Which square has all its boxes marked off first? _____

 **went**

say the word went aloud as you trace it.

_____

went

Now practice writing the word once on each line.

_____

. . . .

_____

. . . .

_____

. . . .

_____

. . . .

_____

I _____ **down the slide.**

Crack the Code

The word **went** is hidden once in each line. Find the word and circle the letters. Then use the code to complete the riddle below.

w	n	t	w	e	n	t	n
*	#	+	@	X	<	=	&

e	w	e	n	t	w	e	n
X	#	&	+	*	<	@	=

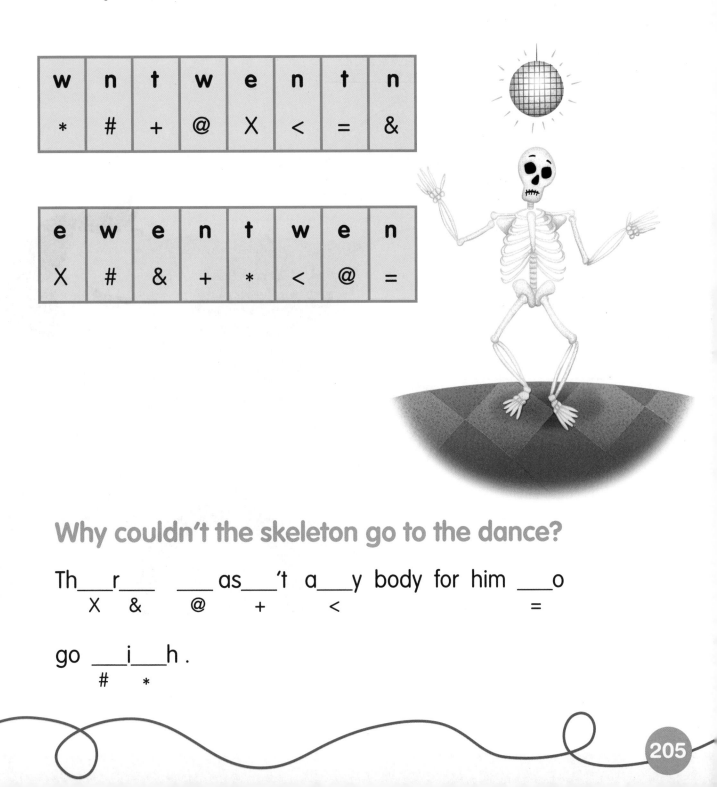

Why couldn't the skeleton go to the dance?

Th___r___ ___ as___'t a___y body for him ___o
    X   &   @   +   <   =

go ___i___h .
   #   *

 **Say the word new aloud as you trace it.**

Now practice writing the word once on each line.

I got a _____ bike.

Tic-Tac-Toe

Circle the row that spells the word **new**.

n	w	n
w	n	e
e	e	w

Circle the row that has the word **new** three times.

new	mew	new
mew	new	new
new	new	now

could Say the word could aloud as you trace it.

could

Now practice writing the word once on each line.

I _____ eat the whole pie!

The Finish Line

Draw a line to link the letters that make the word could.

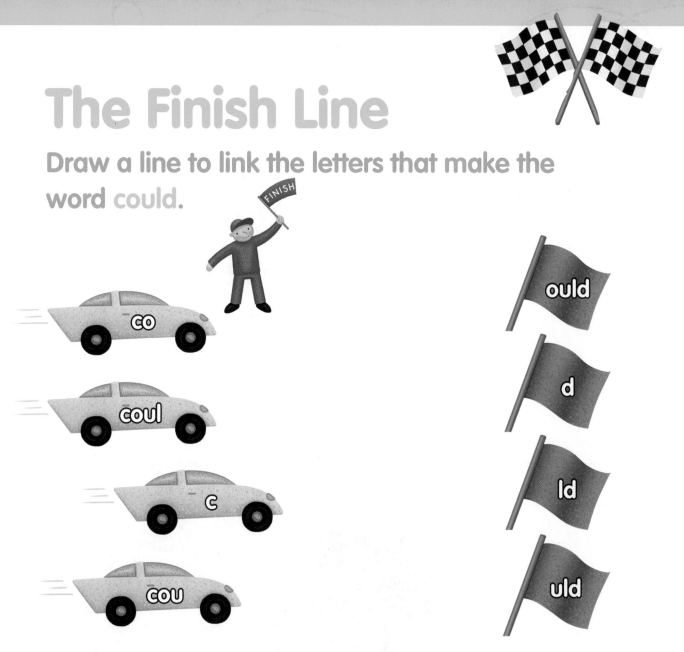

Do the letters in the flags make the word could? Circle Yes or No.

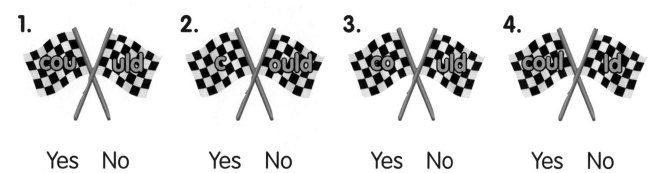

1. Yes   No

2. Yes   No

3. Yes   No

4. Yes   No

 **there**

say the word there aloud as you trace it.

there

Now practice writing the word once on each line.

My shoes are over _____.

Word Hunt

The word **there** is in the story five times. Hunt for the word and circle it each time it appears.

Where did all the cookies go? This morning there were three cookies. They were right there in the jar. Now there aren't any cookies! They're all gone! But I can still smell cookies. It's coming from over there by the oven. There is a new batch of cookies! I can't wait to eat them all up.

Circle the cookie jars with the word **there** inside.

1. there
2. there
3. their
4. thair
5. theer
6. there

 **say the word eat aloud as you trace it.**

eat

Now practice writing the word once on each line.

It's time to _____.

Rhyme Time

Circle the pictures that rhyme with **eat**. Underline the letters **e-a-t** in each word.

heat

neat

ear

skate

tea

seat

meat

read

Review: Word Search

Find each word in the word search.

| went | new | could | there | eat |

```
t  e  a  t  c  o
h  a  w  e  n  c
t  h  e  r  e  o
e  n  a  l  n  u
w  e  w  d  e  l
e  w  e  n  t  d
```

Color the column that has all five words spelled correctly.

1.	2.	3.	4.	5.
went	new	could	there	eat
nev	could	there	eat	went
could	theer	new	went	go
eet	went	weht	new	there
there	mew	eat	could	cuold

214

Review: Story Code

Look for the review words as you read the story. Follow the code each time you see a review word.

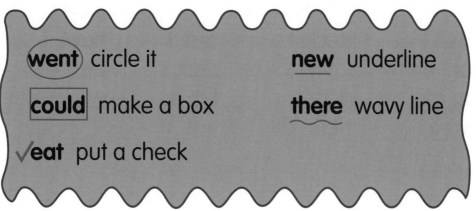

went circle it   new underline

could make a box   there wavy line

eat put a check

Zack could not think of anything fun to do. He wanted to try something new. He decided to bake a pie that he could eat.

Then, his friend Josh came over with a new ball. The boys went outside to play with it. Zack forgot there was a pie baking in the oven.

"I'm so hungry, I could eat a pie," Josh said.

"There is a pie in the oven!" Zack said. The boys went inside. The pie was burned. There was nothing they could do.

"Let's bake a new pie," Josh said.

"And this time, let's make sure we get to eat it!" Zack said.

Review: Riddle

Use the code to fill in the missing letters and answer the knock knock joke.

came: **i**	black: **t**	are: **i**	have: **l**
soon: **o**	so: **n**	ride: **s**	ate: **A**
him: **c**	please: **r**	let: **e**	will: **h**
new: **o**	there: **d**	eat: **a**	

Knock knock.
Who's there?

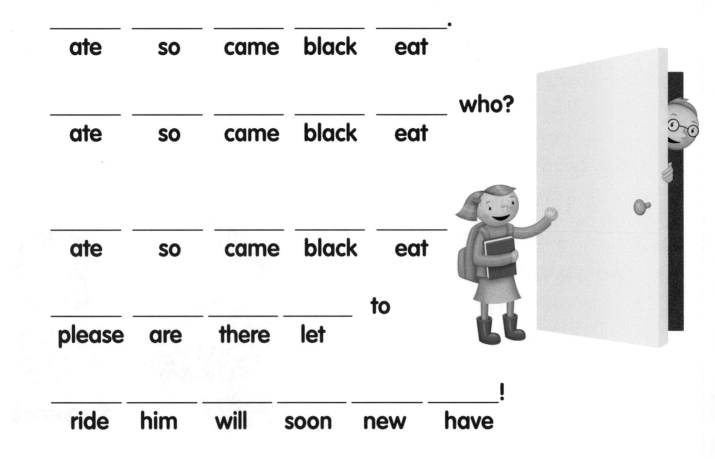

_____ _____ _____ _____ _____ .
ate   so   came   black   eat

_____ _____ _____ _____ _____ who?
ate   so   came   black   eat

_____ _____ _____ _____ _____
ate   so   came   black   eat

_____ _____ _____ _____ to
please   are   there   let

_____ _____ _____ _____ _____ _____ !
ride   him   will   soon   new   have

Review: Race

Look at each set of boxes. Find the word whose letters fit in the boxes.

going   at   under   do   must
brown   they   went   could   get
too   after   into   any   four

1. m u s t

2.

3.

4.

5.

6.

7.

8.

9.

10.

11.

12.

13.

14.

15.

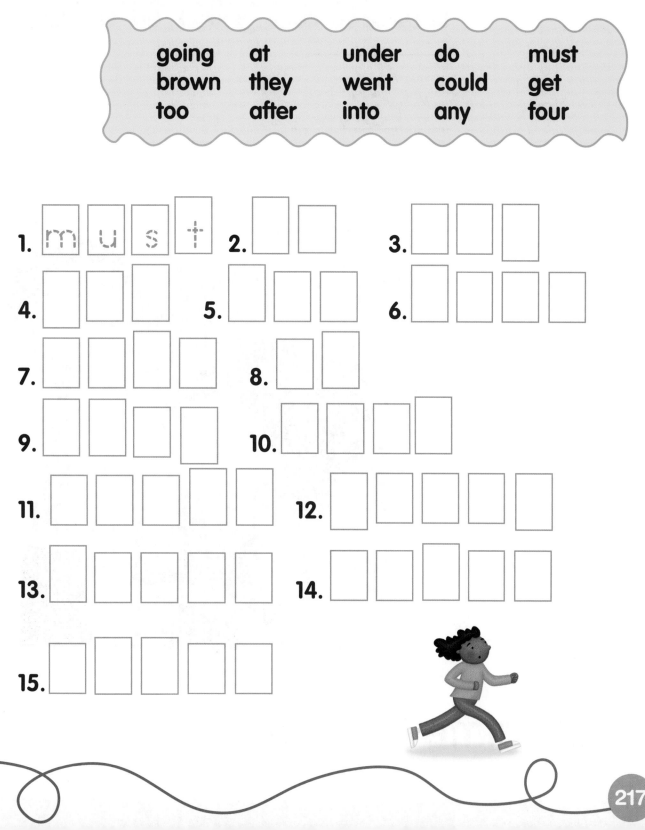

now say the word now aloud as you trace it.

_____

now

Now practice writing the word once on each line.

It's time for bed _____.

Stay on Track

Find the word **now** on each track and circle it.

o n o w n w o w n o

w n o n o n o w n o

n o o w n o n o w n

Circle all the words that spell **now**.

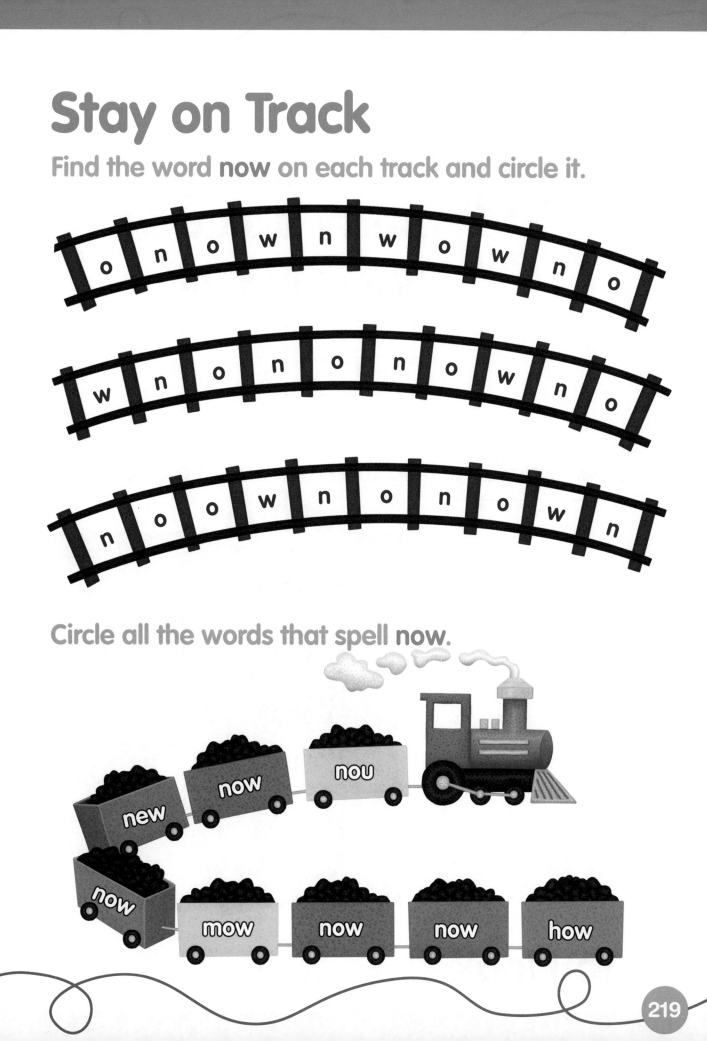

new
now
nou
now
mow
now
now
how

pretty say the word pretty aloud as you trace it.

pretty

Now practice writing the word once on each line.

You look _____!

Maze Craze

Help the kitten find its way through the maze. Connect the letters **p-r-e-t-t-y** to make the word **pretty**.

 **Say the word this aloud as you trace it.**

this

Now practice writing the word once on each line.

I sit at _____ desk.

Out of Order

The letters for the word this are out of order! If the letters can be unscrambled to make the word this, write the word on the line. If not, leave it blank.

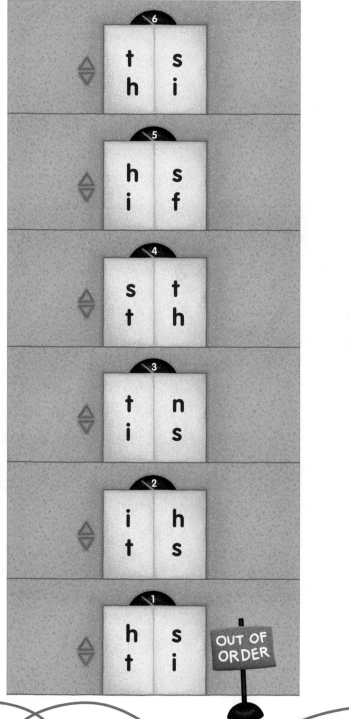

_____

....

_____

....

_____

....

_____

....

_____

....

_____

 **say the word give aloud as you trace it.**

Now practice writing the word once on each line.

I like to _____ my mom flowers.

Three Cheers

Circle the word **give** every time it appears. Count the number of circled words in each cheer and write it in the box.

Give me a W!
Give me an 1!
Give me an N!
What does it spell?
Win!

Put your hands together. Give our team a shout! You can also give a cheer. That's what it's all about!

Team A

Team B

Which team's cheer has the higher number? _____

every

say the word every aloud as you trace it.

_____

`every`

Now practice writing the word once on each line.

_____
....
_____
_____
....
_____
_____
....
_____

I do my homework _____ day.

Hide and Seek

Some of the words in the treetop have **every** hidden inside. Find the words and write them on the lines below. Circle the letters **e-v-e-r-y** in each word.

seven   clever   everybody   everyone

reverse   everywhere

evergreen   never

everything   event

every

_____

_____

_____

_____

Review: Word Search

Find each word in the word search.

now   pretty   this   give   every

```
e  p  g  i  v  e
v  r  i  n  o  r
y  e  v  e  r  y
n  t  i  i  v  t
o  t  h  s  g  t
w  y  t  h  i  s
```

Color the column that has all five words spelled correctly.

1.	2.	3.	4.	5.
evrey	this	prety	now	nuw
this	giv	evry	pretty	this
now	every	give	give	prety
pritty	pretty	this	this	every
give	now	mow	every	giv

Review: Black Out!

Read each sentence, then find the missing word in the boxes. Put an X through all the boxes that show the missing word.

A.

give	pretty
this	every

B.

now	give
every	pretty

1. What can I _____ my mom for Mother's Day?

2. It seems like _____ year I buy flowers.

3. I want to get something new _____ year.

4. A _____ dress would be a nice gift.

5. All I need to do _____ is go buy one!

Which square has all its boxes marked off first? _____

 **say the word she aloud as you trace it.**

she

Now practice writing the word once on each line.

_____ is my sister.

Crack the Code

The word **she** is hidden once in each line. Find the word and circle the letters. Then use the code to complete the riddle below.

h	s	h	e	s	h	s	e
*	#	+	@	X	<	=	&

s	h	h	s	h	e	e	h
X	#	&	=	*	<	@	+

Why did the boy put sugar under his pillow?

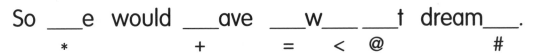

So ___e would ___ave ___w___ ___t dream___.
   *   +   = < @   #

 **say the word saw aloud as you trace it.**

saw

Now practice writing the word once on each line.

I _____ a deer.

Tic-Tac-Toe

Circle the row that spells the word **saw**.

s	w	w
w	a	w
s	w	s

Circle the row that has the word **saw** three times.

saw	saw	swa
suw	saw	saw
sow	sew	saw

again

Say the word *again* **aloud as you trace it.**

Now practice writing the word once on each line.

I want to ride _____!

The Finish Line

Draw a line to the flag with the letters that finish the word **again**.

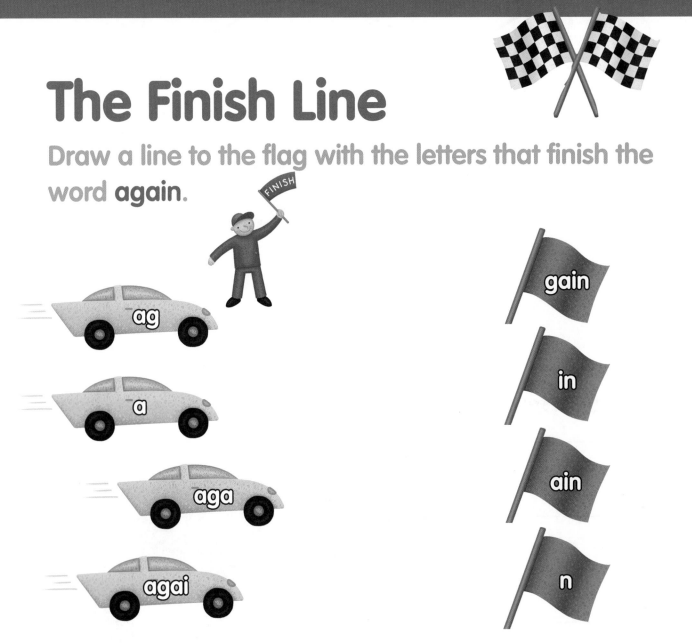

Do the letters in the flags make the word **again**?
Circle Yes or No.

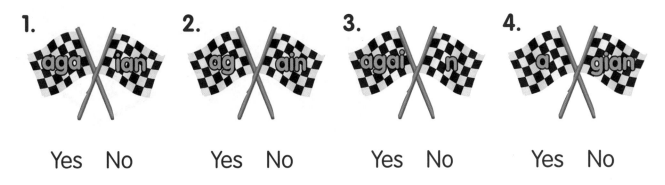

1. Yes   No

2. Yes   No

3. Yes   No

4. Yes   No

of

Say the word of aloud as you trace it.

of

Now practice writing the word once on each line.

My hat is on top _____ the books.

Word Hunt

The word **of** is in the story five times. Hunt for the word and circle it each time it appears.

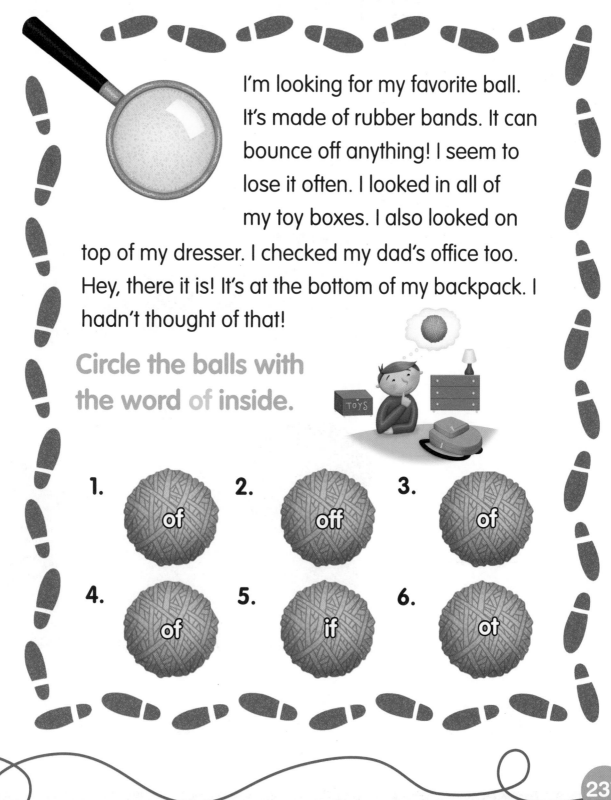

I'm looking for my favorite ball. It's made of rubber bands. It can bounce off anything! I seem to lose it often. I looked in all of my toy boxes. I also looked on top of my dresser. I checked my dad's office too. Hey, there it is! It's at the bottom of my backpack. I hadn't thought of that!

Circle the balls with the word of inside.

1. of
2. off
3. of
4. of
5. if
6. ot

our

say the word **our** aloud as you trace it.

our

Now practice writing the word once on each line.

This is _____ room.

Rhyme Time

Circle the pictures that rhyme with **our**. Underline the letters **o-u-r** in each word.

core

sour

turn

hour

scour

roar

floor

flour

Review: Word Search

Find each word in the word search.

| she | saw | again | of | our |

w	o	e	r	o
h	h	w	e	u
s	a	w	r	r
a	g	a	i	n
f	n	o	f	s

Color the column that has all five words spelled correctly.

1.	2.	3.	4.	5.
again	of	uor	she	saw
swa	our	again	oru	she
she	again	she	saw	af
fo	she	ot	shi	again
our	saw	saw	of	our

Review: Story Code

Look for the review words as you read the story. Follow the code each time you see a review word.

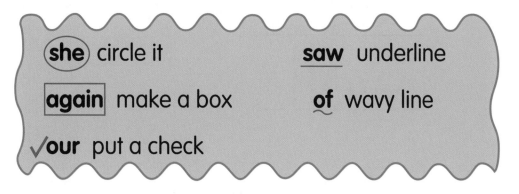

(she) circle it   <u>saw</u> underline

[again] make a box   <u>of</u> wavy line

✓our put a check

This morning we saw a kitten in our backyard. She was playing with a ball of yarn.

"None of our neighbors have a kitten," I said. "She must be lost."

When we looked up again, the kitten was gone.

Later that day, we saw her again. She was sleeping on top of our car.

"I saw a sign about a lost kitten at our bus stop," my dad said.

The sign had a picture of a kitten. It looked just like the kitten we saw!

We called the owners of the kitten. They came to pick her up at our house.

They were so happy to see their kitten again!

 **well** Say the word **well** aloud as you trace it.

well

Now practice writing the word once on each line.

I can sing very _____.

Stay on Track

Find the word **well** on each track and circle it.

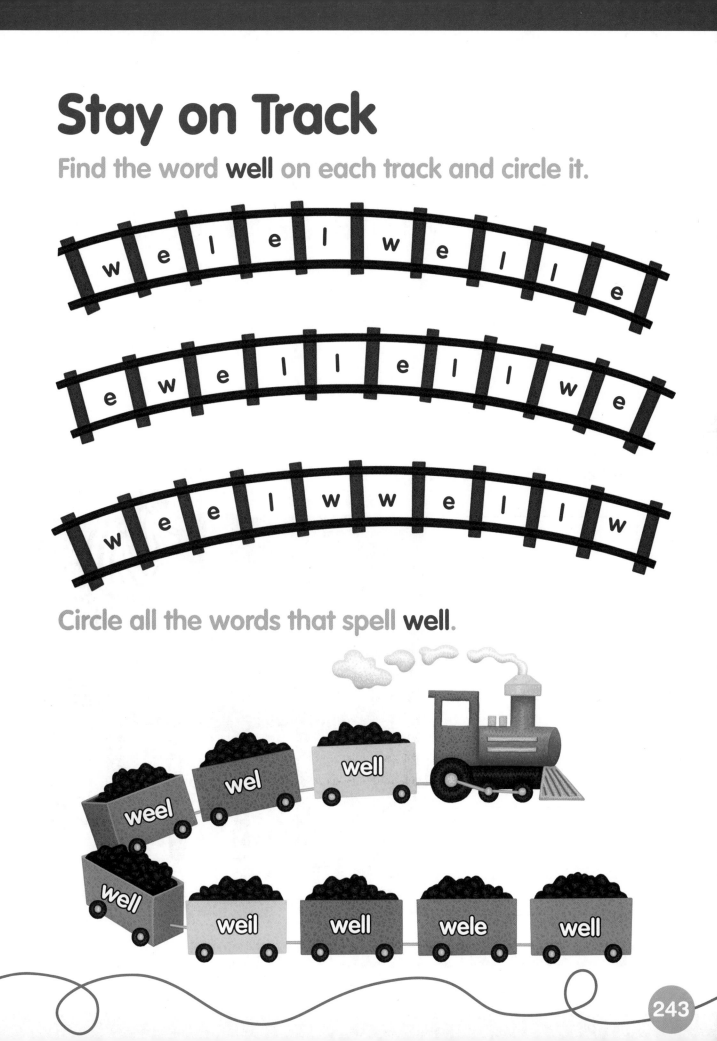

| w | e | l | e | l | w | e | l | l | e |

| e | w | e | l | l | e | l | l | w | e |

| w | e | e | l | w | w | e | l | l | w |

Circle all the words that spell **well**.

weel

wel

well

well

weil

well

wele

well

 **white** say the word white aloud as you trace it.

white

Now practice writing the word once on each line.

The zebra is black and _____.

Maze Craze

Help the rabbit find its way through the maze. Connect the letters w-h-i-t-e to make the word white.

 **want**

Say the word
want aloud as
you trace it.

_____

want

Now practice writing the word once on each line.

_____

....

_____

....

_____

....

_____

_____

....

_____

I _____ this book, please.

Out of Order

The letters for the word **want** are out of order! If the letters can be unscrambled to make the word **want**, write the word on the line. If not, leave it blank.

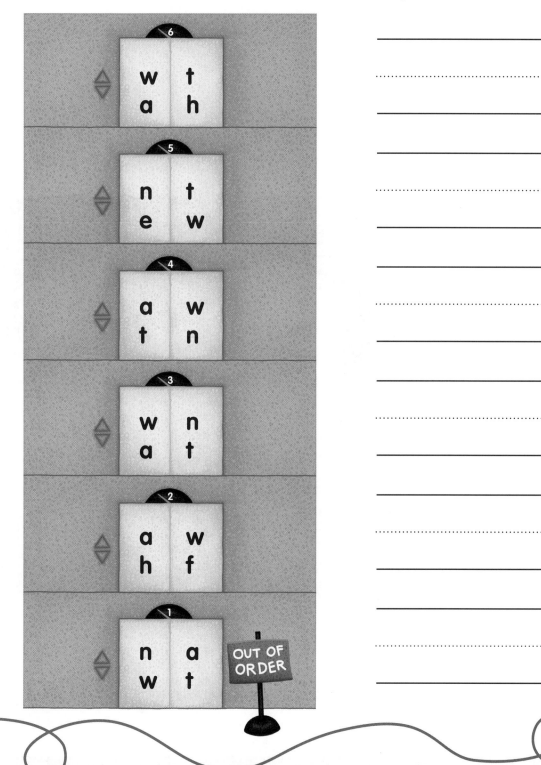

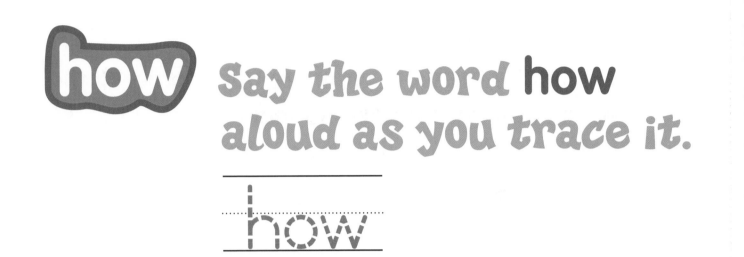

how say the word **how** aloud as you trace it.

how

Now practice writing the word once on each line.

_____ are you doing today?

Three Cheers

Circle the word **how** every time it appears. Count the number of circled words in each cheer and write it in the box.

We know how to play.
We know how to win.
We'll show them how it's done.
Now let's begin!

How will we beat the other team? How will we win tonight? We know how, and starting now, we'll show them how to do it right!

Team A

Team B

Which team's cheer has the higher number? _____

some Say the word some aloud as you trace it.

_____

⁙ some ⁙

Now practice writing the word once on each line.

I have _____ of the apples.

Hide and Seek

Some of the words in the treetop have some hidden inside. Find the words and write them on the lines below. Circle the letters s-o-m-e in each word.

summer sameness smooth somebody

handsome

something someone

somewhere sometimes

summary

some

_____

_____

_____

_____

_____

_____

Review: Word Search

Find each word in the word search.

| well | white | want | some | how |

```
h  o  s  m  w
w  a  n  t  e
s  o  m  e  l
o  h  o  w  l
w  h  i  t  e
```

Color the column that has all five words spelled correctly.

1.	2.	3.	4.	5.
how	well	want	some	whate
want	white	some	whife	some
some	want	white	how	well
weil	some	huw	will	how
white	how	well	whant	want

Review: Black Out!

Read each sentence, then find the missing word in the boxes. Put an X through all the boxes that show the missing word.

A.

want	white
well	How

B.

some	How
want	well

1. Today my dad isn't feeling very _____.

2. He looks pale and _____.

3. _____ can I help him feel better?

4. I _____ to cheer him up.

5. I can make him _____ hot soup.

Which square has all its boxes marked off first? _____

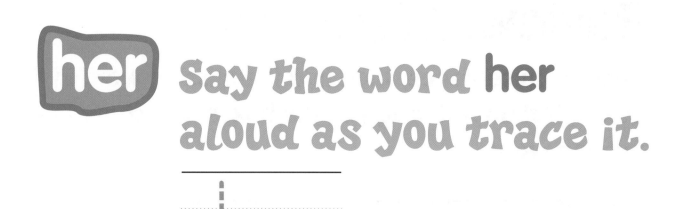

her *say the word* **her** *aloud as you trace it.*

her

Now practice writing the word once on each line.

I threw the ball to _____ .

Crack the Code

The word **her** is hidden once in each line. Find the word and circle the letters. Then use the code to complete the riddle below.

h	r	e	h	h	e	r	e
*	#	+	@	X	<	=	&

e	h	e	r	h	r	e	r
<	#	&	+	*	X	@	=

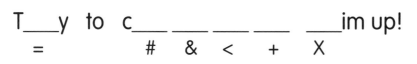

What do you do with a blue whale?

T___y to c___ ___ ___ ___ ___im up!
    =   #   &   <   +   X

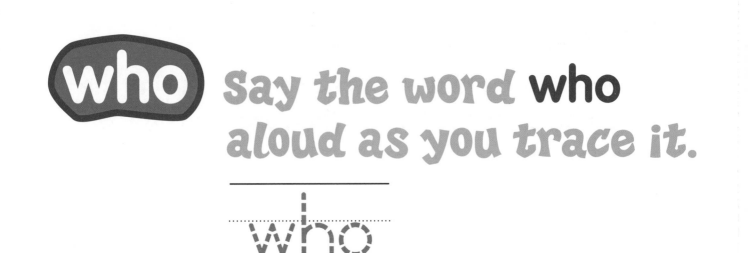

who say the word **who** aloud as you trace it.

who

Now practice writing the word once on each line.

_____ is it?

Tic-Tac-Toe

Circle the row that spells the word **who**.

w	w	h
w	h	w
o	w	o

Circle the row that has the word **who** three times.

wno	who	who
who	hoo	wha
who	who	who

round

say the word round aloud as you trace it.

round

Now practice writing the word once on each line.

The table is _____.

The Finish Line

Draw a line to the flag with the letters that finish the word **round**.

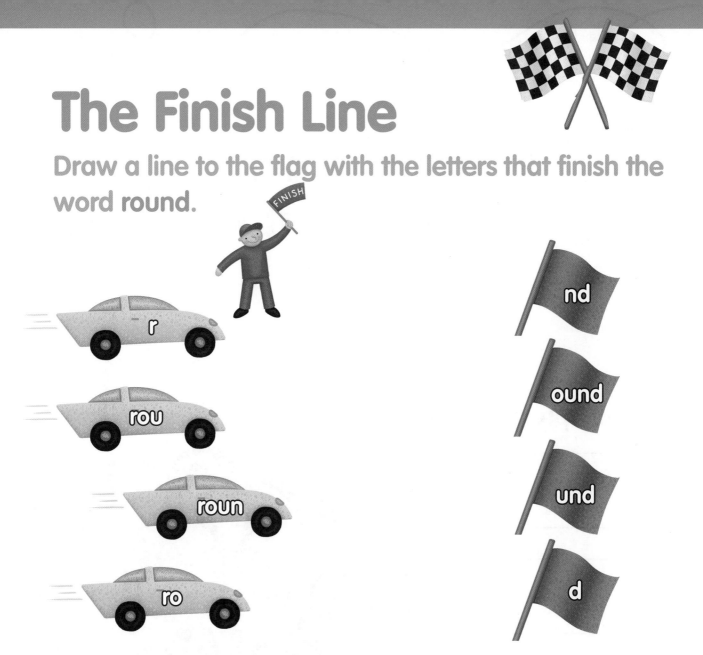

Do the letters in the flags make the word **round**?
Circle Yes or No.

1.

Yes   No

2.

Yes   No

3.

Yes   No

4.

Yes   No

as *say the word* as
aloud as *you trace it.*

_____

_____ a̲s̲ _____

Now practice writing the word once on each line.

I am as tall _____ my brother.

Word Hunt

The word **as** is in the story five times. Hunt for the word and circle it each time it appears.

Today I lost my hamster. She is very small. Her fur is white as snow. I looked all over the house, as did my mom. Just as I was about to give up, I heard a noise.

It sounded as if my hamster was in the bathtub. I looked in the tub, and there she was! She was playing with the bath toys, happy as can be.

Circle the ducks with the word **as** inside.

1. as
2. as
3. is
4. an
5. as
6. az

 **say the word out aloud as you trace it.**

out

Now practice writing the word once on each line.

The dog ran _____ the door.

Rhyme Time

Circle the pictures that rhyme with **out**. Underline the letters **o-u-t** in each word.

shout

coat

spout

pout

sprout

flute

snout

note

Review: Word Search

Find each word in the word search.

her   who   round   as   out

```
r   o   u   r   d
w   s   e   o   n
w   h   e   u   a
r   n   o   n   s
o   u   t   d   h
```

Color the column that has all five words spelled correctly.

1.	2.	3.	4.	5.
as	owt	her	round	who
who	her	rounb	out	as
out	round	as	vho	rounb
her	who	who	as	out
round	az	out	hir	hoo

Review: Story Code

Look for the review words as you read the story.
Follow the code each time you see a review word.

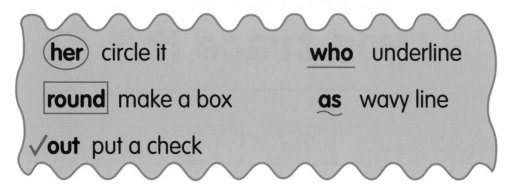

(her) circle it   **who** underline

[round] make a box   **as** wavy line

✓**out** put a check

On my sister's birthday, someone gave her a gift as a surprise.
They left it out on our front steps. The box was big and round.

"Who is it from?" my sister asked.

"It doesn't say who it's from," I told her.

Just as we were about to open it, a puppy jumped out of
the box! The puppy had big round eyes
and fur white as snow. He
licked her face and let out a
bark. He was as cute as could
be. We never found out who
gave her the puppy. We loved
it as one of the family.

from

say the word from aloud as you trace it.

from

Now practice writing the word once on each line.

I got a letter _____ Grandma.

Stay on Track

Find the word **from** on each track and circle it.

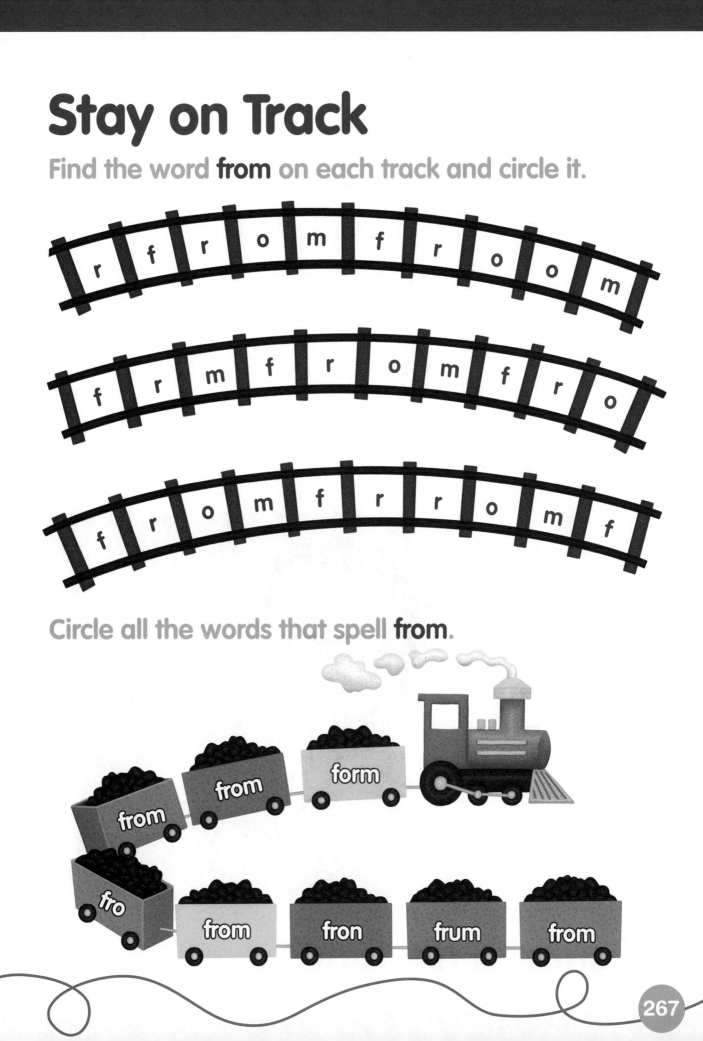

r f r o m f r r o o m

f r m f r o m f r o

f r o m f r r r o m f

Circle all the words that spell **from**.

from
from
form
fro
from
fron
frum
from

267

with say the word with aloud as you trace it.

Now practice writing the word once on each line.

I shared my lunch _____ him.

Out of Order

The letters for the word **with** are out of order! If the letters can be unscrambled to make the word **with**, write the word on the line. If not, leave it blank.

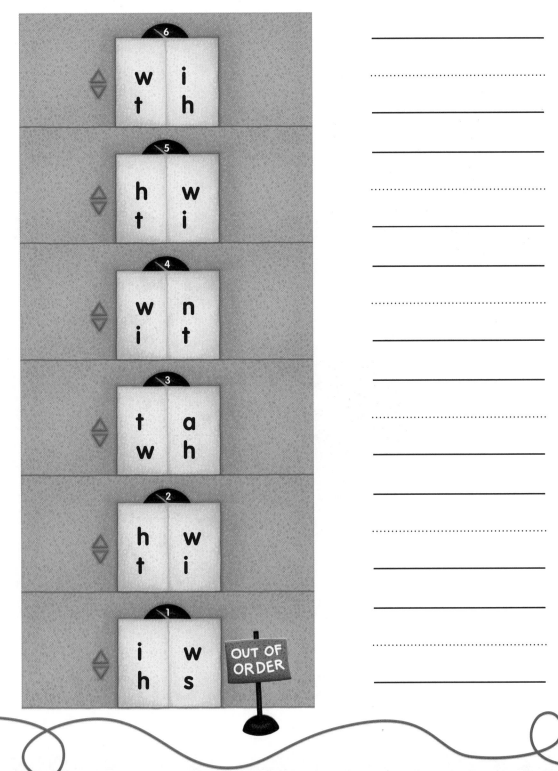

 **had**

say the word had aloud as you trace it.

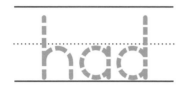

Now practice writing the word once on each line.

I ＿＿＿＿ pizza for dinner.

Tic-Tac-Toe

Circle the row that spells the word **had**.

a	h	a
d	a	d
h	d	h

Circle the row that has the word **had** three times.

had	had	had
had	had	hand
dad	bad	hod

 **thank**

say the word thank aloud as you trace it.

Now practice writing the word once on each line.

I want to _____ you for helping me.

The Finish Line

Draw a line to the flag with the letters that finish the word **thank**.

than

tha

t

th

nk

ank

k

hank

Do the letters in the flags make the word **thank**?
Circle Yes or No.

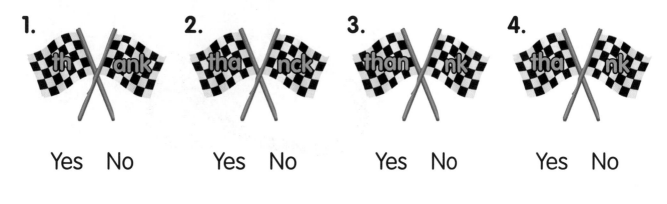

1. th ank

Yes   No

2. tha nck

Yes   No

3. than nk

Yes   No

4. tha nk

Yes   No

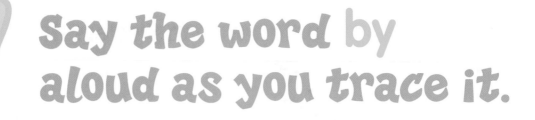

by

Say the word by aloud as you trace it.

by

Now practice writing the word once on each line.

My bag is _____ the chair.

Word Hunt

The word **by** is in the story five times. Hunt for the word and circle it each time it appears.

I lost my book. It's written by my favorite author. I can read the whole book by myself. I like to read it before I go to bed. By the time I find it, it will be too late to read it. I have to go to bed by eight o'clock. Maybe tomorrow I can buy a new book. Wait! I found it! It was right by my bed all along.

Circle the books with the word by inside.

1. by
2. buy
3. busy
4. dy
5. by
6. by

Review: Word Search

Find each word in the word search.

a   from   with   had   thank   by

i	w	i	t	h
f	h	b	h	i
r	i	h	a	d
o	m	a	n	r
m	b	y	k	f

Color the column that has all five words spelled correctly.

1.	2.	3.	4.	5.
bv	thank	with	had	from
thank	had	thanx	for	with
from	wifh	had	dy	had
with	by	fron	from	thank
hab	from	by	thank	by

Review: Black Out!

Read each sentence, then find the missing word in the boxes. Put an X through all the boxes that show the missing word.

A.

from	had
by	with

B.

with	thank
had	by

1. A new boy moved into the house _____ mine.

2. He moved here _____ Japan.

3. We asked him to have dinner _____ us.

4. We _____ a great dinner.

5. He gave us a gift to _____ us.

Which square has all its boxes marked off first? _____

Review: Riddle

Use the code to fill in the missing letters and answer the knock knock joke.

pretty: **t**	our: **i**	her: **i**	out: **e**
this: **n**	white: **c**	who: **s**	with: **u**
every: **t**	how: **n**	round: **m**	had: **h**
saw: **J**	some: **u**	as: **l**	

Knock knock.
Who's there?

____ ____ ____ ____ ____ ____.
saw   some   who   every   our   how

____ ____ ____ ____ ____ ____ who?
saw   some   who   every   our   how

____ ____ ____ ____ ____ ____
saw   some   who   every   our   how

____ ____ ____ ____
pretty   her   round   out

for ____ ____ ____ ____ ____ !
      as   with   this   white   had

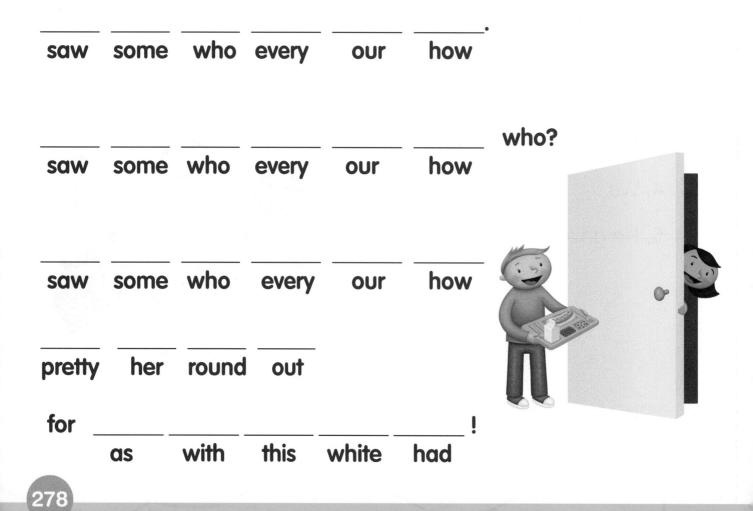

Review: Race

Look at each set of boxes. Find the word whose letters fit in the boxes.

of	she	want	from	again
by	now	give	well	thank

1. of

2. ⬚⬚⬚

3. ⬚⬚

4. ⬚⬚⬚⬚

5. ⬚⬚⬚

6. ⬚⬚⬚⬚

7. ⬚⬚⬚⬚

8. ⬚⬚⬚⬚

9. ⬚⬚⬚⬚⬚

10. ⬚⬚⬚⬚⬚

Level C

The sight words included in this section are:

an	found	made	put	think
ask	gave	many	read	those
been	goes	may	right	use
best	green	off	sit	very
buy	has	old	sleep	walk
cold	his	once	stop	warm
does	its	open	take	wash
don't	jump	or	tell	were
first	just	over	them	when
five	know	own	then	why
fly	live	pull	these	your

fly

say the word fly aloud as you trace it.

fly

Now practice writing the word once on each line.

The bird can _____.

Keep on Track

Look for the word **fly** in each track. Circle it each time you see it. Then count the number of circled words in each track and write it in the sign.

f l i f l y f l y l

f l y l f y f y l y

y f l y f l y f l y

fly   fli   fly   fwy   tly   fly   fly   fiy

found

say the word found aloud as you trace it.

found

Now practice writing the word once on each line.

I _____ the key.

Maze Craze

Help the dog find its way through the maze. Connect the letters f-o-u-n-d to make the word found.

 **very** say the word **very** aloud as you trace it.

Now practice writing the word once on each line.

It is _____ cold.

Solve the Puzzle

Circle the puzzle pieces that have the word **very** inside. Put an X through the other puzzle pieces. Use the code inside the circled puzzle pieces to solve the word puzzle below.

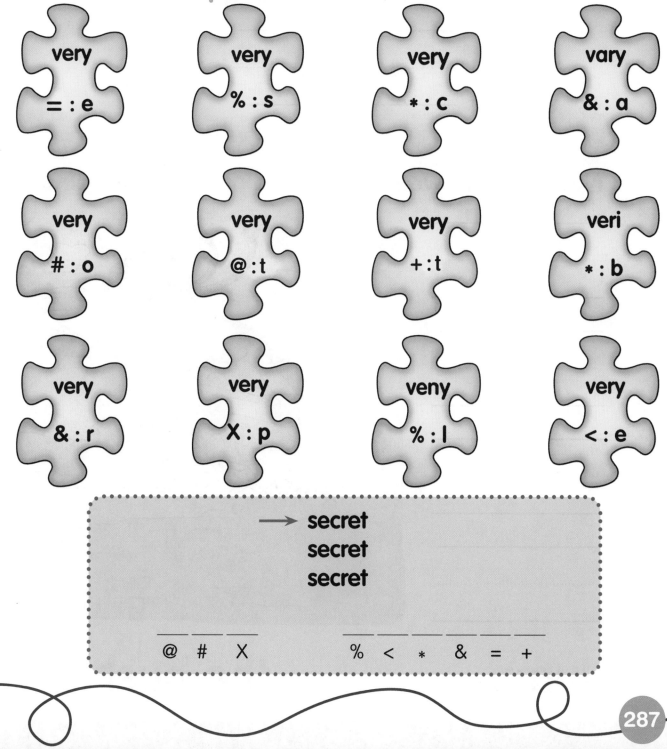

very = : e

very % : s

very * : c

vary & : a

very # : o

very @ : t

very + : t

veri * : b

very & : r

very X : p

veny % : l

very < : e

→ secret
secret
secret

___ ___ ___   ___ ___ ___ ___ ___ ___
@   #   X   %   <   *   &   =   +

 **say the word over aloud as you trace it.**

over

Now practice writing the word once on each line.

Jump _____ the bush.

Target Words

Circle the words that have **over** hidden inside.
Underline the letters **o-v-e-r** in each circled word.

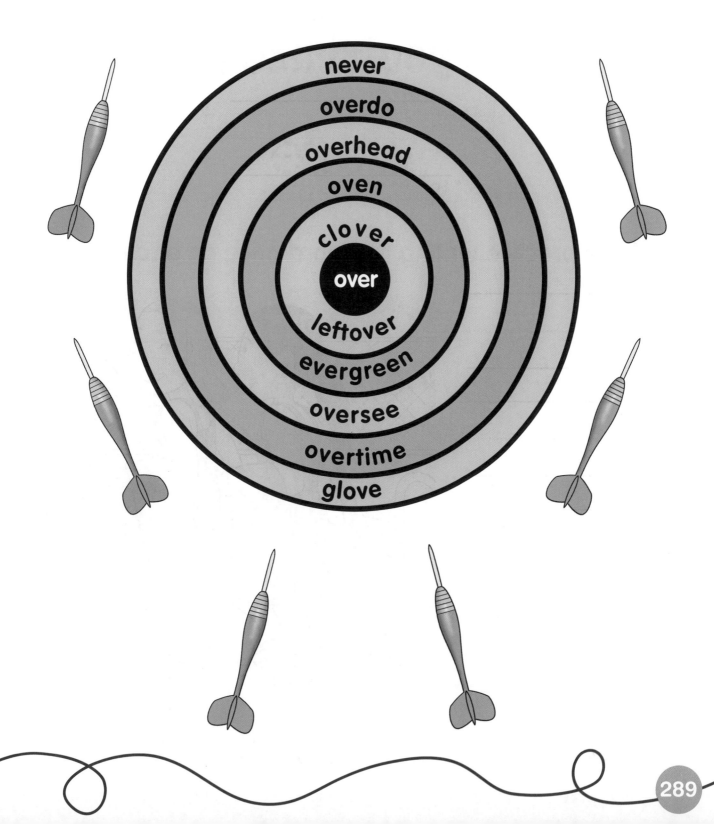

never
overdo
overhead
oven
clover
over
leftover
evergreen
oversee
overtime
glove

 **were** **say the word were aloud as you trace it.**

‾‾‾‾‾‾‾‾‾‾‾‾‾‾‾‾

were

Now practice writing the word once on each line.

We _____ at the pool.

Q Versus A

Circle the word **were** every time it appears. When you circle the word **were** in a question, give the Q Team a point. When you circle the word **were** in an answer, give the A Team a point. See how many points the Qs and As get!

Q: Were Bill and Tim at school today? **A:** Yes, they were both at school.	**Q:** Why were you cold? **A:** I didn't wear my coat.
Q: What were you doing at the park? **A:** We were having a picnic.	**Q:** Where were you today? **A:** I was at work.

Q: A:

Review: Crossword Puzzle!

Use the sentence clues below to solve the crossword puzzle.

fly   found   very   over   were

Across

1. We _____ it under the bed.

3. The bug is _____ small.

4. The bird flew _____ my head.

Down

1. Airplanes can _____ very high.

2. Yesterday, we _____ at the zoo.

Review: Black Out!

Read each sentence, and find the missing word in the boxes. Put an X through all the boxes that show the missing word.

A.

very	were
found	fly

B.

fly	over
very	were

1. We decided to _____ our kite at the park.

2. It was _____ windy, so our kite blew away.

3. The wind carried it high _____ the tree tops.

4. Our kite was gone and we _____ upset.

5. We _____ the kite stuck in a tree.

Which square has all of its boxes marked off first? _____

 **Say the word cold aloud as you trace it.**

cold

Now practice writing the word once on each line.

The ice is _____.

Sport Search

Find the word **cold** three times in the word search.

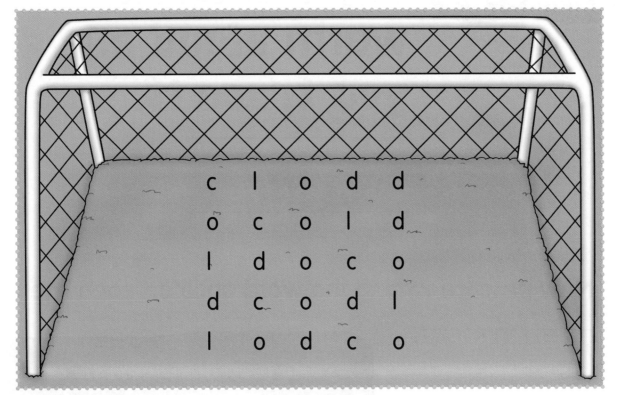

```
c   l   o   d   d
o   c   o   l   d
l   d   o   c   o
d   c   o   d   l
l   o   d   c   o
```

Cross out all the soccer balls that don't show the word **cold**.

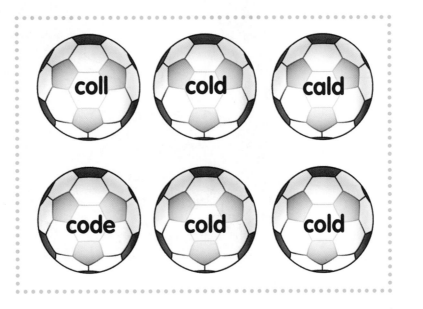

coll   cold   cald

code   cold   cold

warm

say the word **warm** aloud as you trace it.

warm

Now practice writing the word once on each line.

The fire is _____.

Scrambled Eggs

Look at the eggs inside each nest. Can the letters be unscrambled to make the word **warm**? If they can, write **warm** on the line. If not, leave the line blank.

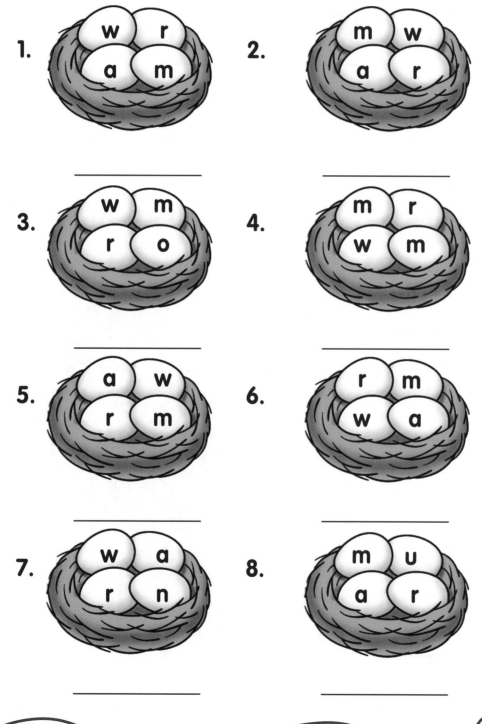

1.
2.
3.
4.
5.
6.
7.
8.

once

Say the word **once** aloud as you trace it.

once

Now practice writing the word once on each line.

I drink milk _____ a day.

Match Patch

Look at the letters in each wheelbarrow and find the matching pumpkin to complete the word **once**. As you draw lines to the pumpkins, see which letters you pass through. Write the letters below to answer the riddle.

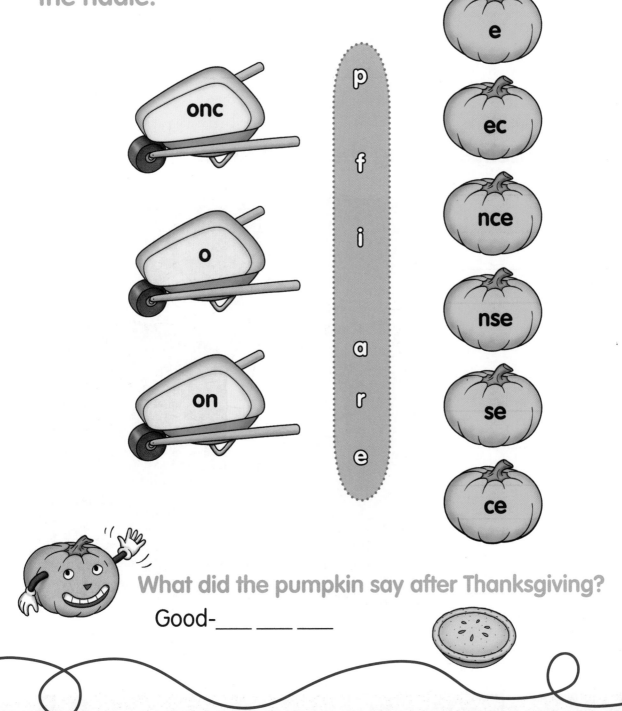

What did the pumpkin say after Thanksgiving?

Good-___ ___ ___

been

say the word
been aloud as
you trace it.

been

Now practice writing the word once on each line.

I've _____ to the moon.

Word Hunt

The word **been** is in the story five times. Hunt for the word and circle it each time it appears. Then circle the chairs with the word **been** inside.

We've been playing hide and seek today. I hid under a chair. I had to bend down very low. Nobody has been able to find me. They have been looking for a long time. Everyone else has been found. Finally, somebody looked beneath the chair. I've been found too!

1. been
2. bene
3. beep
4. heen
5. been
6. been

 **old**

Say the word old aloud as you trace it.

old

Now practice writing the word once on each line.

I am eight years _____.

Ring Around the Rhyme

Draw a line to the words that rhyme with **old**.
Underline the letters **o-l-d** in each word.

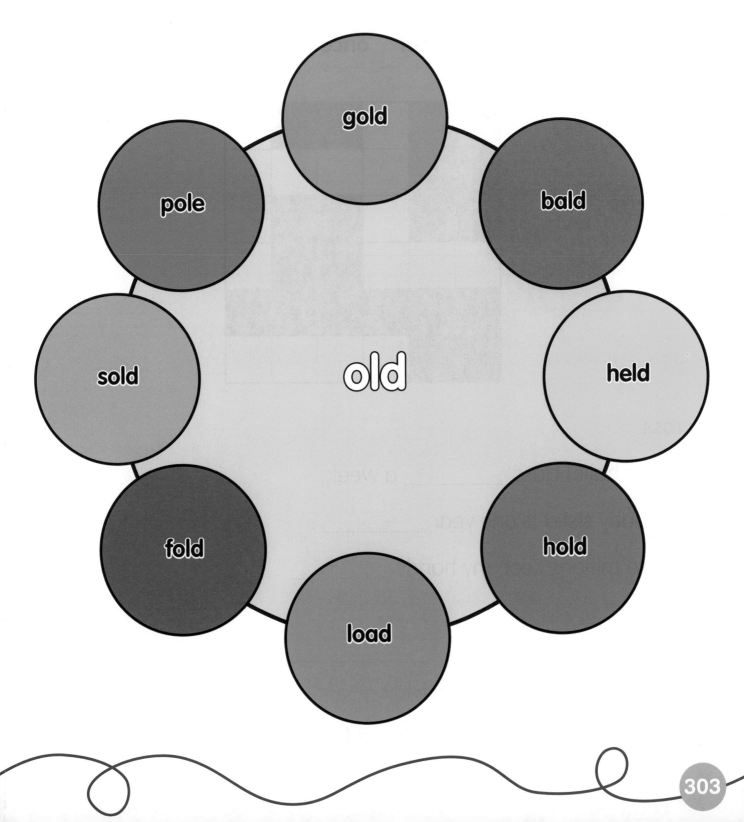

Review: Crossword Puzzle!

Use the sentence clues below to solve the crossword puzzle.

cold   warm   once   been   old

Across

3. I have ballet class _____ a week.

4. My baby sister is one year _____ .

5. These mittens keep my hands _____ .

Down

1. It's rainy and _____ outside.

2. I've never _____ to the Grand Canyon.

Review: High Five

Look for the review words as you read the sentences inside each box. Put a check in the box that uses all five review words.

☐ **1.** I've been to see the snow once. I was six years old. I wore warm clothes, but I was still cold!

☐ **2.** I've been visiting my grandma once a week. She's very old. I bring her warm soup.

☐ **3.** I've been sick with a cold all week. I feel warm and dizzy. I take a pill once a day.

☐ **4.** Once I visited an old house. It had been empty for a long time. It was cold inside.

 **say the word his aloud as you trace it.**

his

Now practice writing the word once on each line.

This is _____ ball.

Keep on Track

Look for the word **his** in each track. Circle it each time you see it. Then count the number of circled words in each track and write it in the sign.

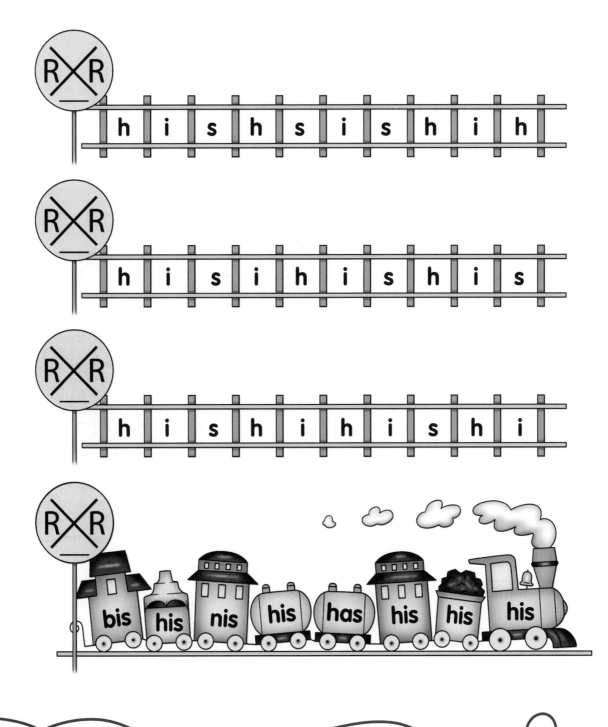

h i s h s i s h i h

h i s i h i s h i s

h i s h i h i s h i

bis his nis his has his his his

say the word
these **aloud as
you trace it.**

these

Now practice writing the word once on each line.

I got _____ at the beach.

Maze Craze

Help the bird find its way through the maze. Connect the letters t-h-e-s-e to make the word these.

goes

say the word
goes aloud as
you trace it.

_____

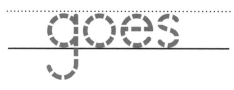

Now practice writing the word once on each line.

My bike _____ very fast.

Solve the Puzzle

Circle the puzzle pieces that have the word **goes** inside. Put an X through the other puzzle pieces. Use the code inside the circled puzzle pieces to solve the word puzzle below.

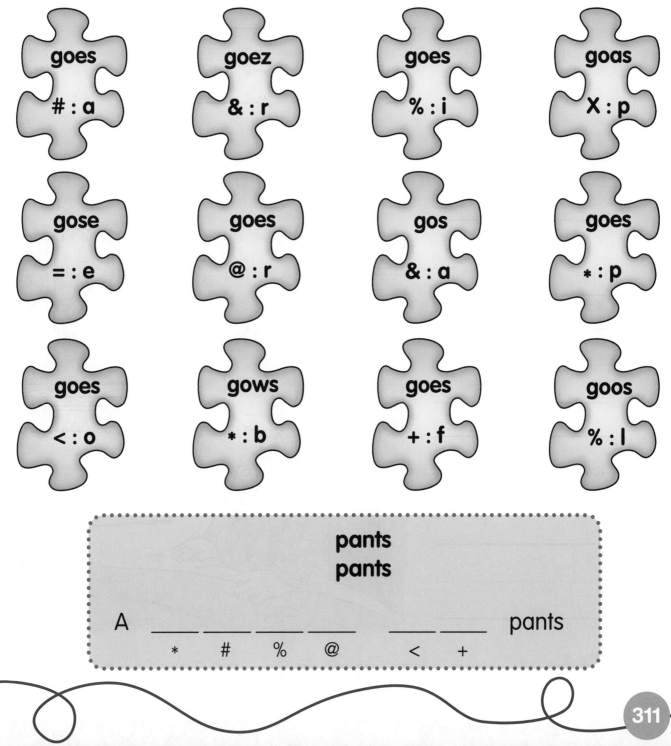

goes # : a

goez & : r

goes % : i

goas X : p

gose = : e

goes @ : r

gos & : a

goes * : p

goes < : o

gows * : b

goes + : f

goos % : l

pants
pants

A ___ ___ ___ ___ ___ ___ pants
       *   #   %   @   <   +

 **sleep**

Say the word sleep aloud as you trace it.

sleep

Now practice writing the word once on each line.

It's time to go to _____.

Target Words

Circle the words that have **sleep** hidden inside.
Underline the letters **s-l-e-e-p** in each circled word.

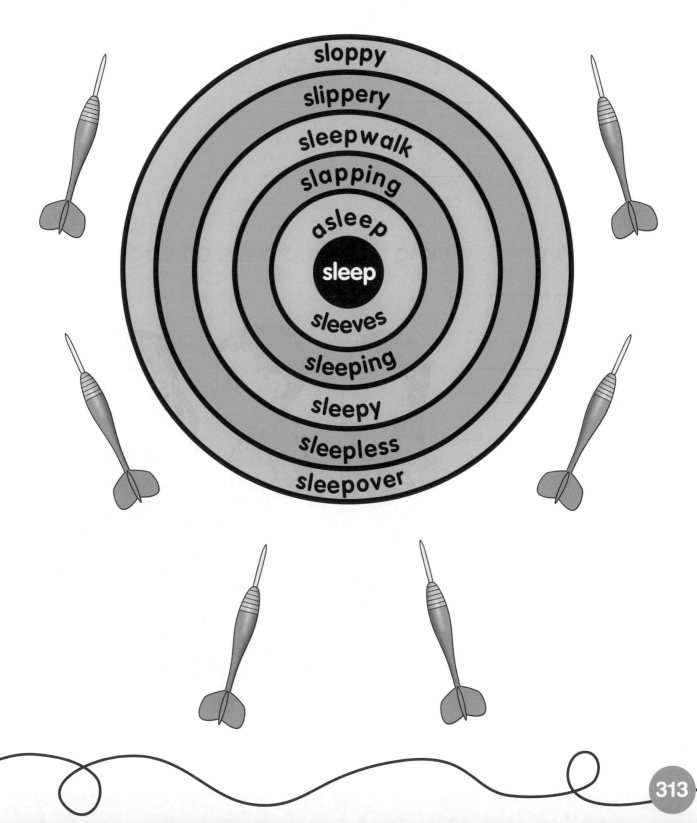

sloppy

slippery

sleepwalk

slapping

asleep

sleep

sleeves

sleeping

sleepy

sleepless

sleepover

**first**

say the word
first aloud as
you trace it.

first

Now practice writing the word once on each line.

I am _____ in line.

Q Versus A

Circle the word **first** every time it appears. When you circle the word **first** in a question, give the Q Team a point. When you circle the word **first** in an answer, give the A Team a point. See how many points the Qs and As get!

Q: What is your first name?

A: My first name is Kim.

Q: Who was first in line?

A: She was in line first.

Q: Is it time for us to eat lunch?

A: Yes, but first we need to wash our hands.

Q: Can I try the new toy first?

A: First your little brother gets a turn.

Review: Crossword Puzzle!

Use the sentence clues below to solve the crossword puzzle.

his   these   goes   sleep   first

Across

1. I want to have the _____ turn!

3. We found _____ coins on the floor.

5. My sister _____ to bed at eight o'clock.

Down

2. I like to _____ with my teddy bear.

4. He gave me _____ pencil.

Review: Black Out!

Read each sentence, and find the missing word in the boxes. Put an X through all the boxes that show the missing word.

A.

these	goes
sleep	his

B.

goes	first
his	sleep

1. I like to _____ in late.

2. My dad is the _____ one to wake up.

3. He _____ to get fresh muffins.

4. Banana muffins are _____ favorite.

5. We eat _____ for breakfast.

Which square has all of its boxes marked off first? _____

 **your**

say the word your aloud as you trace it.

 your

Now practice writing the word once on each line.

Is this _____ **dollar?**

Sport Search

Find the word **your** three times in the word search. Then cross out all the baseballs that don't show the word **your**.

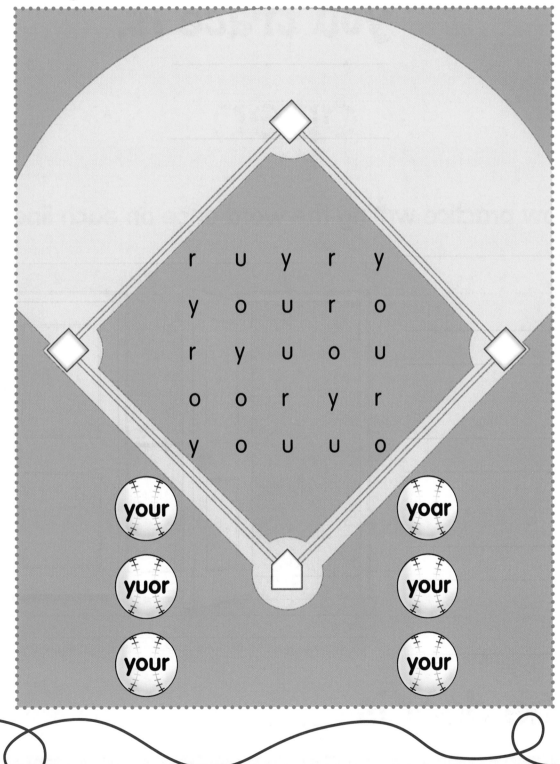

r u y r y
y o u r o
r y u o u
o o r y r
y o u u o

your   yoar

yuor   your

your   your

 **open**

say the word open aloud as you trace it.

Now practice writing the word once on each line.

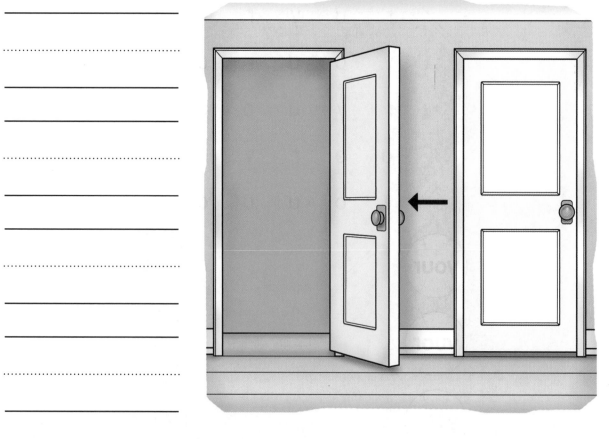

The door is _____.

Scrambled Eggs

Look at the eggs inside each nest. Can the letters be unscrambled to make the word **open**? If they can, write **open** on the line. If not, leave the line blank.

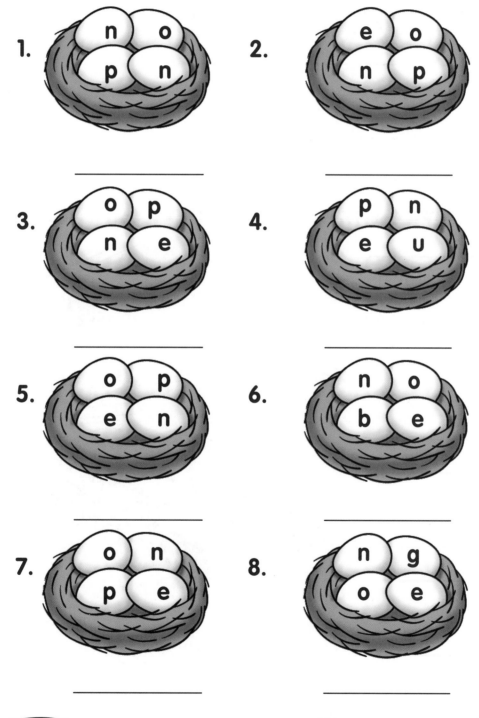

1. n o p n
_____

2. e o n p
_____

3. o p n e
_____

4. p n e u
_____

5. o p e n
_____

6. n o b e
_____

7. o n p e
_____

8. n g o e
_____

 **Say the word stop aloud as you trace it.**

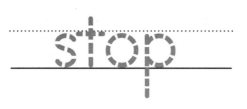

Now practice writing the word once on each line.

You must _____ at the red light.

Match Patch

Look at the letters in each wheelbarrow and find the matching pumpkin to complete the word stop. As you draw lines to the pumpkins, see which letters you pass through. Write the letters below to answer the riddle.

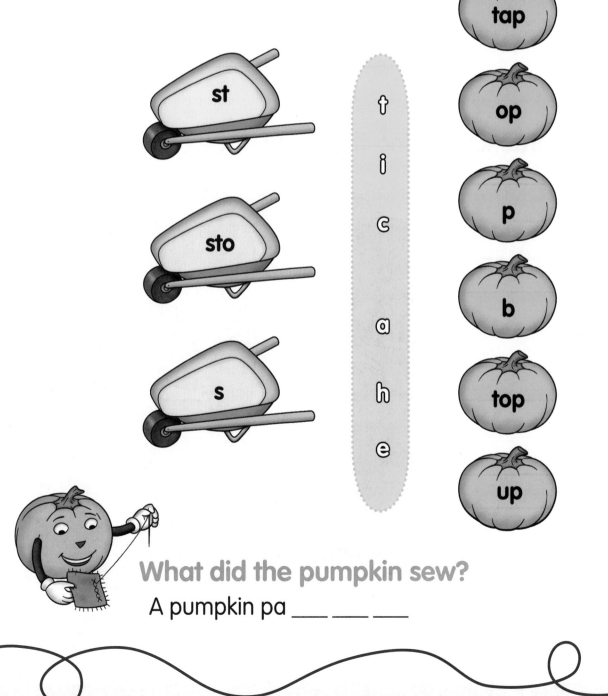

What did the pumpkin sew?

A pumpkin pa ___ ___ ___

 **say the word don't aloud as you trace it.**

don't

Now practice writing the word once on each line.

Please _____ step on the flowers

Word Hunt

The word **don't** is in the story five times. Hunt for the word and circle it each time it appears. Then circle the bills with the word **don't** inside.

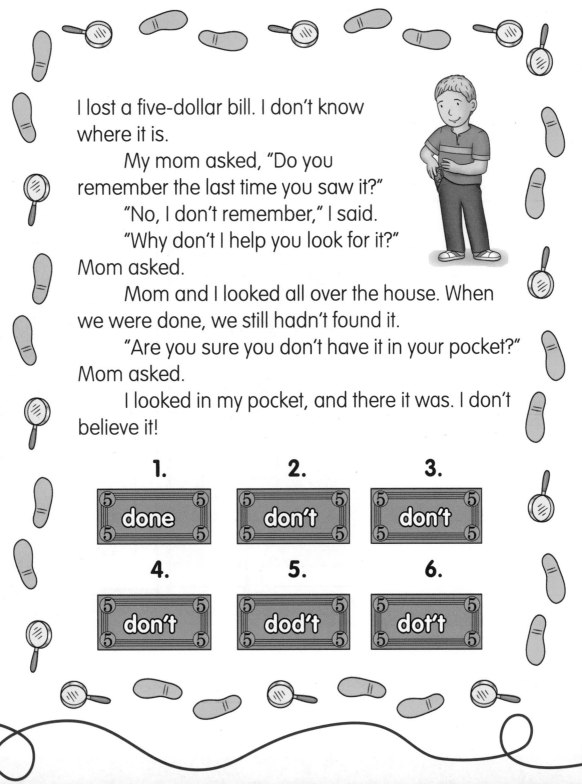

I lost a five-dollar bill. I don't know where it is.

My mom asked, "Do you remember the last time you saw it?"

"No, I don't remember," I said.

"Why don't I help you look for it?" Mom asked.

Mom and I looked all over the house. When we were done, we still hadn't found it.

"Are you sure you don't have it in your pocket?" Mom asked.

I looked in my pocket, and there it was. I don't believe it!

1. done

2. don't

3. don't

4. don't

5. dod't

6. dot't

own say the word **own** aloud as you trace it.

own

Now practice writing the word once on each line.

ANN'S ROOM

I have my _____ room.

Ring Around the Rhyme

Draw a line to the words that rhyme with **own**.
Underline the letters **o-w-n** in each word.

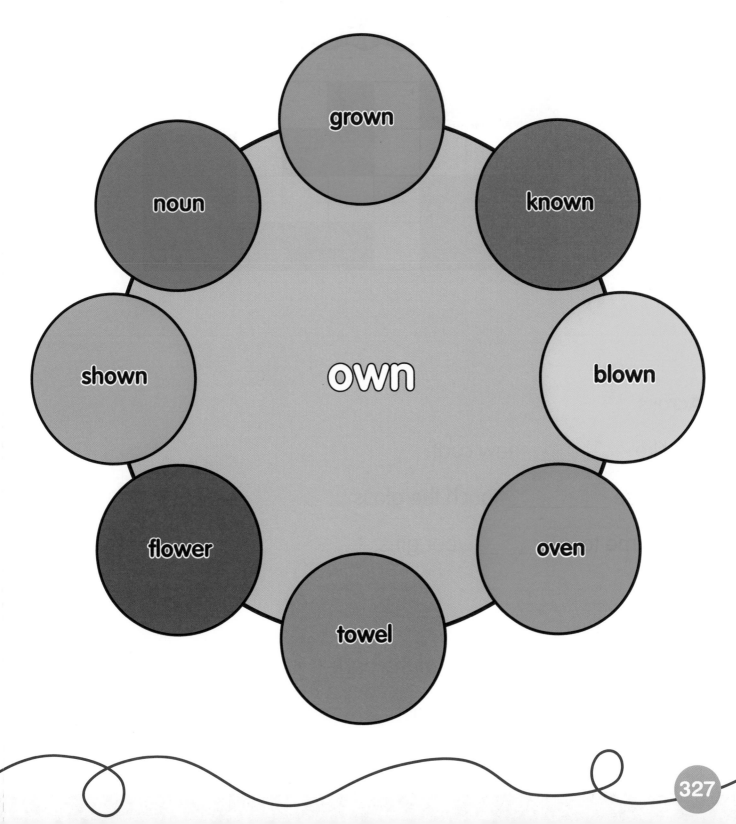

grown

noun

known

shown

own

blown

flower

oven

towel

Review: Crossword Puzzle!

Use the sentence clues below to solve the crossword puzzle.

your   open   stop   don't   own

Across

2. I like _____ new coat!

4. Please _____ touch the glass.

5. It's time to _____ your gifts.

Down

1. Let's _____ and play at the park.

3. I brought my _____ lunch.

Review: High Five

Look for the review words as you read the sentences inside each box. Put a check in the box that uses all five review words.

1. Please don't open your door. Wait until we stop the car.

2. Can I use your scissors to open this box? I don't own any scissors.

3. Why don't you stop talking and open your own book?

4. Don't stop at the park on the way home. You will be late for your piano lesson.

 **may** say the word may aloud as you trace it.

may

Now practice writing the word once on each line.

_____ I have some milk?

Keep on Track

Look for the word **may** in each track. Circle it each time you see it. Then count the number of circled words in each track and write it in the sign.

 **think**

say the word think aloud as you trace it.

think

Now practice writing the word once on each line.

I need to _____ about it.

Maze Craze

Help the monkey find its way through the maze.
Connect the letters **t-h-i-n-k** to make the word **think**.

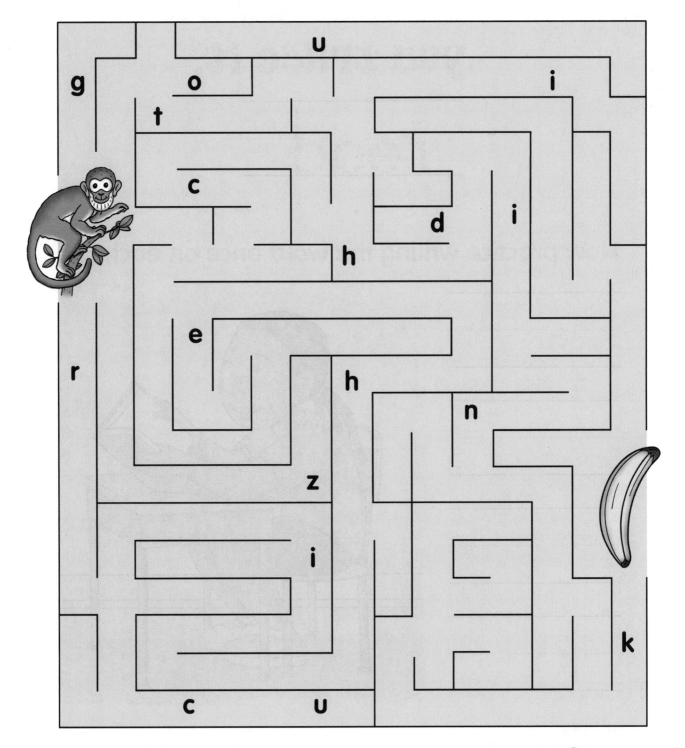

read

Say the word **read** aloud as you trace it.

read

Now practice writing the word once on each line.

I like to _____ books.

Solve the Puzzle

Circle the puzzle pieces that have the word **read** inside. Put an X through the other puzzle pieces. Use the code inside the circled puzzle pieces to solve the word puzzle below.

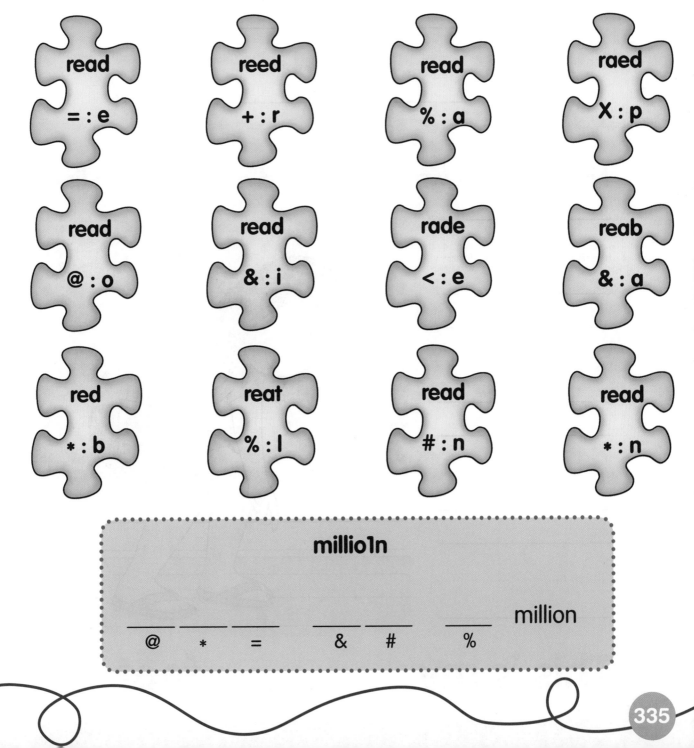

read	reed	read	raed
= : e	+ : r	% : a	X : p

read	read	rade	reab
@ : o	& : i	< : e	& : a

red	reat	read	read
* : b	% : l	# : n	* : n

millio1n

___ ___ ___   ___ ___ ___ million
@   *   =   &   #   %

335

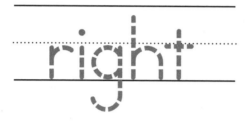 **right** **say the word right aloud as you trace it.**

right

Now practice writing the word once on each line.

This is my _____ foot.

Target Words

Circle the words that have right hidden inside.
Underline the letters r-i-g-h-t in each circled word.

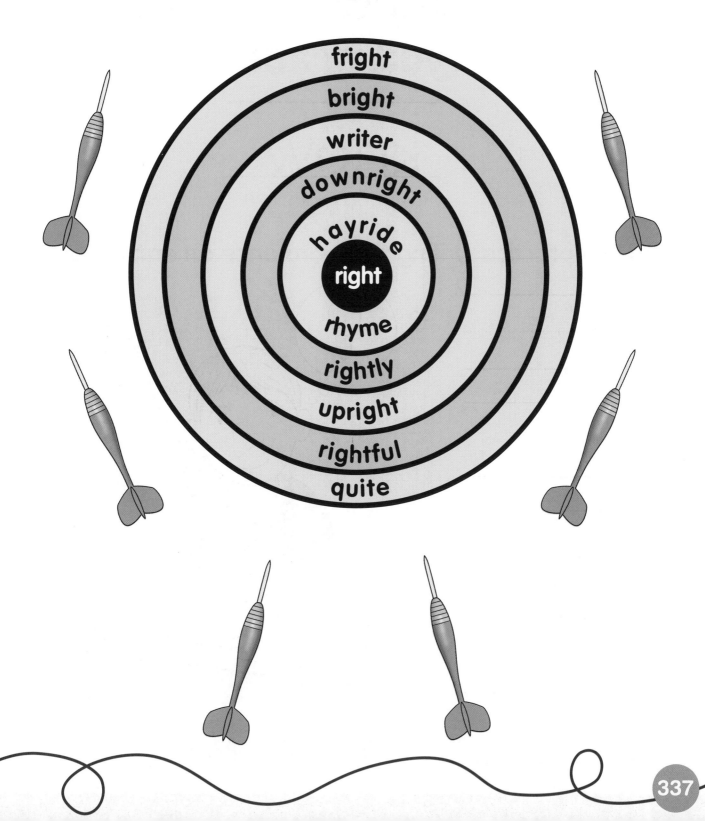

fright
bright
writer
downright
hayride
right
rhyme
rightly
upright
rightful
quite

**know**

say the word **know** aloud as you trace it.

know

Now practice writing the word once on each line.

I _____ the answer.

Q Versus A

Circle the word **know** every time it appears. When you circle the word **know** in a question, give the Q Team a point. When you circle the word **know** in an answer, give the A Team a point. See how many points the Qs and As get!

Q: Do you know how to swim?

A: I know how to swim very well.

Q: Have you met Chris before?

A: Yes, we already know each other.

Q: How do you know Susan?

A: I know her from my class.

Q: Which way is the park?

A: I don't know.

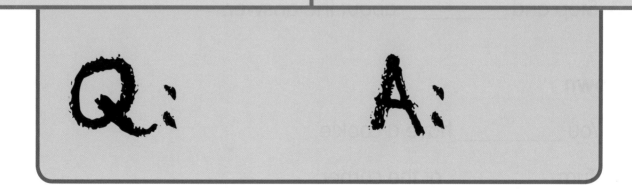

Q: A:

Review: Crossword Puzzle!

Use the sentence clues below to solve the crossword puzzle.

may   think   read   right   know

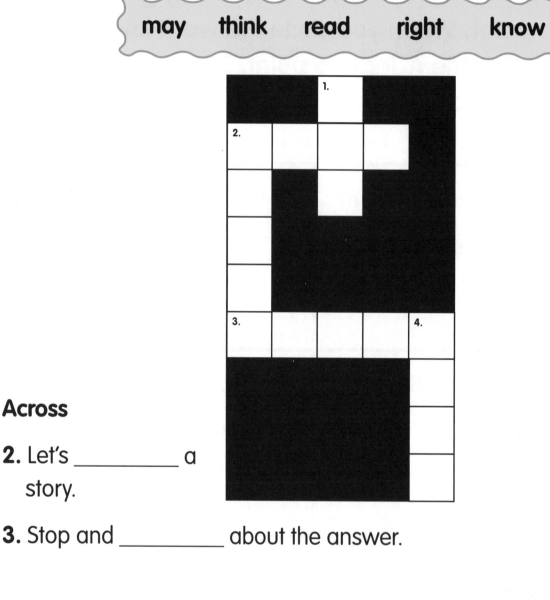

Across

2. Let's _____ a story.

3. Stop and _____ about the answer.

Down

1. You _____ have a cookie.

2. Turn _____ at the corner.

4. I _____ how to ride a bike.

Review: Black Out!

Read each sentence, and find the missing word in the boxes. Put an X through all the boxes that show the missing word.

A.

may	read
think	right

B.

read	think
right	know

1. Mom said I _____ go to the library.

2. It is _____ around the corner.

3. I like to _____ new books.

4. I _____ I have read almost every book there.

5. The more I read, the more I will _____ !

Which square has all of its boxes marked off first? _____

 **say the word sit aloud as you trace it.**

sit

Now practice writing the word once on each line.

Please _____ down.

Sport Search

Find the word **sit** three times in the word search.

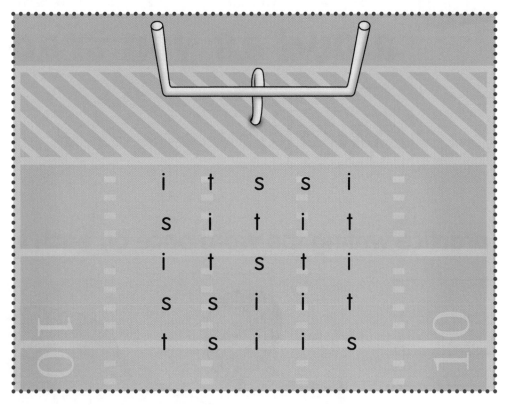

i t s s i
s i t i t
i t s t i
s s i i t
t s i i s

Cross out all the footballs that don't show the word **sit**.

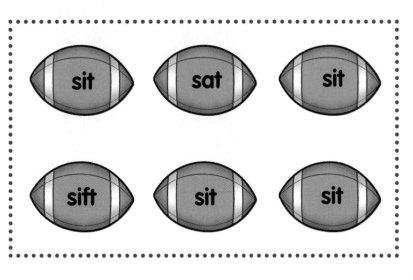

sit   sat   sit

sift   sit   sit

walk say the word walk aloud as you trace it.

walk

Now practice writing the word once on each line.

I like to _____ with my dog.

Scrambled Eggs

Look at the eggs inside each nest. Can the letters be unscrambled to make the word **walk**? If they can, write **walk** on the line. If not, leave the line blank.

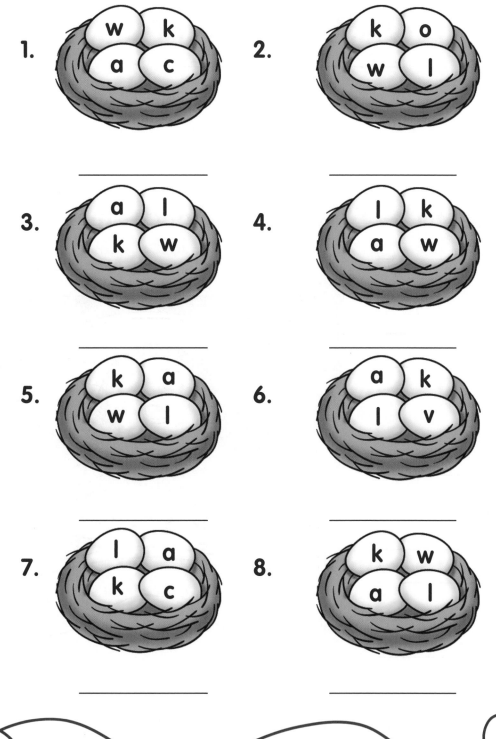

1. w k a c _____

2. k o w l _____

3. a l k w _____

4. l k a w _____

5. k a w l _____

6. a k l v _____

7. l a k c _____

8. k w a l _____

just say the word **just** aloud as you trace it.

just

Now practice writing the word once on each line.

I _____ woke up.

346

Match Patch

Look at the letters in each wheelbarrow and find the matching pumpkin to complete the word **just**. As you draw lines to the pumpkins, see which letters you pass through. Write the letters below to answer the riddle.

What do you call a chubby pumpkin?

A p___ ___ ___ pkin

 **then** say the word **then** aloud as you trace it.

Now practice writing the word once on each line.

It rained, _____ the sun came out.

Word Hunt

The word **then** is in the story five times. Hunt for the word and circle it each time it appears. Then circle the tents with the word **then** inside.

My family likes to camp more than anything. Last time we camped, I lost my flashlight. I looked in our tent, then I looked outside. It was so dark, I bumped into my dad! Then we both bumped into my mom.

"If we had a flashlight, then we could find our way!" I told them.

"We don't need a flashlight," Dad said. Then he lit a match to give us light.

We found our way back to the tent. Only then did we find the flashlight. It was inside my sleeping bag!

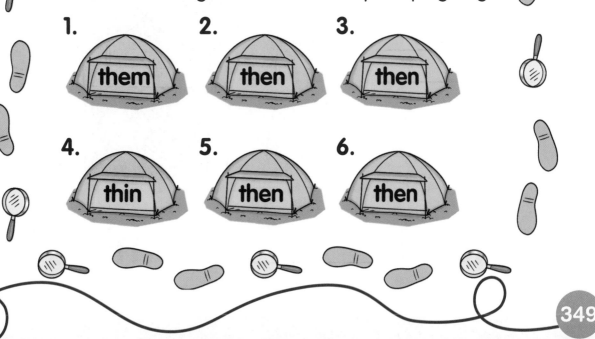

1. them

2. then

3. then

4. thin

5. then

6. then

 **Say the word an
aloud as you trace it.**

_____

⋯⋯⋯an⋯⋯⋯

Now practice writing the word once on each line.

I need _____ umbrella.

Ring Around the Rhyme

Draw a line to the words that rhyme with an.
Underline the letters a-n in each word.

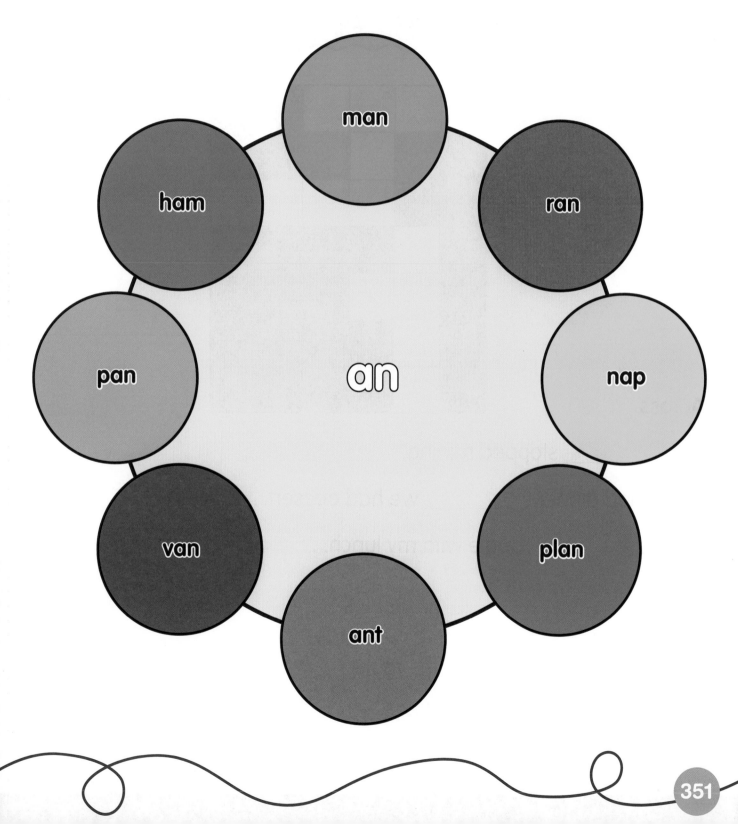

Review: Crossword Puzzle!

Use the sentence clues below to solve the crossword puzzle.

then   just   an   walk   sit

Across

1. It _____ stopped raining.

3. We had dinner, _____ we had dessert.

5. I ate _____ apple with my lunch.

Down

2. Let's _____ down at the table.

4. I like to _____ along the beach.

Review: High Five

Look for the review words as you read the sentences inside each box. Put a check in the box that uses all five review words.

1. Find an empty chair and sit down. Then we will start the movie.

2. If I don't have an egg, then I can't bake cookies. I'll just walk to the store and buy one.

3. I was just about to go on a walk. Then Mom told me to sit down and do an art project.

4. The bus was an hour late. I was just about to walk home!

Review: ABC Gumballs

Write the review words in alphabetical order.

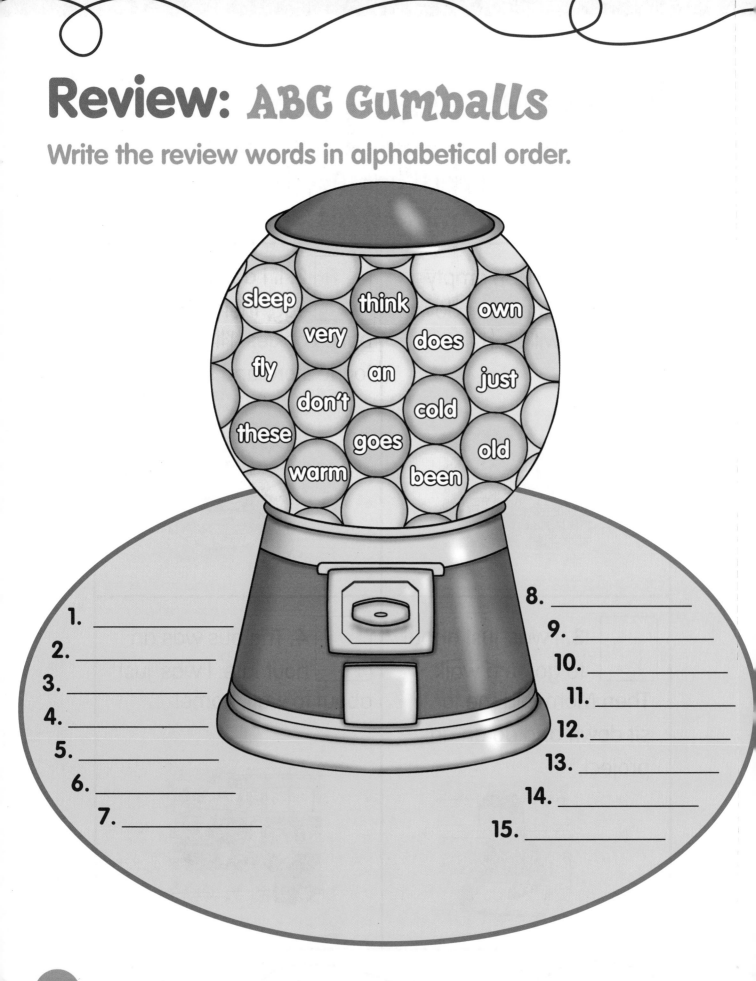

sleep · think · own · very · does · fly · an · just · don't · cold · these · goes · old · warm · been

1. _____

2. _____

3. _____

4. _____

5. _____

6. _____

7. _____

8. _____

9. _____

10. _____

11. _____

12. _____

13. _____

14. _____

15. _____

Review: Super Sentences

Use the review words to complete the sentences.

1. You _____ have the toy _____ , and _____ it's _____ turn.

his   **may**

first   **then**

2. I try to _____ down and _____ a story _____ a day.

read   **sit**   **once**

3. To get to the park, _____ to the _____ sign at the corner. Turn _____ and go _____ the bridge.

right   **stop**

over   **walk**

4. I _____ the keys that _____ the door. They _____ under _____ coat.

were   **found**

your   **open**

 **buy** **say the word buy aloud as you trace it.**

Now practice writing the word once on each line.

I'd like to _____ some milk.

Keep on Track

Look for the word **buy** in each track. Circle it each time you see it. Then count the number of circled words in each track and write it in the sign.

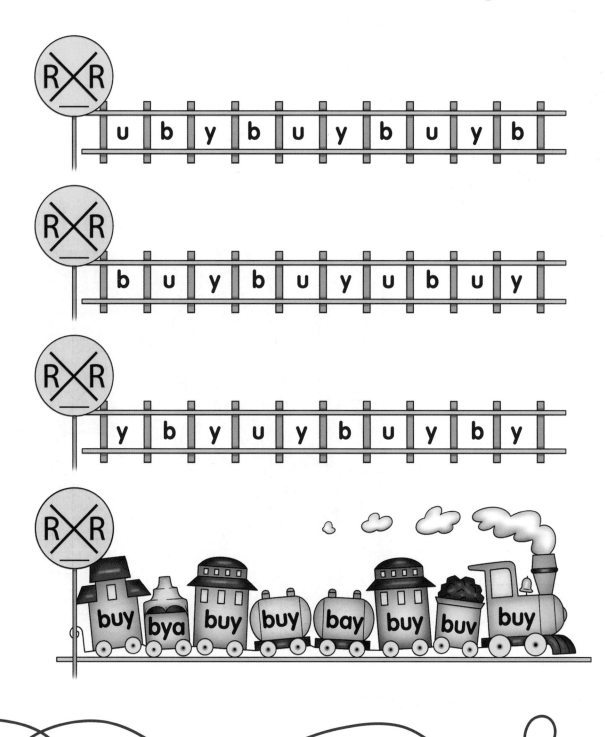

u b y b u y b u y b

b u y b u y u b u y

y b y u y b u y b y

buy bya buy buy bay buy buv buy

 **those** say the word those aloud as you trace it.

those

Now practice writing the word once on each line.

I want to wear _____ shoes.

Maze Craze

Help the bear find its way through the maze. Connect the letters t-h-o-s-e to make the word those.

 **Say the word many aloud as you trace it.**

_____

many

Now practice writing the word once on each line.

How _____ apples do I have?

Solve the Puzzle

Circle the puzzle pieces that have the word **many** inside. Put an X through the other puzzle pieces. Use the code inside the circled puzzle pieces to solve the word puzzle below.

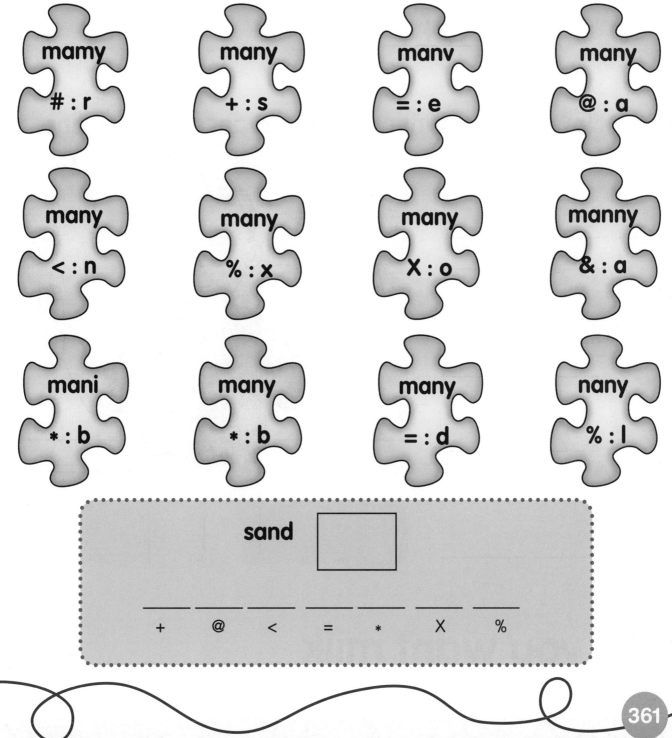

mamy
: r

many
+ : s

manv
= : e

many
@ : a

many
< : n

many
% : x

many
X : o

manny
& : a

mani
* : b

many
* : b

many
= : d

nany
% : l

sand ☐

___ ___ ___ ___ ___ ___ ___
\+ @ < = * X %

or Say the word **or** aloud as you trace it.

or

Now practice writing the word once on each line.

Do you want milk _____ juice?

Target Words

Circle the words that have **or** hidden inside.
Underline the letters **o-r** in each circled word.

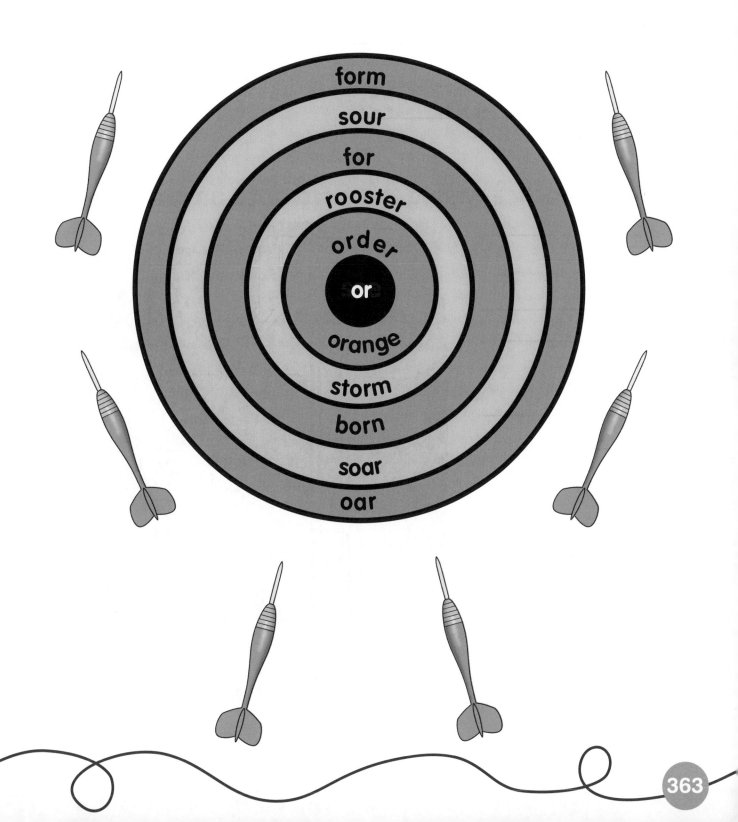

form
sour
for
rooster
order
or
orange
storm
born
soar
oar

 **say the word** does
aloud as you trace it.

does

Now practice writing the word once on each line.

When _____ the mail come?

Q Versus A

Circle the word does every time it appears. When you circle the word does in a question, give the Q Team a point. When you circle the word does in an answer, give the A Team a point. See how many points the Qs and As get!

Q: Where does Mom keep the cookies?

A: She keeps them in the jar.

Q: Does Emily know how to swim?

A: Yes, she does.

Q: How does your dad wash the car?

A: He does it with a hose.

Q: When does the mall open?

A: It opens at 10:00 AM.

Review: Crossword Puzzle!

Use the sentence clues below to solve the crossword puzzle.

buy   those   many   or   does

Across

2. Do you want the blue _____ the red one?

3. When _____ lunch time start?

5. How _____ kids are in this class?

Down

1. Please pass me _____ books.

4. We _____ milk at the market.

Review: Black Out!

Read each sentence, and find the missing word in the boxes. Put an X through all the boxes that show the missing word.

A.

buy	those
many	or

B.

or	many
does	buy

1. What _____ everyone want for dessert?

2. Let's go _____ some ice cream.

3. Do you want a cone _____ a cup?

4. How _____ scoops do you want?

5. Please pass us _____ napkins!

Which square has all of its boxes marked off first? _____

 **why** say the word **why** aloud as you trace it.

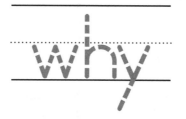

Now practice writing the word once on each line.

I don't know _____ the sky is blue.

Sport Search

Find the word **why** three times in the word search.

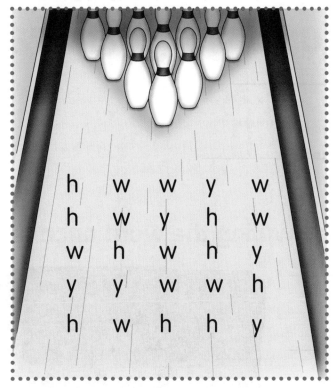

h w w y w
h w y h w
w h w h y
y y w w h
h w h h y

Cross out all the bowling balls that don't show the word **why**.

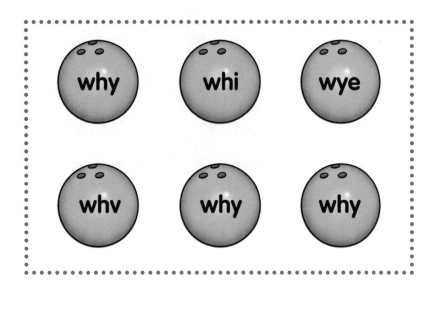

why   whi   wye

whv   why   why

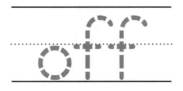 **Say the word off aloud as you trace it.**

off

Now practice writing the word once on each line.

Turn the lights _____, please.

Scrambled Eggs

Look at the eggs inside each nest. Can the letters be unscrambled to make the word **off**? If they can, write **off** on the line. If not, leave the line blank.

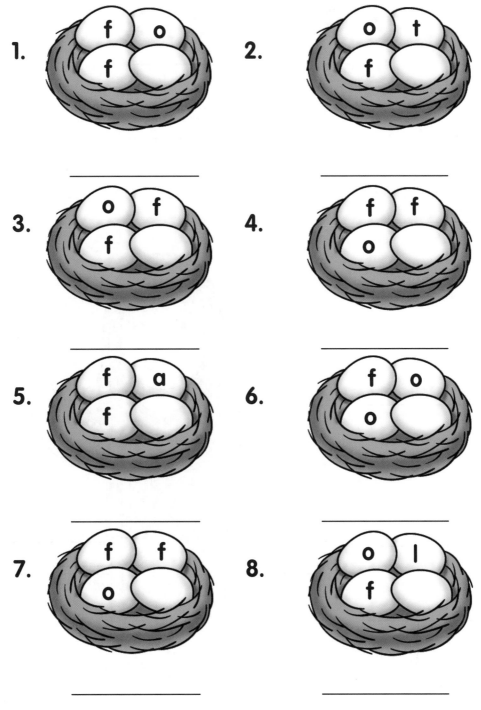

1. f o f

_____

2. o t f

_____

3. o f f

_____

4. f f o

_____

5. f a f

_____

6. f o o

_____

7. f f o

_____

8. o l f

_____

 **five**

say the word
five aloud as
you trace it.

five

Now practice writing the word once on each line.

I have _____ fingers on
this hand.

Match Patch

Look at the letters in each wheelbarrow and find the matching pumpkin to complete the word **five**. As you draw lines to the pumpkins, see which letters you pass through. Write the letters below to answer the riddle.

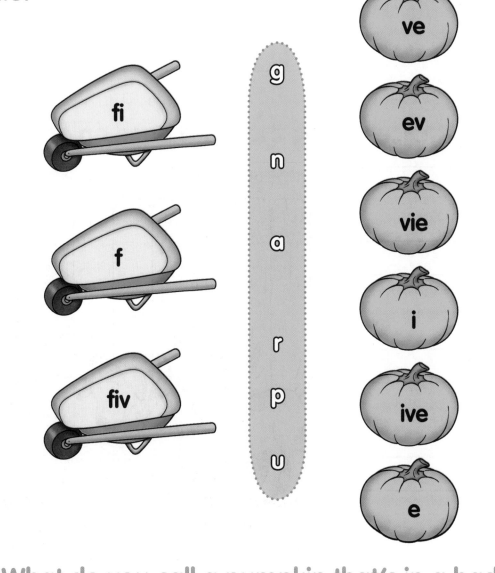

What do you call a pumpkin that's in a bad mood?

A ___ ___ ___mpkin

them

say the word them aloud as you trace it.

them

Now practice writing the word once on each line.

I have two dogs. I like to play with _____.

Word Hunt

The word **them** is in the story five times. Hunt for the word and circle it each time it appears. Then circle the umbrellas with the word **them** inside.

I can't find my rain boots. It's raining outside, so I need to wear them. They are usually in my closet. I looked in the closet, but they weren't there. Then I looked under my bed. I can't find them anywhere. The last time I wore them was yesterday. I took them off when I put down my umbrella. I know where they are now! I put them under my umbrella!

1. then
2. theme
3. them
4. thumb
5. them
6. them

its

say the word its aloud as you trace it.

its

Now practice writing the word once on each line.

Let's help the bird find _____ nest.

Ring Around the Rhyme

Draw a line to the words that rhyme with **its**.
Underline the letters **i-t-s** in each word.

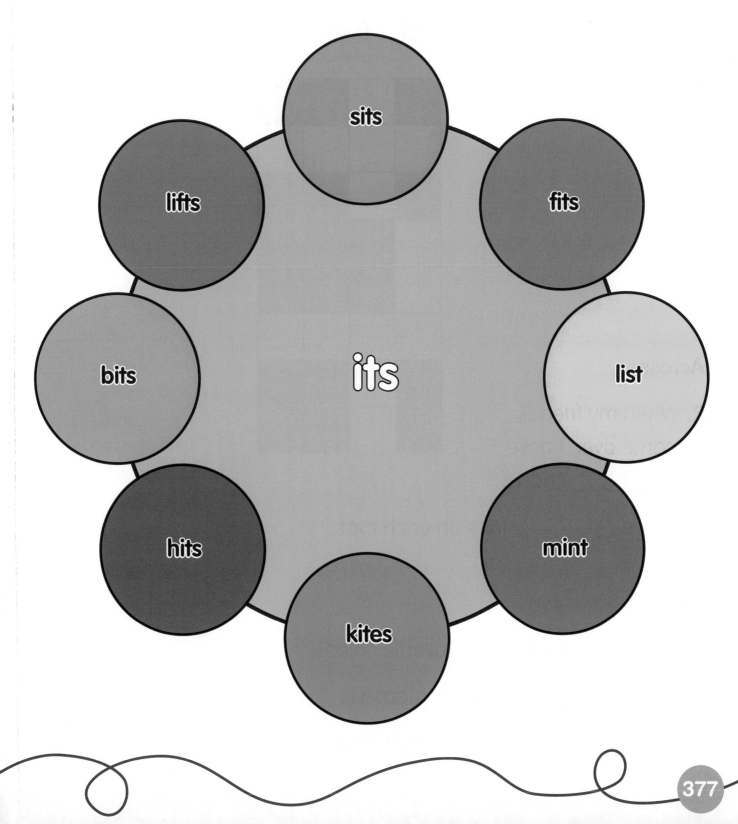

Review: Crossword Puzzle!

Use the sentence clues below to solve the crossword puzzle.

why   off   five   them   its

Across

2. When my friends came over, I gave _____ snacks.

4. I have _____ toes on each foot.

Down

1. _____ is blue your favorite color?

3. Turn _____ the radio, please.

5. The bus is on _____ way to the city.

Review: High Five

Look for the review words as you read the sentences inside each box. Put a check in the box that uses all five review words.

1. Why do you have five hats on? Take four of them off!	**2.** There are five cookies in the box. Why don't we take its lid off and eat them?
3. Why is my coat on the floor? I think it fell off its hook.	**4.** Why did you wear muddy shoes in the house? Please take them off right away.

has

Say the word has aloud as you trace it.

has

Now practice writing the word once on each line.

He _____ a ball and a bat.

Keep on Track

Look for the word **has** in each track. Circle it each time you see it. Then count the number of circled words in each track and write it in the sign.

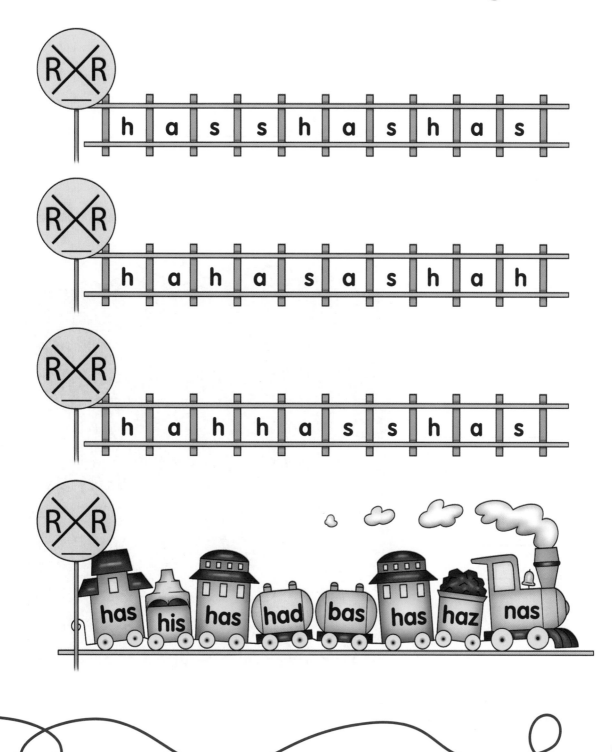

| h | a | s | s | h | a | s | h | a | s |

| h | a | h | a | s | a | s | h | a | h |

| h | a | h | h | a | s | s | h | a | s |

has · his · has · had · bas · has · haz · nas

green

say the word green aloud as you trace it.

green

Now practice writing the word once on each line.

The grass is _____.

Maze Craze

Help the ant find its way through the maze. Connect the letters **g-r-e-e-n** to make the word **green**.

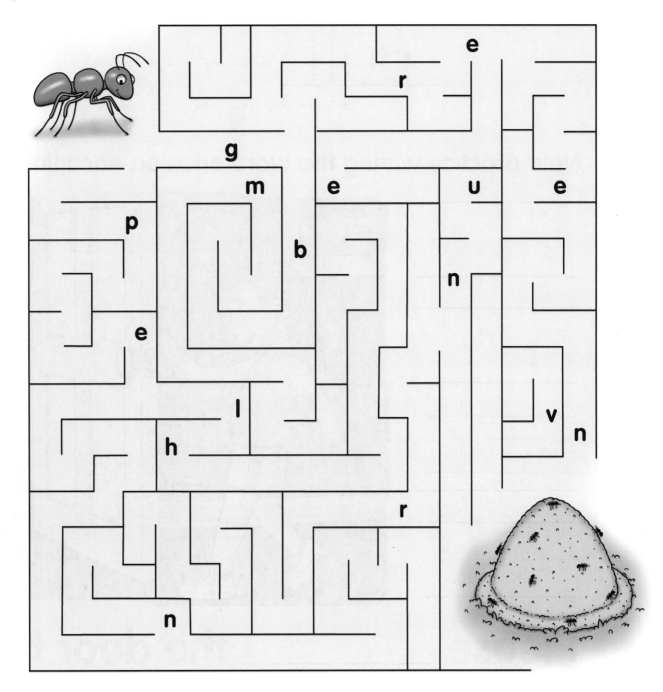

 **say the word pull aloud as you trace it.**

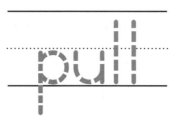

Now practice writing the word once on each line.

Please _____ the door to open it.

Solve the Puzzle

Circle the puzzle pieces that have the word **pull** inside. Put an X through the other puzzle pieces. Use the code inside the circled puzzle pieces to solve the word puzzle below.

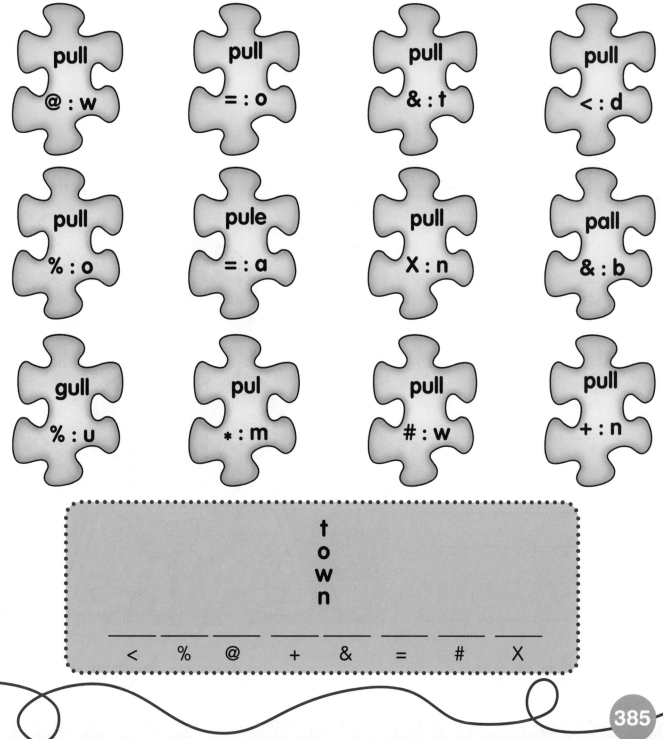

pull @ : w

pull = : o

pull & : t

pull < : d

pull % : o

pule = : a

pull X : n

pall & : b

gull % : u

pul * : m

pull # : w

pull + : n

t
o
w
n

___ ___ ___ ___ ___ ___ ___ ___
 <   %   @   +   &   =   #   X

 **wash**

say the word wash aloud as you trace it.

wash

Now practice writing the word once on each line.

Please _____ your hands.

Target Words

Circle the words that have **wash** hidden inside.
Underline the letters **w-a-s-h** in each circled word.

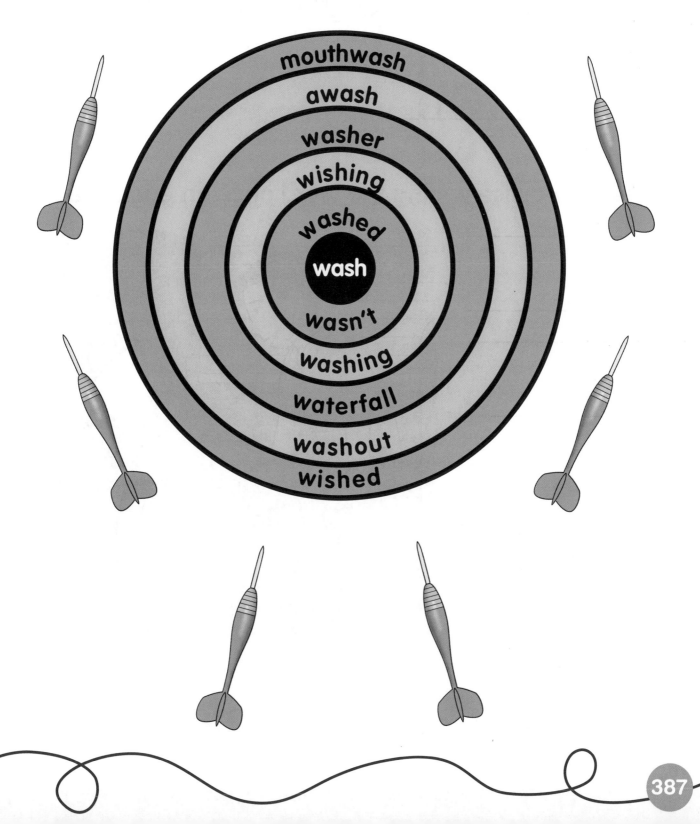

mouthwash
awash
washer
wishing
washed
wash
wasn't
washing
waterfall
washout
wished

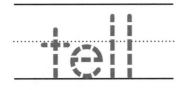 **say the word tell aloud as you trace it.**

tell

Now practice writing the word once on each line.

Will you _____ me a story?

Q Versus A

Circle the word **tell** every time it appears. When you circle the word **tell** in a question, give the Q Team a point. When you circle the word **tell** in an answer, give the A Team a point. See how many points the Qs and As get!

Q: May I tell you a secret?

A: Sure, you may tell me a secret.

Q: Will you tell me where the cookies are?

A: I can't tell you until after lunch!

Q: Should we tell Dad about this?

A: Of course we should tell him.

Q: Would you tell Mom I'm ready?

A: I already told her!

Q: A:

Review: Crossword Puzzle!

Use the sentence clues below to solve the crossword puzzle.

has   green   pull   wash   tell

Across

2. In spring, the leaves are _____ .

3. Please _____ a chair up to the table.

5. The car is dirty so we need to _____ it.

Down

1. Please _____ me about yourself.

4. My sister _____ pretty hair.

Review: Black Out!

Read each sentence, and find the missing word in the boxes. Put an X through all the boxes that show the missing word.

A.

green	**wash**
has	**tell**

B.

pull	**tell**
has	**green**

1. Our teacher _____ a new game for us to play.

2. She will _____ us how to play.

3. Everyone has to _____ on a long rope.

4. If you fall in the grass, you could get a _____ stain.

5. We can _____ it off in the sink.

Which square has all of its boxes marked off first? _____

 **say the word best aloud as you trace it.**

best

Now practice writing the word once on each line.

I baked the _____ pie.

Sport Search

Find the word best three times in the word search.

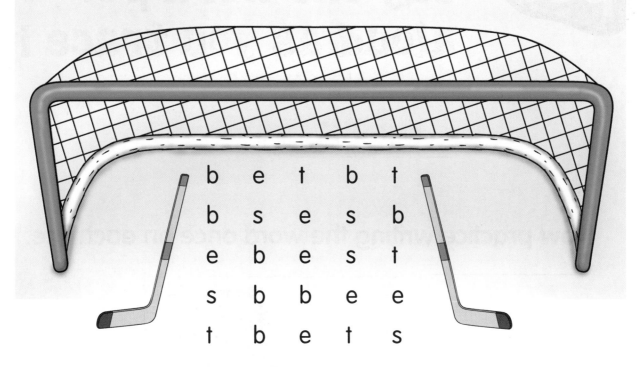

b e t b t
b s e s b
e e b e s t
s b b e e
t b e t s

Cross out all the hockey sticks that don't show the word best.

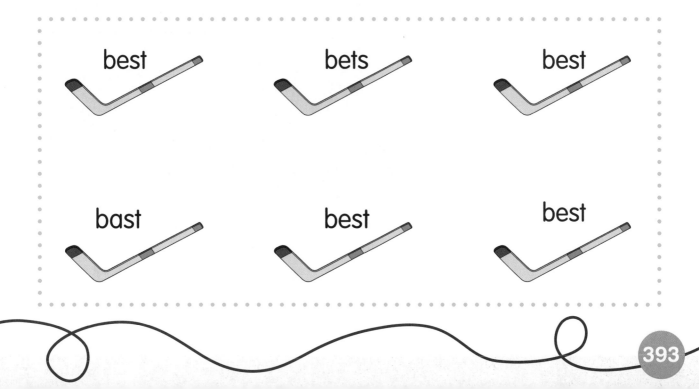

best   bets   best

bast   best   best

 **put**

say the word **put** aloud as you trace it.

Now practice writing the word once on each line.

I _____ my toy in the box.

Scrambled Eggs

Look at the eggs inside each nest. Can the letters be unscrambled to make the word **put**? If they can, write **put** on the line. If not, leave the line blank.

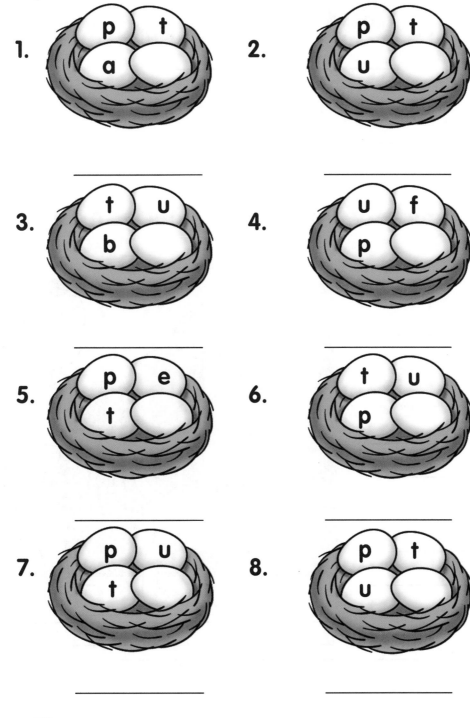

1. p t a

2. p t u

3. t u b

4. u f p

5. p e t

6. t u p

7. p u t

8. p t u

take say the word **take** aloud as you trace it.

take

Now practice writing the word once on each line.

I _____ my dog to the park.

Match Patch

Look at the letters in each wheelbarrow and find the matching pumpkin to complete the word **take**. As you draw lines to the pumpkins, see which letters you pass through. Write the letters below to answer the riddle.

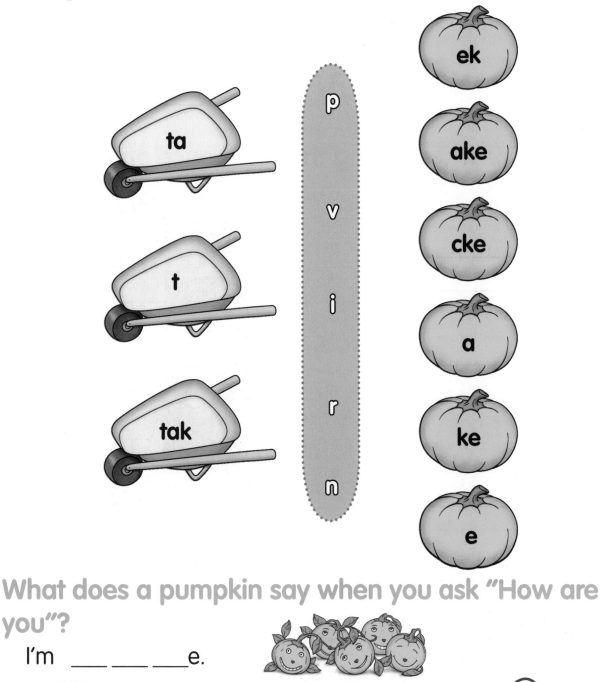

What does a pumpkin say when you ask "How are you"?

I'm ___ ___ ___e.

 **say the word when aloud as you trace it.**

when

Now practice writing the word once on each line.

The bell rings _____ it's time for lunch.

Word Hunt

The word **when** is in the story five times. Hunt for the word and circle it each time it appears. Then circle the lunch boxes with the word **when** inside.

I don't know where my lunch box is. When all the kids are eating, I'll have no lunch! I went to the lost and found. It wasn't there. When was the last time I had my lunch box? I know I had it when I got to school. I was on the playground before school. Maybe I left it by the swings when I was playing there. When I went and looked by the swings, my lunchbox was there! I can hardly wait to eat lunch!

1. whem
2. when
3. when
4. when
5. whin
6. wenn

 **say the word ask aloud as you trace it.**

Now practice writing the word once on each line.

I'll _____ my teacher for help.

Ring Around the Rhyme

Draw a line to the words that rhyme with **ask**.
Underline the letters **a-s-k** in each word.

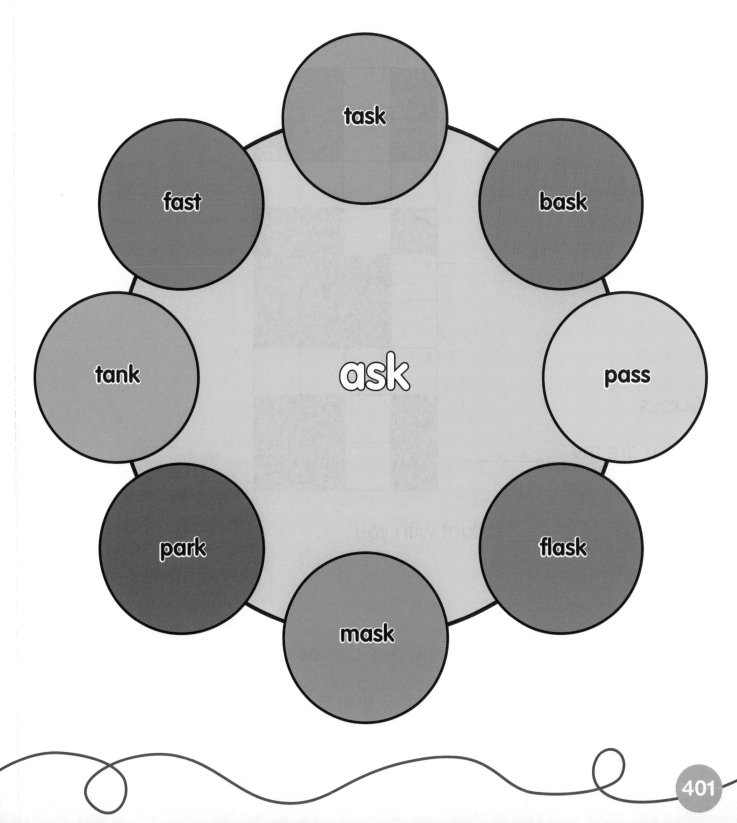

Review: Crossword Puzzle!

Use the sentence clues below to solve the crossword puzzle.

best   put   take   when   ask

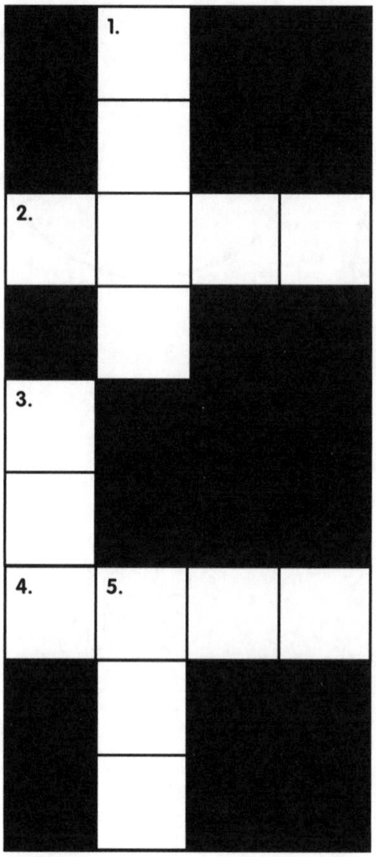

Across

2. You are my _____ friend.

4. Please _____ a coat with you.

Down

1. Do you know _____ the bus comes?

3. It's time to _____ away the game.

5. Let's _____ Dad for some help.

Review: High Five

Look for the review words as you read the sentences inside each box. Put a check in the box that uses all five review words.

☐ **1.** Let's ask Mom if we can take out the toys. We'll do our best to put them all away.

☐ **2.** Remember to put on your best dress when we go to the party.

☐ **3.** When we go camping, take your best tent. Ask Dad to help you put it up.

☐ **4.** I take the bus to school when it's raining. We have the best bus driver.

 **use** *say the word* **use** *aloud as you trace it.*

Now practice writing the word once on each line.

May I _____ your markers?

Keep on Track

Look for the word **use** in each track. Circle it each time you see it. Then count the number of circled words in each track and write it in the sign.

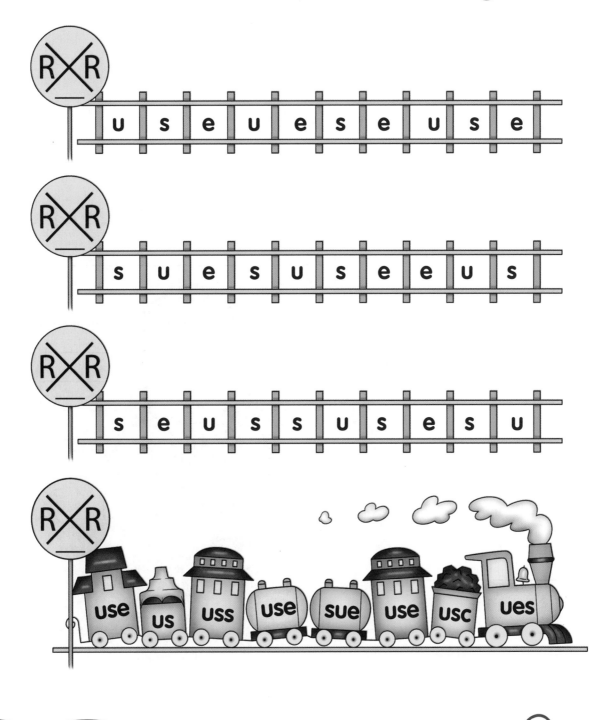

| u | s | e | u | e | s | e | u | s | e |

| s | u | e | s | u | s | e | e | u | s |

| s | e | u | s | s | u | s | e | s | u |

use   US   uss   use   sue   use   usc   ues

gave

Say the word gave aloud as you trace it.

gave

Now practice writing the word once on each line.

My dad _____ me these flowers.

Q Versus A

Circle the word gave every time it appears. When you circle the word gave in a question, give the Q Team a point. When you circle the word gave in an answer, give the A Team a point. See how many points the Qs and As get!

Q: Who gave you that hat?

A: My brother gave it to me.

Q: How did you get home so fast?

A: My friend gave me a ride home.

Q: Who gave you gifts for your birthday?

A: My family and friends gave me gifts.

Q: Where did all the cookies go?

A: I gave them to my friends.

jump

Say the word jump aloud as you trace it.

jump

Now practice writing the word once on each line.

I like to _____ in the air.

Scrambled Eggs

Look at the eggs inside each nest. Can the letters be unscrambled to make the word **jump**? If they can, write **jump** on the line. If not, leave the line blank.

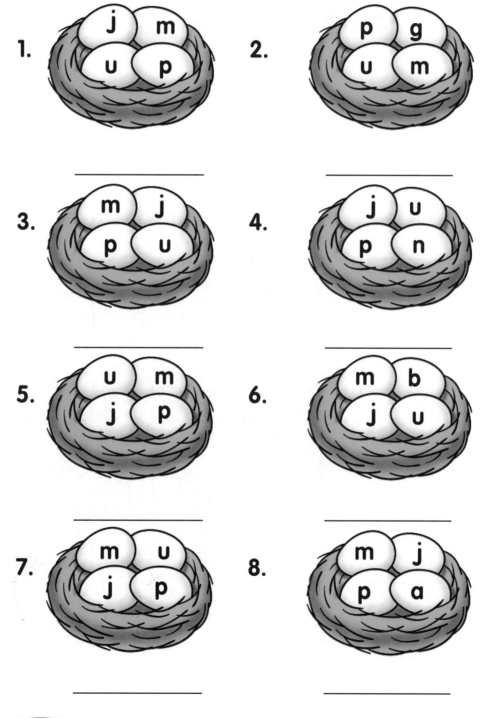

1. j m u p

2. p g u m

3. m j p u

4. j u p n

5. u m j p

6. m b j u

7. m u j p

8. m j p a

live

say the word
live aloud as
you trace it.

live

Now practice writing the word once on each line.

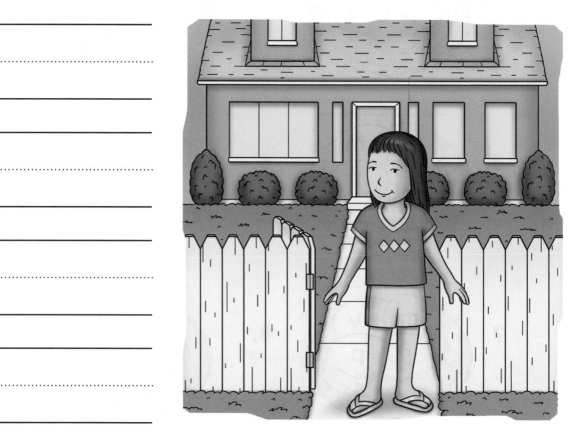

I _____ in this house.

Match Patch

Look at the letters in each wheelbarrow and find the matching pumpkin to complete the word **live**. As you draw lines to the pumpkins, see which letters you pass through. Write the letters below to answer the riddle.

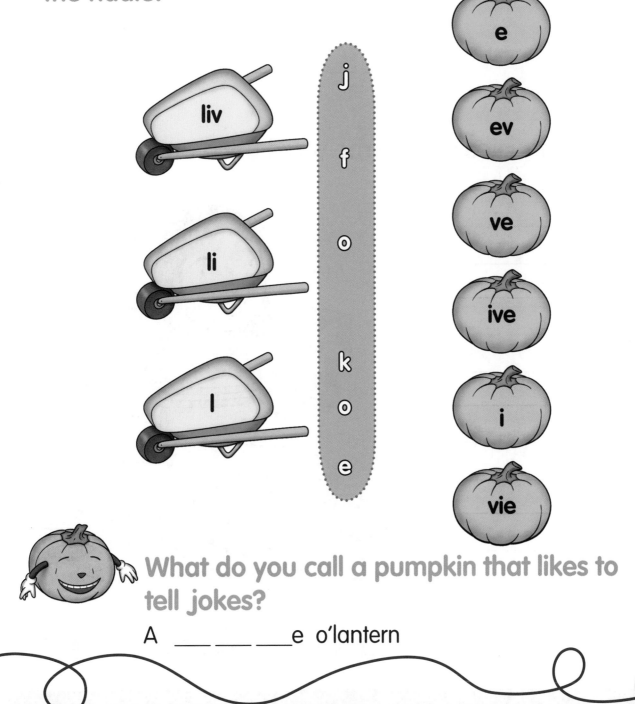

What do you call a pumpkin that likes to tell jokes?

A ___ ___ ___e o'lantern

made *say the word* **made** *aloud as you trace it.*

made

Now practice writing the word once on each line.

I _____ a card for my mom.

Word Hunt

The word **made** is in the story five times. Hunt for the word and circle it each time it appears. Then circle the scarves with the word **made** inside.

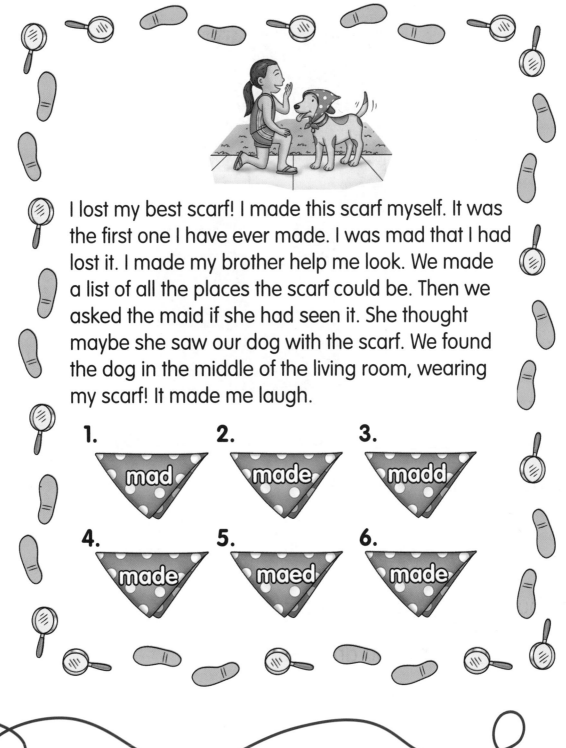

I lost my best scarf! I made this scarf myself. It was the first one I have ever made. I was mad that I had lost it. I made my brother help me look. We made a list of all the places the scarf could be. Then we asked the maid if she had seen it. She thought maybe she saw our dog with the scarf. We found the dog in the middle of the living room, wearing my scarf! It made me laugh.

1. mad
2. made
3. madd
4. made
5. maed
6. made

Review: Crossword Puzzle!

Use the sentence clues below to solve the crossword puzzle.

use   gave   jump   live   made

Across

3. My brother _____ me books for my birthday.

5. We need to ask before we _____ it.

Down

1. Do you _____ on my street?

2. We _____ crafts in art class.

4. Try to _____ over the bush.

Review: Black Out!

Read each sentence, and find the missing word in the boxes. Put an X through all the boxes that show the missing word.

A.

use	made
live	jump

B.

gave	made
use	live

1. My grandparents _____ down the street.

2. They _____ me a long, thick rope.

3. My grandmother _____ it herself!

4. We _____ it to play a game.

5. The game we play is _____ rope!

Which square has all of its boxes marked off first? _____

Review: ABC Gumballs

Write the review words in alphabetical order.

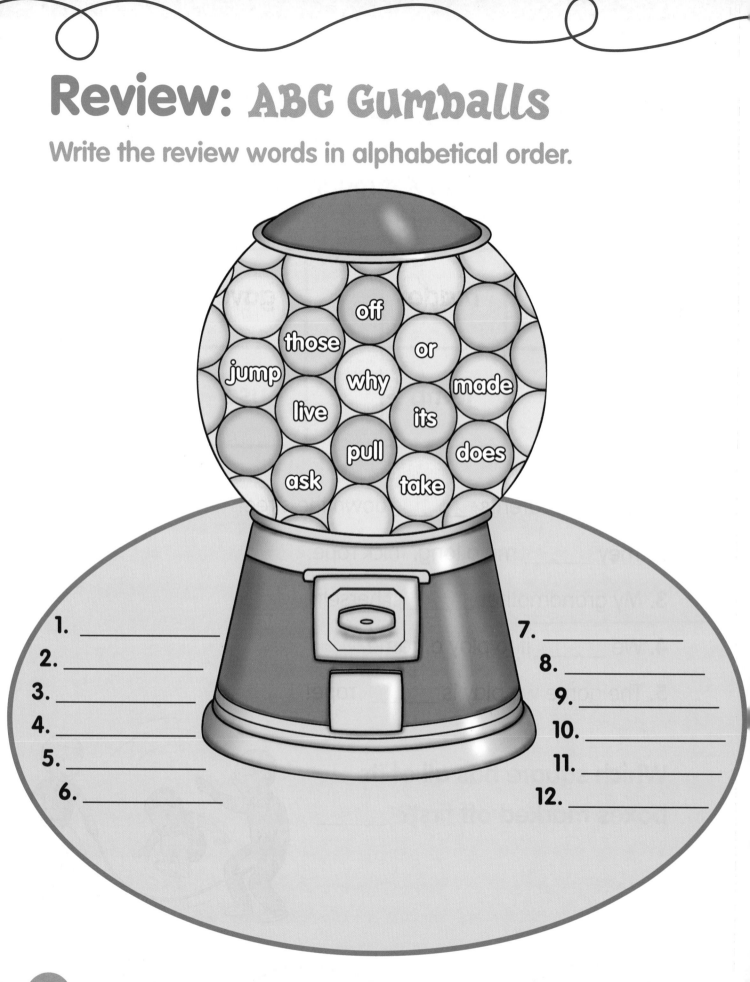

off **those** **or** **jump** **why** **made** **live** **its** **pull** **does** **ask** **take**

1. _____

2. _____

3. _____

4. _____

5. _____

6. _____

7. _____

8. _____

9. _____

10. _____

11. _____

12. _____

Review: Super Sentences

Use the review words to complete the sentences.

1. How _____ toys did you _____? Make sure to _____ them all away.

many   **put**   **buy**

2. My neighbor _____ a long hose. Maybe we can _____ it to _____ the car.

wash   **use**   **has**

3. I saw _____ ducks _____ we were at the pond. I watched _____ walk across the _____ grass.

green   when
five   them

4. My dad _____ me the _____ birthday gift! I want to _____ all my friends about it.

tell   gave   best

Level D

The sight words included in this section are:

about	cut	hold	never	their
always	done	hot	only	today
around	draw	hurt	pick	together
because	drink	if	seven	try
before	eight	keep	shall	upon
better	fall	kind	show	us
both	far	laugh	sing	which
bring	fast	light	six	wish
call	full	long	small	work
carry	got	much	start	would
clean	grow	myself	ten	write

 **say the word try aloud as you trace it.**

try

Now practice writing the word once on each line.

I'll _____ a bite.

Keep on Track

Look for the word **try** in each track. Circle it each time you see it. Then count the number of circled words in each track and write it in the sign.

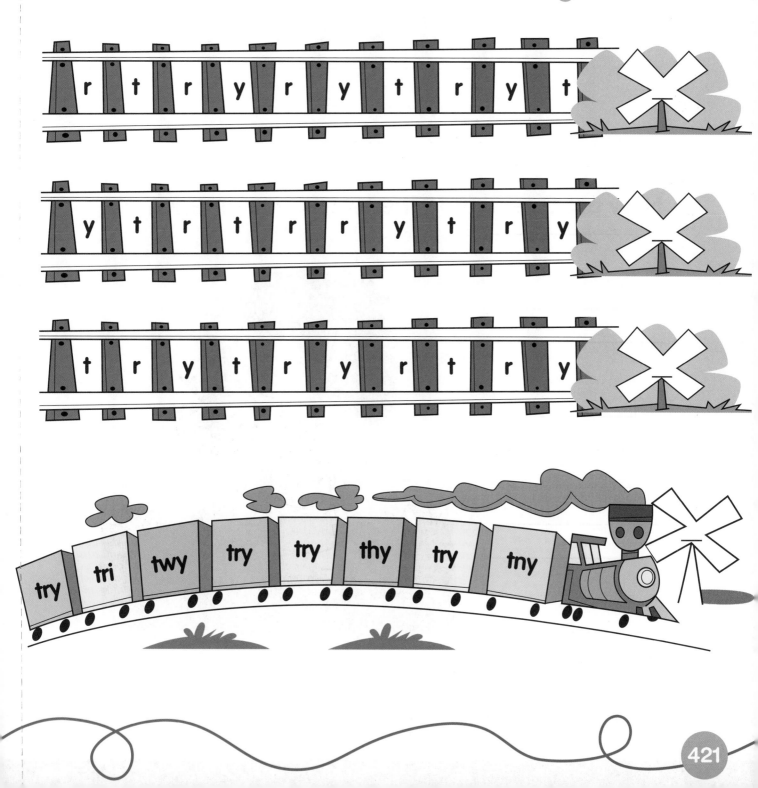

r t r y r y t r y t

y t r t r r y t r y

t r y t r y r t r y

try tri twy try try thy try tny

 **better** say the word **better** aloud as you trace it.

better

Now practice writing the word once on each line.

I like apples _____ than oranges.

Word Watch

Circle the birds that have the word **better** inside.

bedder

better

beter

better

beteer

better

detter

better

better

beterr

 **Say the word sing aloud as you trace it.**

Now practice writing the word once on each line.

Let's _____ a song.

Crack the Code

The word **sing** is hidden once in each column. Find the word and circle the letters. Then use the code to complete the riddle below.

n	**1: h**	s	**1: c**	s	**1: d**
g	**2: c**	i	**2: l**	n	**2: o**
s	**3: l**	n	**3: e**	g	**3: i**
i	**4: a**	g	**4: a**	i	**4: f**
s	**5: n**	s	**5: b**	s	**5: h**
i	**6: g**	i	**6: p**	g	**6: u**
n	**7: e**	g	**7: f**	i	**7: r**
g	**8: t**	n	**8: i**	g	**8: g**
i	**9: y**	i	**9: o**	s	**9: a**
s	**10: e**	n	**10: v**	i	**10: w**
n	**11: t**	g	**11: r**	n	**11: a**
g	**12: h**	s	**12: y**	g	**12: y**

Why did the burglar take a shower?

He wanted to make a ___ ___ ___ ___ ___
           1   2   3   4   5

___ ___ ___ ___ ___ ___ ___!
6   7   8   9   10   11   12

 **say the word ten aloud as you trace it.**

ten

Now practice writing the word once on each line.

I have _____ fingers.

Target Words

Circle the words that have **ten** hidden inside.
Underline the letters t-e-n in each circled word.

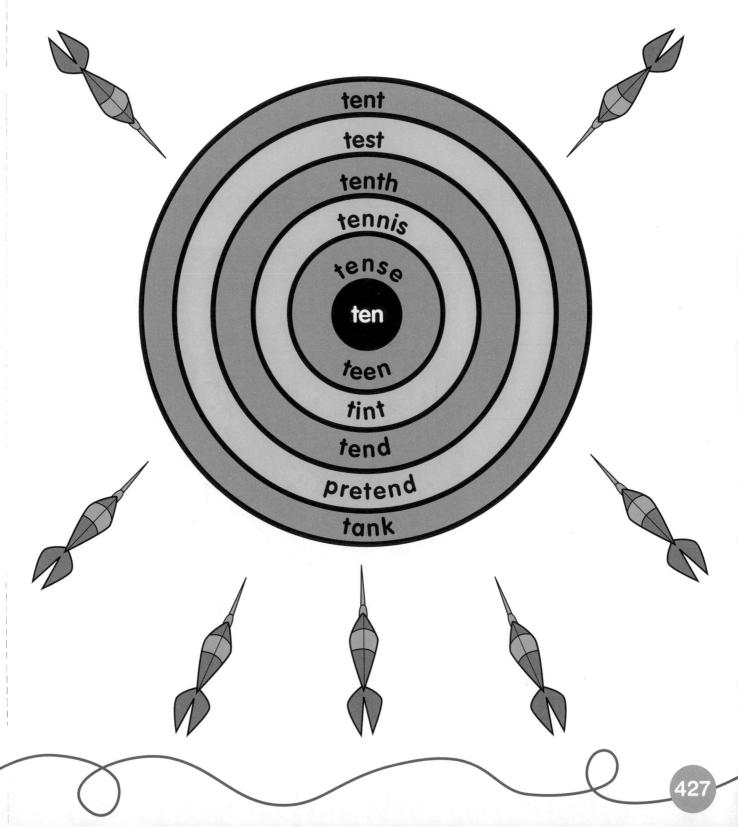

tent
test
tenth
tennis
tense
ten
teen
tint
tend
pretend
tank

 **US** *say the word* **us** *aloud as you trace it.*

 us

Now practice writing the word once on each line.

This gift is for _____.

Pen Pals

Circle the word **us** every time it appears in the letters. Count how many circled words are in each letter, and write the number in the box. Find out which pen pal used the word **us** more.

Dear Alex,

I hope you can visit me this summer. There are so many things for us to do. My dad will make us pancakes every day. Our tree house is big enough for us to sleep in. You can stay with us as long as you want!

Sincerely,

Justin

Dear Justin,

You've planned a lot of fun things for us! My parents want you to come camping with us. They will take us to the mountains. There is a tent just for us. Call us and let us know if you can come.

Sincerely,

Alex

Review: Crossword Puzzle!

Use the sentence clues below to solve the crossword puzzle.

try   better   sing   ten   us

Across

1. Dad gave _____ a ride to school.

3. I have _____ toes.

4. Yesterday I was sick, but today I feel _____ .

Down

2. I can _____ very loud.

3. Let's _____ our best to win the game.

Review: High Five

Look for the review words as you read the sentences inside each box. Put a check in the box that uses all five review words.

☐ **1.** I was sick for ten days. I decided to sing a happy song. It made me feel better.

☐ **2.** Mom told us to try a new food. It tasted better than I thought it would! I ate ten bites.

☐ **3.** There are ten of us in the choir. We try to sing even better every day.

☐ **4.** Our teacher helped us learn to sing better. We practice for ten minutes a day.

wish

say the word **wish** aloud as you trace it.

wish

Now practice writing the word once on each line.

I _____ for a new doll.

Search and Splash

Find the word **wish** three times in the word search.

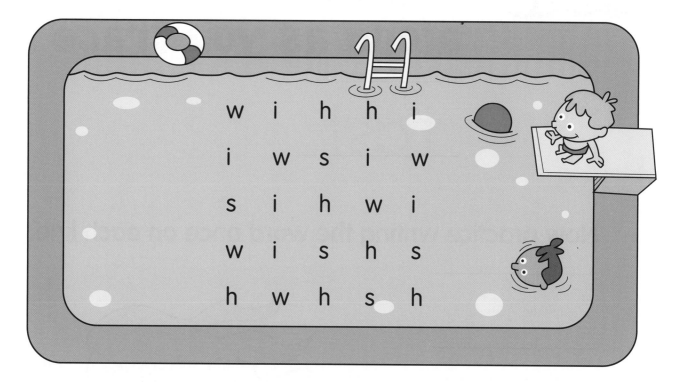

w	i	h	h	i
i	w	s	i	w
s	i	h	w	i
w	i	s	h	s
h	w	h	s	h

Do the letters go together to make the word **wish**?
Circle Yes or No.

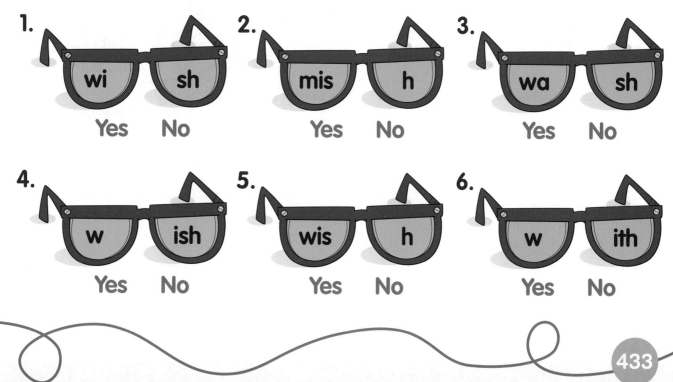

1. wi sh — Yes No

2. mis h — Yes No

3. wa sh — Yes No

4. w ish — Yes No

5. wis h — Yes No

6. w ith — Yes No

 **fast** say the word **fast** aloud as you trace it.

fast

Now practice writing the word once on each line.

I can run _____!

What's the Order?

If the letters can be unscrambled to make the word **fast**, write it on the line. If the letters don't make the word **fast**, leave the line blank.

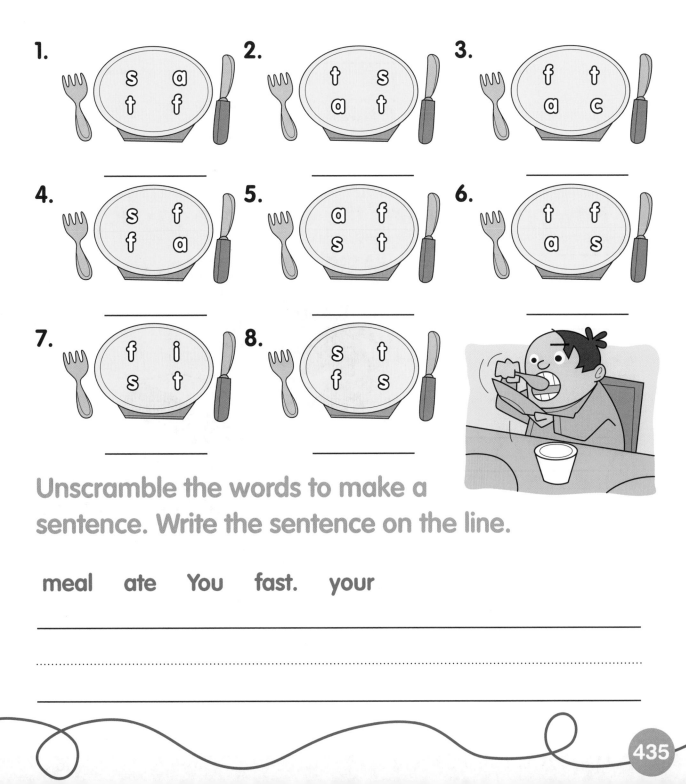

1. s a t f

2. t s a t

3. f t a c

4. s f f a

5. a f s t

6. t f a s

7. f i s t

8. s t f s

Unscramble the words to make a sentence. Write the sentence on the line.

meal   ate   You   fast.   your

_____

_____

_____

before say the word **before** aloud as you trace it.

┊ b e f o r e

Now practice writing the word once on each line.

You can go _____ me.

Stop and Go

Draw a line to connect the letters and make the word **before**.

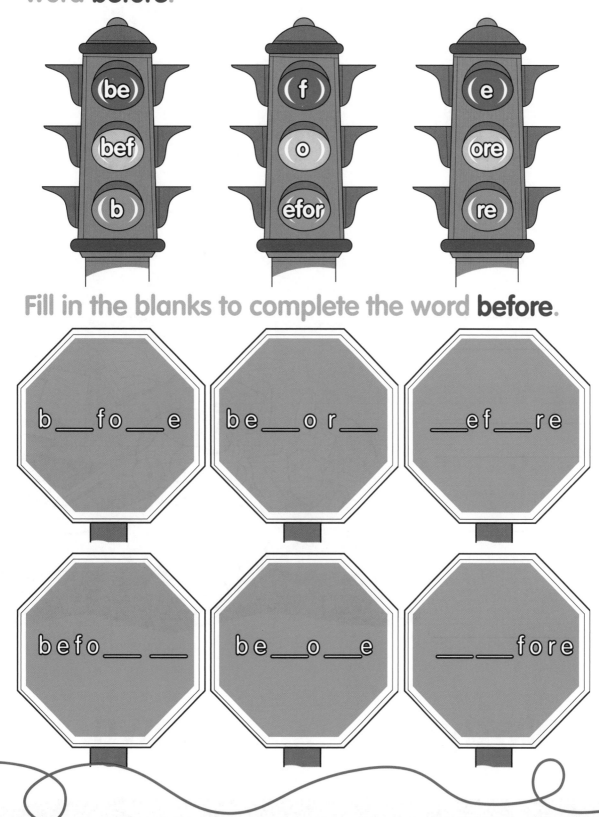

Fill in the blanks to complete the word **before**.

b__fo__e

be__or__

__ef__re

befo____

be__o__e

____fore

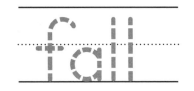 **say the word fall aloud as you trace it.**

fall

Now practice writing the word once on each line.

I always _____ down.

Amazing Maze

Look for the word **fall** in the maze. Connect all the words that spell **fall** to find your way out of the maze.

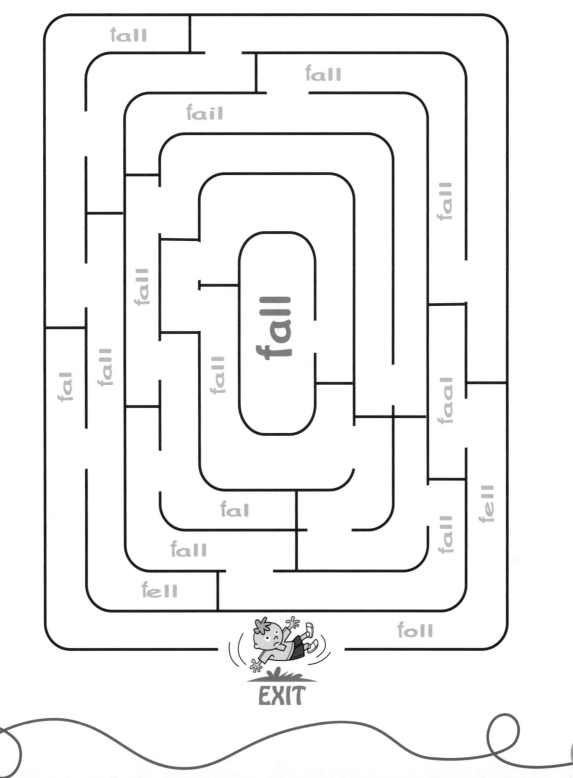

fall   fall   fail   fall

fall   fall   **fall**   faal

fal   fall   fall   fell

fal   fall   fall

fell   foll

EXIT

 **never** *Say the word never aloud as you trace it.*

_____

⋯⋯⋯⋯⋯⋯⋯⋯⋯
never
_____

Now practice writing the word once on each line.

_____

⋯⋯⋯⋯⋯⋯⋯⋯⋯

_____

_____

⋯⋯⋯⋯⋯⋯⋯⋯⋯

_____

_____

⋯⋯⋯⋯⋯⋯⋯⋯⋯

_____

You should _____ touch a hot stove.

Picture Puzzle

Find the word **never** in each sentence and circle it. Draw a line to connect the circled words in each sentence and see which letter your line passes through. Write the letters below to solve the picture puzzle.

1. I have never been to New York.

   l   d   b   g   n

2. I told my mom I would never do it again.

   w   e   r   a   i

3. I never wake up on time.

   c   a   b   o   m

4. The snow is something I have never seen.

   d   l   m   n   w

5. I would never tell a lie.

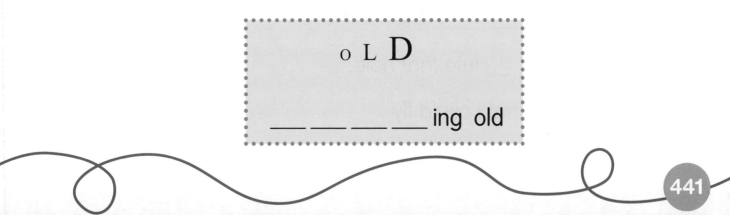

o L D

___ ___ ___ ___ing old

Review: Crossword Puzzle!

Use the sentence clues below to solve the crossword puzzle.

wish   fast   before   fall   never

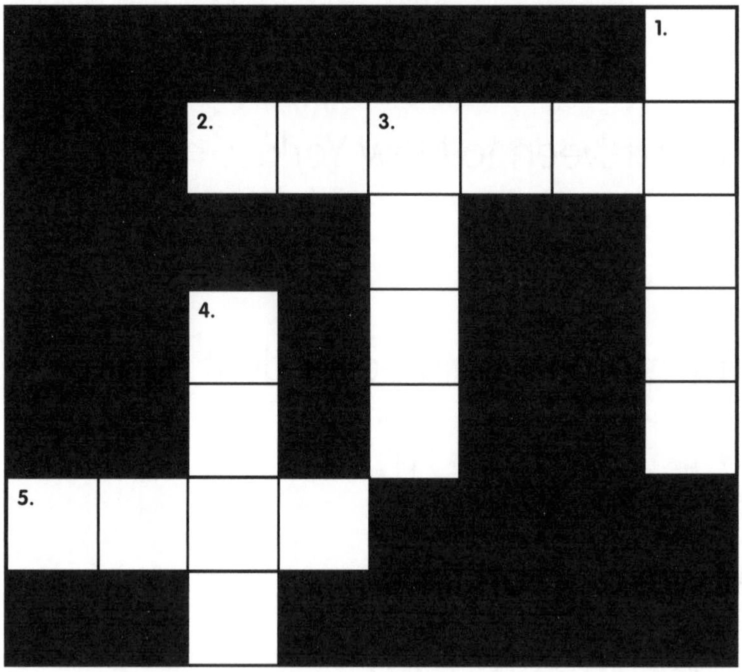

Across

2. Please wash your hands _____ dinner.

5. I can ride my bike _____ .

Down

1. You should _____ play with fire.

3. Don't _____ into that hole!

4. I _____ that I could fly.

Review: Story Code

Crack the code by writing the correct review word in each blank. Write the word that goes with each symbol in the box below.

My birthday _____ was to go to the lake. I had
            #

_____ been there _____ . My _____ came true.
   *   &   #

_____ we left, my brother said, "Be careful not to _____
  &   @

in the lake!"

We got to the lake, and _____ anyone could stop me,
                          &

I ran to the water very _____ . I was running so _____ , I
                     !   !

fell into the water.

"I knew you would _____ in!" said my brother.
                     @

I _____ I had _____ gone to the lake!
   #   *

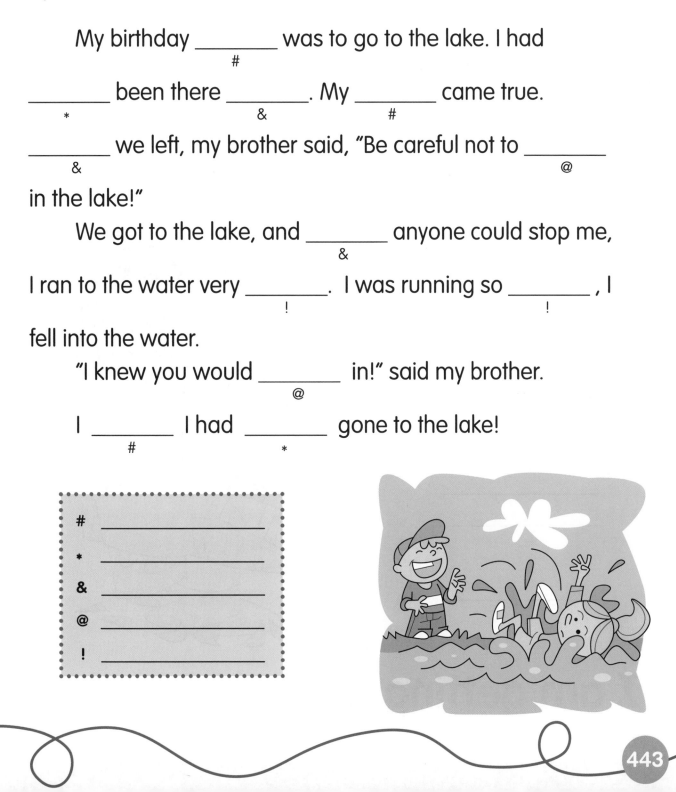

_____

* _____

& _____

@ _____

! _____

 **Say the word cut aloud as you trace it.**

Now practice writing the word once on each line.

I am getting my hair _____.

Keep on Track

Look for the word cut in each track. Circle it each time you see it. Then count the number of circled words in each track and write it in the sign.

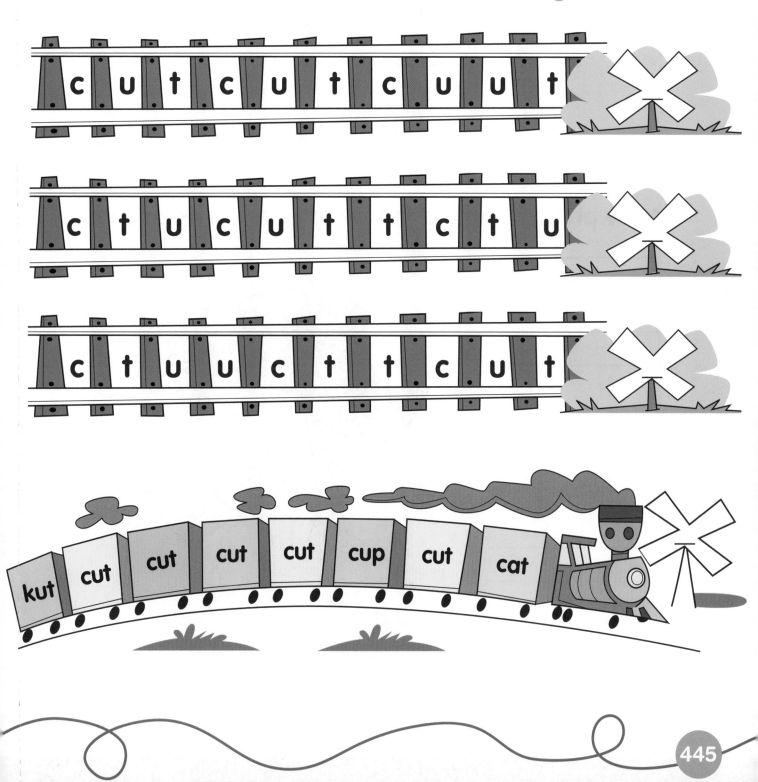

c u t c u t c u u t

c t u c u t t c t u

c t u u c t t c u t

kut   cut   cut   cut   cut   cup   cut   cat

myself say the word **myself** aloud as you trace it.

myself

Now practice writing the word once on each line.

I kept one cookie for _____.

Word Watch

Circle the birds that have the word **myself** inside.

hurt

say the word hurt aloud as you trace it.

hurt

Now practice writing the word once on each line.

I _____ my knee.

Crack the Code

The word **hurt** is hidden once in each column. Find the word and circle the letters. Then use the code to complete the riddle below.

Col 1		Col 2		Col 3	
r	1: c	u	1: y	h	1: H
h	2: k	r	2: e	u	2: e
t	3: l	t	3: s	r	3: f
u	4: a	h	4: S	t	4: e
h	5: r	h	5: l	r	5: a
u	6: e	u	6: t	h	6: t
n	7: n	r	7: c	u	7: h
t	8: o	t	8: r	t	8: e
h	9: u	h	9: w	r	9: s
u	10: m	u	10: a	t	10: r
r	11: m	r	11: s	h	11: e
t	12: y	r	12: n	u	12: t

Why did the cookie go to the doctor?

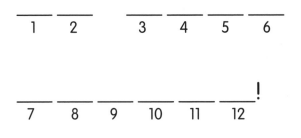

$\underline{\text{H}}_{1} \underline{\text{e}}_{2} \quad \underline{\text{f}}_{3} \underline{\text{e}}_{4} \underline{\text{l}}_{5} \underline{\text{t}}_{6}$

$\underline{\text{c}}_{7} \underline{\text{r}}_{8} \underline{\text{u}}_{9} \underline{\text{m}}_{10} \underline{\text{m}}_{11} \underline{\text{y}}_{12}!$

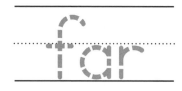 **say the word far aloud as you trace it.**

far

Now practice writing the word once on each line.

How _____ away is the beach?

Target Words

Circle the words that have **far** hidden inside.
Underline the letters **f-a-r** in each circled word.

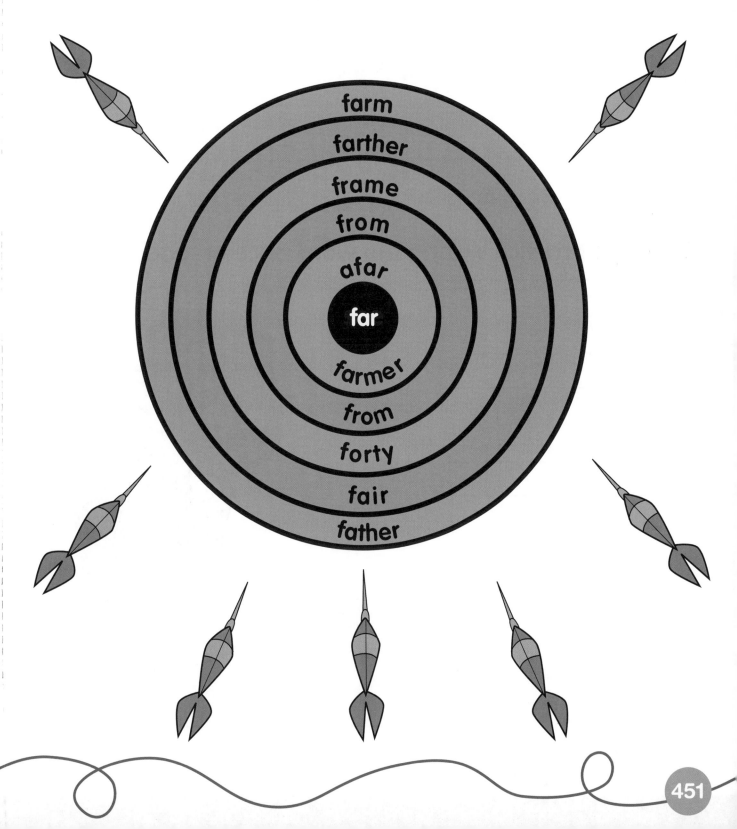

because *say the word because aloud as you trace it.*

because

Now practice writing the word once on each line.

A vase broke _____ I
dropped it.

Pen Pals

Circle the word **because** every time it appears in the letters. Count how many circled words are in each letter, and write the number in the box. Find out which pen pal used the word **because** more.

Dear Emily,

I can't go to the beach today because it's raining. Rainy days are nice because I can stay inside and write letters. I am excited because I can use my new pen. My dad gave it to me because I did well on my spelling test. I hope to become the best speller in my class! I study every night because I want to be in the spelling bee!

Sincerely,

Anna

Dear Anna,

I like getting your letters because they are always fun to read. I like rainy days too, but not because I can write letters. I like rainy days because I can read by the fire. Sometimes on rainy days I read old letters from my pen pals. I never throw away a letter because I might want to read it again. I keep all my letters in a box right beside my bed.

Sincerely,

Emily

Review: Crossword Puzzle!

Use the sentence clues below to solve the crossword puzzle.

cut   myself   hurt   far   because

Across

2. I'm sleepy _____ it's very late.

4. When I fell off my bike, I _____ my foot.

5. My grandma lives very _____ away.

Down

1. I did the dishes all by _____ .

3. Please _____ the paper into two pieces.

Review: High Five

Look for the review words as you read the sentences inside each box. Put a check in the box that uses all five review words.

☐ **1.** I cut my sandwich in half because my friend had no lunch. I gave half to him and ate the other half myself.

☐ **2.** We take the bus to school because it's too far to walk. I read quietly to myself while I'm on the bus.

☐ **3.** I need to see the nurse because I hurt myself. I cut my hand playing outside.

☐ **4.** I stepped on some glass and cut myself. I couldn't walk very far because my foot hurt.

clean

say the word clean aloud as you trace it.

clean

Now practice writing the word once on each line.

I need to put on some _____ clothes.

Search and Splash

Find the word **clean** three times in the word search.

```
c   n   c   l   e
e   l   l   e   n
c   l   e   a   n
l   a   a   a   c
e   n   n   l   n
```

Do the letters go together to make the word **clean**?
Circle Yes or No.

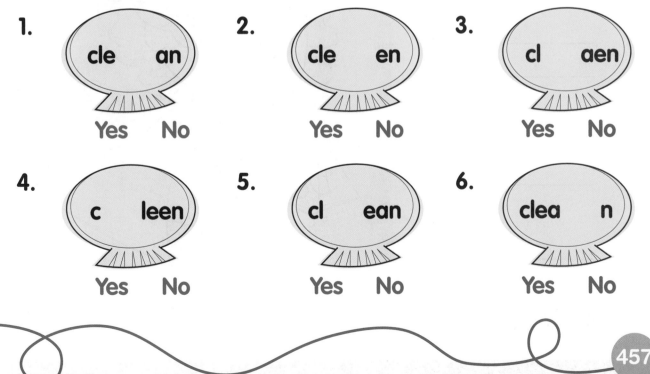

1. cle an
   Yes   No

2. cle en
   Yes   No

3. cl aen
   Yes   No

4. c leen
   Yes   No

5. cl ean
   Yes   No

6. clea n
   Yes   No

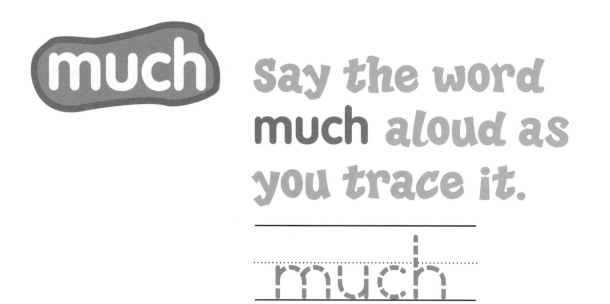

much

say the word **much** aloud as you trace it.

much

Now practice writing the word once on each line.

How _____ does it cost?

458

What's the Order?

If the letters can be unscrambled to make the word **much**, write it on the line. If the letters don't make the word **much**, leave the line blank.

1. c h m a

_____

2. m u c k

_____

3. u h m c

_____

4. m h c u

_____

5. c u m h

_____

6. c h n u

_____

7. h m u c

_____

8. c n m u

_____

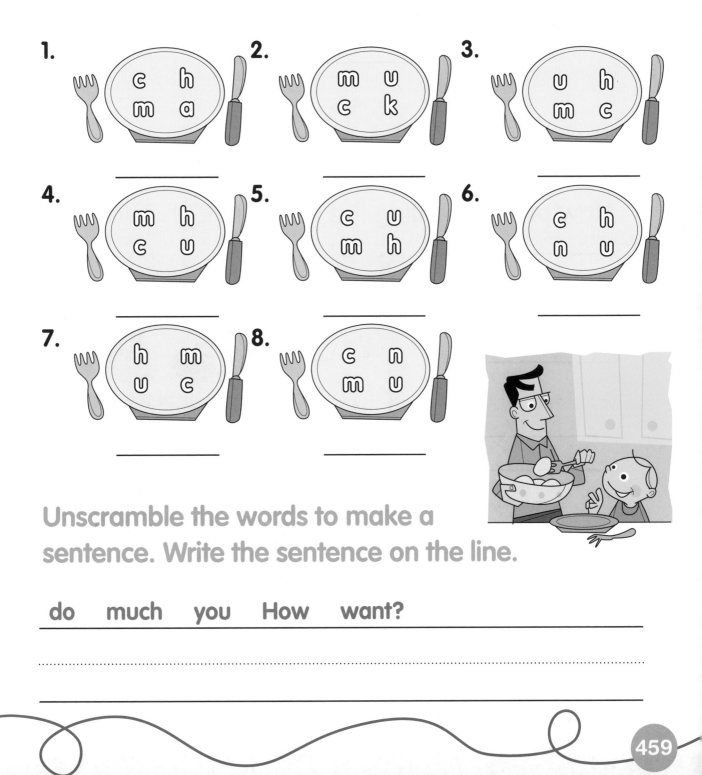

Unscramble the words to make a sentence. Write the sentence on the line.

do   much   you   How   want?

_____

....

_____

would *say the word* **would** *aloud as you trace it.*

would

Now practice writing the word once on each line.

What flavor _____ you like?

Stop and Go

Draw a line to connect the letters and make the
word **would**.

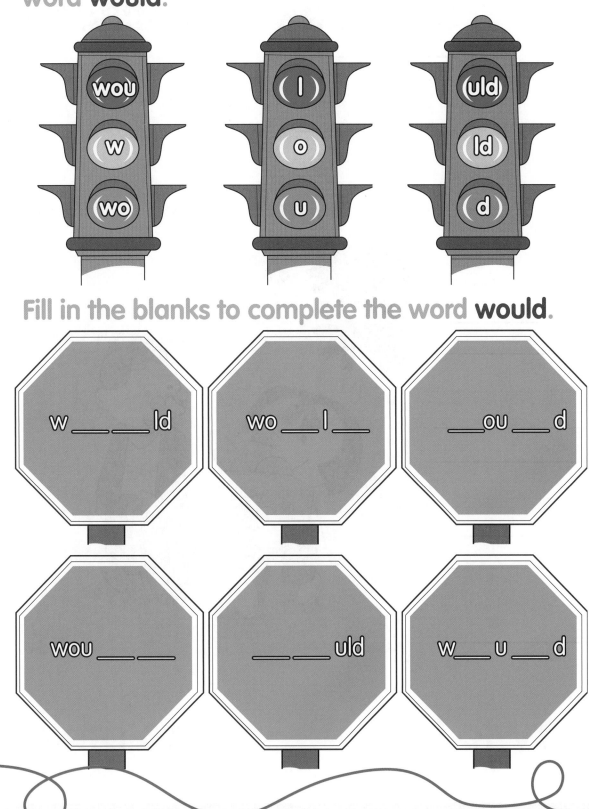

Fill in the blanks to complete the word **would**.

w _____ ld

wo ___ l ___

___ ou ___ d

wou _____ _____

_____ ___ uld

w ___ u ___ d

461

kind say the word kind aloud as you trace it.

kind

Now practice writing the word once on each line.

I try to be _____ to others.

Amazing Maze

Look for the word **kind** in the maze. Connect all the words that spell **kind** to find your way out of the maze.

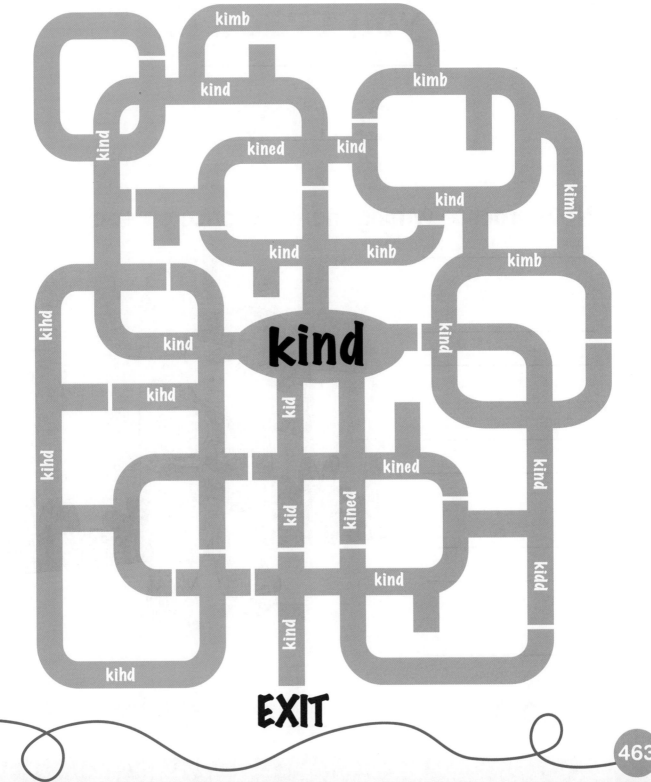

EXIT

carry Say the word carry aloud as you trace it.

carry

Now practice writing the word once on each line.

I can _____ my baby sister.

Picture Puzzle

Find the word **carry** in each sentence and circle it. Draw a line to connect the circled words in each sentence and see which letter your line passes through. Write the letters below to solve the picture puzzle.

1. Please carry your plate to the sink.

      l   a   s   t   i

2. My bag is too heavy to carry.

      w   g   y   a   i

3. I like to carry my brother on my back.

      c   g   y   i   l

4. There are too many books to carry.

      d   e   p   l   w

5. I can't carry this to the car!

T
A
L
E   ___ ___ ___ ___ tale

Review: Crossword Puzzle!

Use the sentence clues below to solve the crossword puzzles.

clean   much   carry   kind   would

Across

3. Can you _____ the box outside?

5. What _____ you like to watch on TV?

Down

1. We need to _____ up our room.

2. It was _____ of you to help me.

4. I have too _____ work to do!

Review: Story Code

Crack the code by writing the correct review word in each blank. Write the word that goes with each symbol in the box below.

I have a very _____ neighbor. She always helps us
     #

_____ the groceries in from the car. My family likes
!

her very _____ .
    @

  One day, she asked if I _____ help her. She needed to
          *

_____ out her garage. There was too _____ stuff for
  &   @

her to _____ . I told her I _____ help her.
    !   *

  When we were done, her garage was so _____ ! It felt
               &

good to do something _____ for her.
        #

_____

*   _____

&   _____

@   _____

!   _____

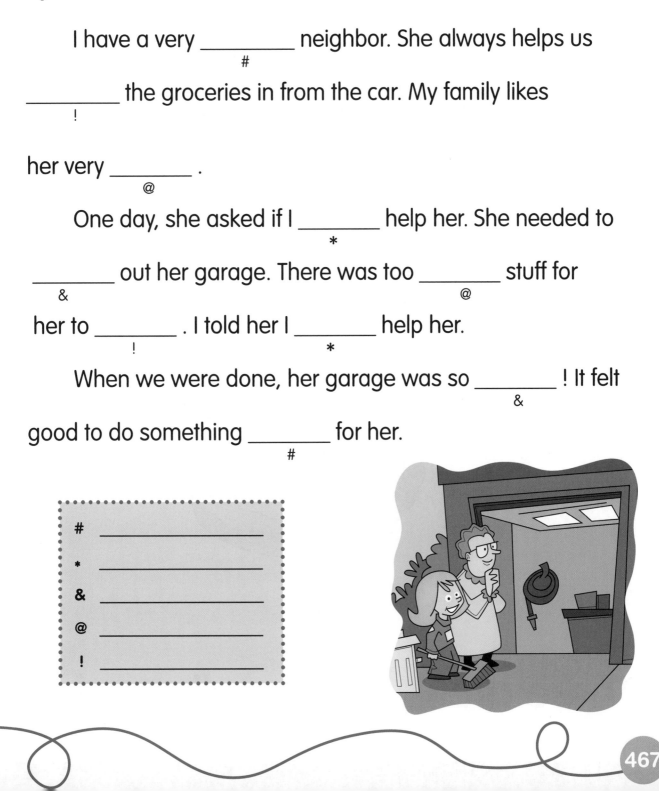

467

 **six**

say the word six aloud as you trace it.

_____

⠄⠄⠄⠄⠄⠄⠄⠄⠄⠄⠄⠄⠄⠄⠄⠄⠄⠄

six

_____

Now practice writing the word once on each line.

_____

⠄⠄⠄⠄⠄⠄⠄⠄⠄⠄⠄⠄⠄⠄⠄⠄⠄⠄

_____

_____

⠄⠄⠄⠄⠄⠄⠄⠄⠄⠄⠄⠄⠄⠄⠄⠄⠄⠄

_____

_____

⠄⠄⠄⠄⠄⠄⠄⠄⠄⠄⠄⠄⠄⠄⠄⠄⠄⠄

_____

_____

⠄⠄⠄⠄⠄⠄⠄⠄⠄⠄⠄⠄⠄⠄⠄⠄⠄⠄

_____

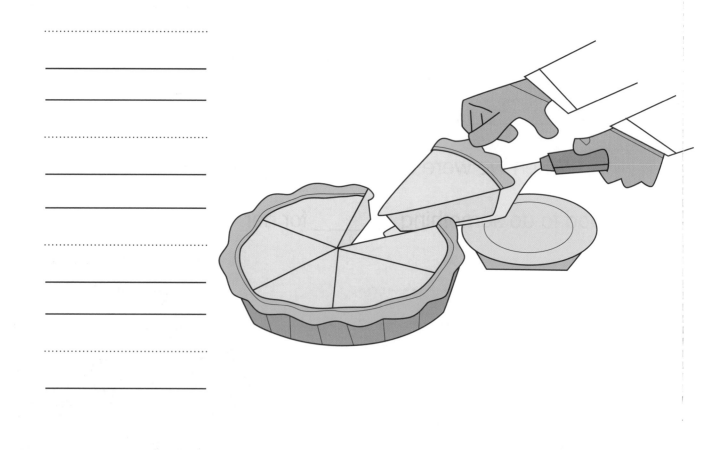

There are _____ slices of pie.

Keep Track

Look for the word **six** in each track. Circle it each time you see it. Then count the number of circled words in each track and write it in the sign.

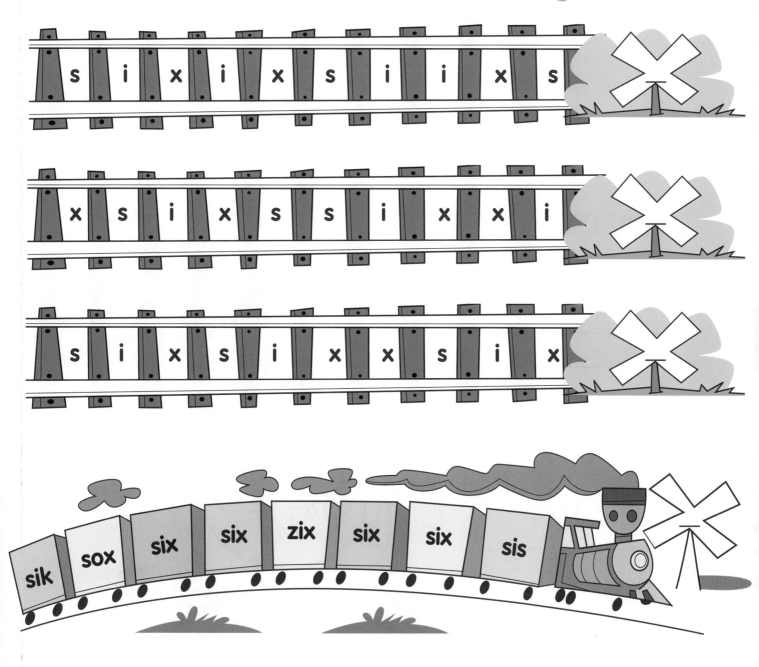

s i x i x s i i x s

x s i x s s i x x i

s i x s i x x s i x

sik sox six six zix six six sis

say the word show aloud as you trace it.

Now practice writing the word once on each line.

_____

....

_____

....

_____

_____

....

_____

....

_____

Let me _____ you my picture.

Word Watch

Circle the birds that have the word **show** inside.

shoe

shaw

show

show

show

show

shov

zhow

shoow

show

Say the word done aloud as you trace it.

done

Now practice writing the word once on each line.

I am all _____ eating.

Crack the Code

The word **done** is hidden once in each column. Find the word and circle the letters. Then use the code to complete the riddle below.

d	1: F	d	1: c	o	1: V
o	2: i	o	2: o	d	2: e
n	3: r	n	3: d	n	3: r
e	4: e	n	4: e	e	4: y
d	5: a	d	5: g	d	5: c
o	6: t	o	6: A	o	6: r
e	7: h	e	7: t	n	7: a
n	8: i	n	8: h	e	8: c
e	9: t	d	9: k	n	9: l
d	10: r	o	10: e	o	10: a
o	11: u	n	11: r	d	11: r
n	12: n	e	12: s	e	12: b

What do firemen put in their soup?

___ ___ ___ ___   ___ ___ ___ ___ ___ ___ ___ ___ !
 1   2   3   4   5   6   7   8   9 10 11 12

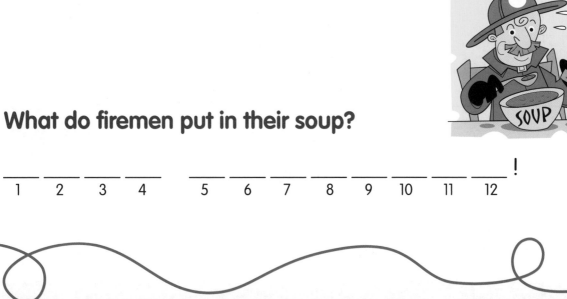

say the word long aloud as you trace it.

long

Now practice writing the word once on each line.

My hair is very _____.

Target Words

Circle the words that have **long** hidden inside.
Underline the letters l-o-n-g in each circled word.

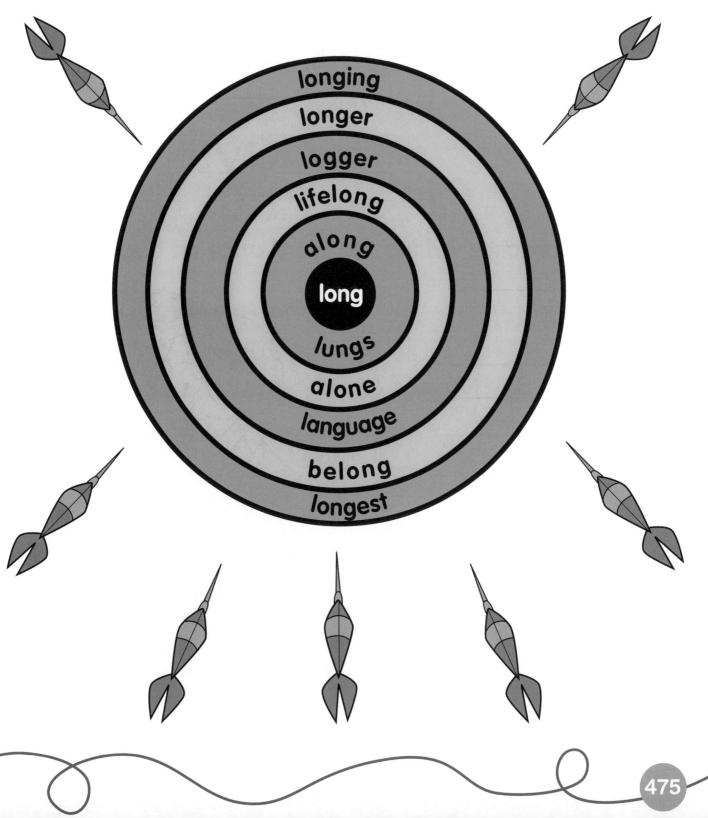

longing
longer
logger
lifelong
along
long
lungs
alone
language
belong
longest

 **always**

say the word always aloud as you trace it.

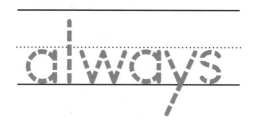

Now practice writing the word once on each line.

I _____ do my chores.

Pen Pals

Circle the word **always** every time it appears in the letters. Count how many circled words are in each letter, and write the number in the box. Find out which pen pal used the word **always** more.

Dear Noah,

Whenever I go on a trip, I always bring a pen and paper along. It's always fun to send you a letter about my trip. My family always camps at the same place every year. This year, the place we always go to is full. So we drove around until we found a new place to camp. I like the new place even better!

Sincerely,

Gabe

Dear Gabe,

I always like reading your letters. You always have a fun story to tell. My family always camps at the same place too. Whenever we camp, we always go on a hike. I wanted to go on the hike alone, but my parents wouldn't allow it. They said you should always hike with a buddy.

Sincerely,

Noah

Review: Crossword Puzzle!

Use the sentence clues below to solve the crossword puzzle.

six   show   done   long   always

Across

3. There is a _____ line for the restroom.

4. Will you _____ me your new dress?

5. We eat dinner at _____ o'clock.

Down

1. Put the game away when you're _____ playing.

2. I _____ wear a helmet when I ride my bike.

Review: High Five

Look for the review words as you read the sentences inside each box. Put a check in the box that uses all five review words.

1. We always have dinner at six o'clock. When we're done, we take a long walk.

2. I always show my paintings to my mom. I've done this since I was six years old.

3. When I'm done surfing, I always show people that my board is six feet long.

4. How long will it be until the pie is done? I always show it to the family before we eat it.

shall

Say the word shall aloud as you trace it.

shall

Now practice writing the word once on each line.

When _____ we have dinner?

Search and Splash

Find the word shall three times in the word search.

s	s	h	a	l
s	h	a	l	l
h	a	a	a	s
a	l	h	l	h
l	l	s	l	l

Do the letters go together to make the word shall?
Circle Yes or No.

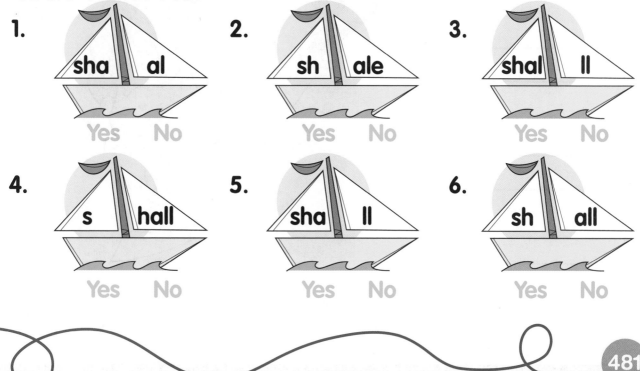

1. sha al
   Yes   No

2. sh ale
   Yes   No

3. shal ll
   Yes   No

4. s hall
   Yes   No

5. sha ll
   Yes   No

6. sh all
   Yes   No

which say the word **which** aloud as you trace it.

which

Now practice writing the word once on each line.

_____ hat should I wear?

What's the Order?

If the letters can be unscrambled to make the word **which**, write it on the line. If the letters don't make the word **which**, leave the line blank.

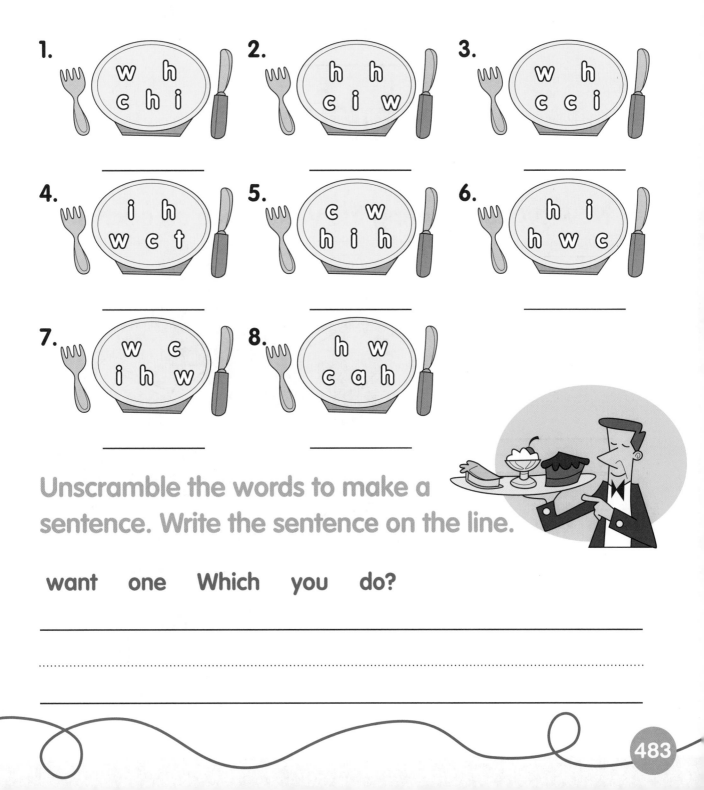

1. w h c i h _____

2. h h c i w _____

3. w h c c i _____

4. i h w c t _____

5. c w h i h _____

6. h i h w c _____

7. w c i h w _____

8. h w c a h _____

Unscramble the words to make a sentence. Write the sentence on the line.

want   one   Which   you   do?

_____

....

_____

 **bring**

say the word bring aloud as you trace it.

Now practice writing the word once on each line.

You should _____ a warm coat.

Stop and Go

Draw a line to connect the letters and make the word **bring**.

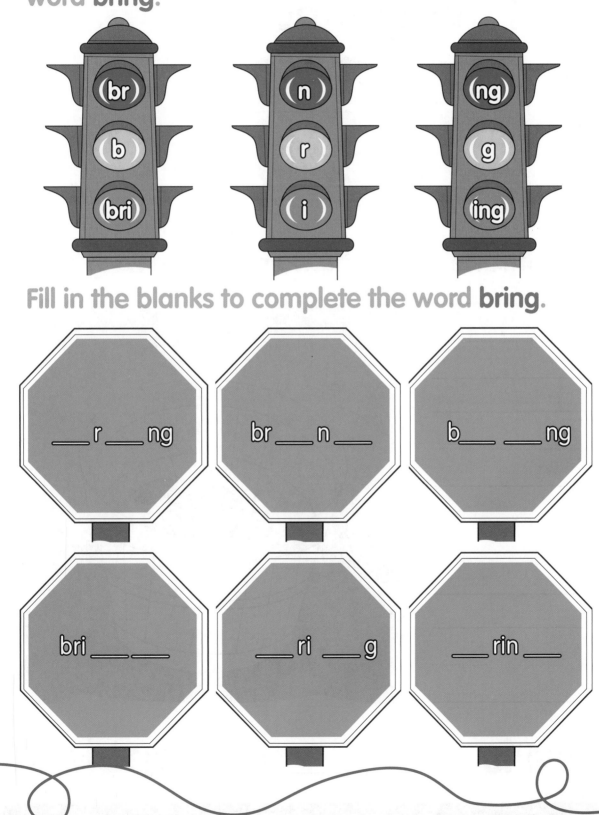

Fill in the blanks to complete the word **bring**.

___r___ng

br___n___

b___ ___ng

bri___ ___

___ri ___g

___rin___

 **only** say the word **only** aloud as you trace it.

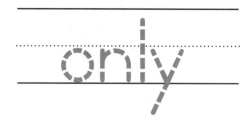

Now practice writing the word once on each line.

There is _____ one apple left.

Amazing Maze

Look for the word **only** in the maze. Connect all the words that spell **only** to find your way out of the maze.

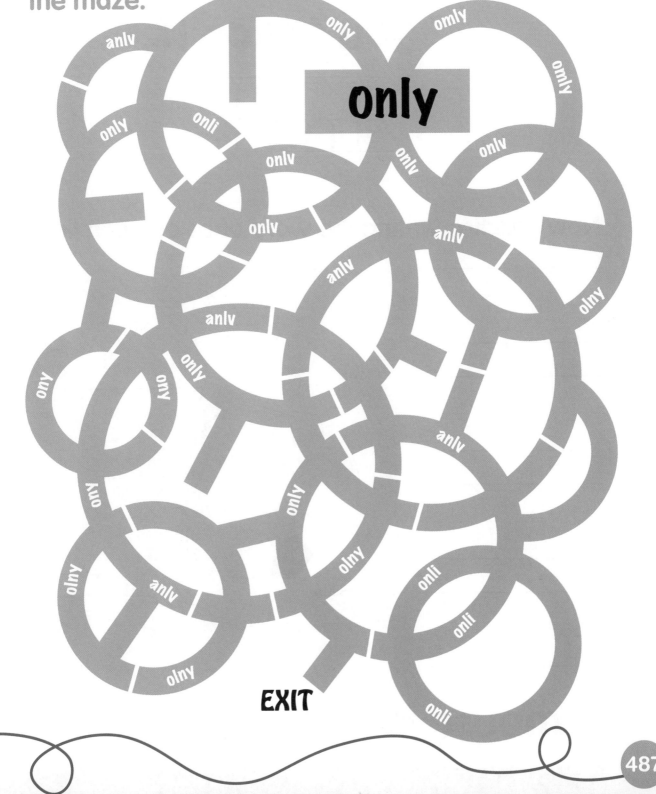

only

EXIT

 **small**

say the word small aloud as you trace it.

small

Now practice writing the word once on each line.

A mouse is very _____.

Picture Puzzle

Find the word **small** in each sentence and circle it. Draw a line to connect the circled words in each sentence and see which letter your line passes through. Write the letters below to solve the picture puzzle.

1. This shirt is too small.

s   i   f   g   r

2. A small bug was on the ground.

o   e   a   t   b

3. I would like to order a small drink.

c   o   v   l   y

4. I'm too small to go on that ride.

h   t   w   l   s

5. These shoes are too small.

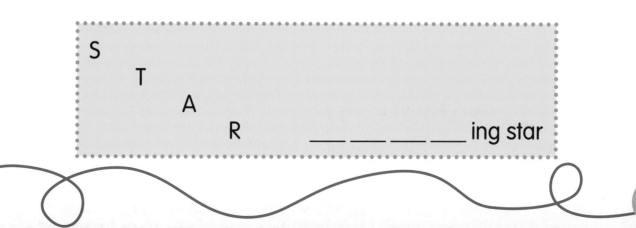

S

T

A

R   ___ ___ ___ ___ ing star

489

Review: Crossword Puzzle!

Use the sentence clues below to solve the crossword puzzle.

shall   which   small   only   bring

Across

2. You need to _____ the box over here.

3. What _____ we do today?

4. I am the _____ one who hit a home run.

Down

1. _____ way should we go?

3. I would like a _____ bowl of soup.

Review: Story Code

Crack the code by writing the correct review word in each blank. Write the word that goes with each symbol in the box below.

What _____ we do when Grandpa comes to visit? He
            #

will _____ be here for a few days. I told him to _____
        @   *

his favorite game. I wonder _____ game he will _____.
                              &   *

_____ room will Grandpa sleep in? My room is,
   &

very _____ and I _____ have one pillow. Grandpa says
        !   @

that my room is not too _____ for him. He will _____ his
                           !   *

own pillow. So, we _____ be roommates!
                       #

_____

* _____

& _____

@ _____

! _____

Review: ABC Gumballs

Write the review words in alphabetical order.

1. _____ 2. _____ 3. _____

4. _____ 5. _____ 6. _____

7. _____ 8. _____ 9. _____

10. _____ 11. _____ 12. _____

13. _____ 14. _____ 15. _____

Review: sentence squares

Read each group of sentences. Then find the group of words below that completes the sentences. Fill the missing words in the blanks.

1. When Grandma comes to visit _____ , she likes to _____ gifts. She has _____ this for a _____ time, and we like it very _____ .

2. My sister _____ does _____ things. When I _____ my foot, she helped _____ me home. I will _____ to be kind to her, too.

3. I needed to _____ my room _____ I made a mess. My room looked so much _____ , so I wanted to _____ it to my family. I was very proud of _____ .

| because | clean | myself | | carry | kind | always |
| better | show | | | try | hurt |

| bring | long | us |
| much | done |

493

 **hot**

say the word hot
aloud as you trace it.

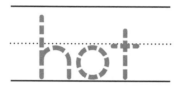

Now practice writing the word once on each line.

The water is too _____!

Keep on Track

Look for the word hot in each track. Circle it each time you see it. Then count the number of circled words in each track and write it in the sign.

Say the word drink aloud as you trace it.

drink

Now practice writing the word once on each line.

I like to _____ milk.

496

Word Watch

Circle the birds that have the word **drink** inside.

drink

brink

drank

drink

drink

dnink

drink

drink

drinc

drihk

their

say the word **their** *aloud as you trace it.*

······tḥ€iͬ

Now practice writing the word once on each line.

The boys are walking _____ dogs.

Crack the Code

The word **their** is hidden once in each column. Find the word and circle the letters. Then use the code to complete the riddle below.

t	1: F	t	1: g	t	1: W
h	2: o	h	2: r	h	2: i
e	3: r	e	3: l	e	3: t
r	4: t	r	4: b	i	4: h
e	5: h	e	5: n	r	5: t
t	6: o	t	6: t	h	6: e
h	7: m	h	7: k	t	7: r
e	8: a	r	8: o	e	8: s
i	9: t	e	9: a	i	9: l
r	10: o	i	10: d	r	10: a
t	11: a	t	11: p	t	11: r
h	12: n	h	12: a	h	12: b
i	13: d	e	13: s	e	13: r
e	14: g	i	14: t	i	14: a
r	15: o	r	15: e	e	15: d

How do you repair a broken tomato?

__ __ __ __   __ __ __ __ __ __
1   2   3   4   5   6   7   8   9   10

__ __ __ __ __!
11   12   13   14   15

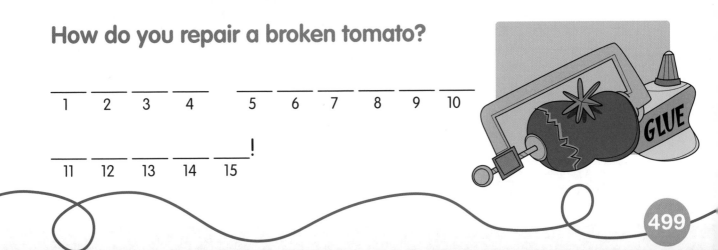

 **light** **say the word** **light** **aloud as** **you trace it.**

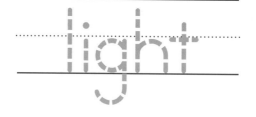

Now practice writing the word once on each line.

Turn on the _____ .

Target Words

Circle the words that have **light** hidden inside.
Underline the letters **l-i-g-h-t** in each circled word.

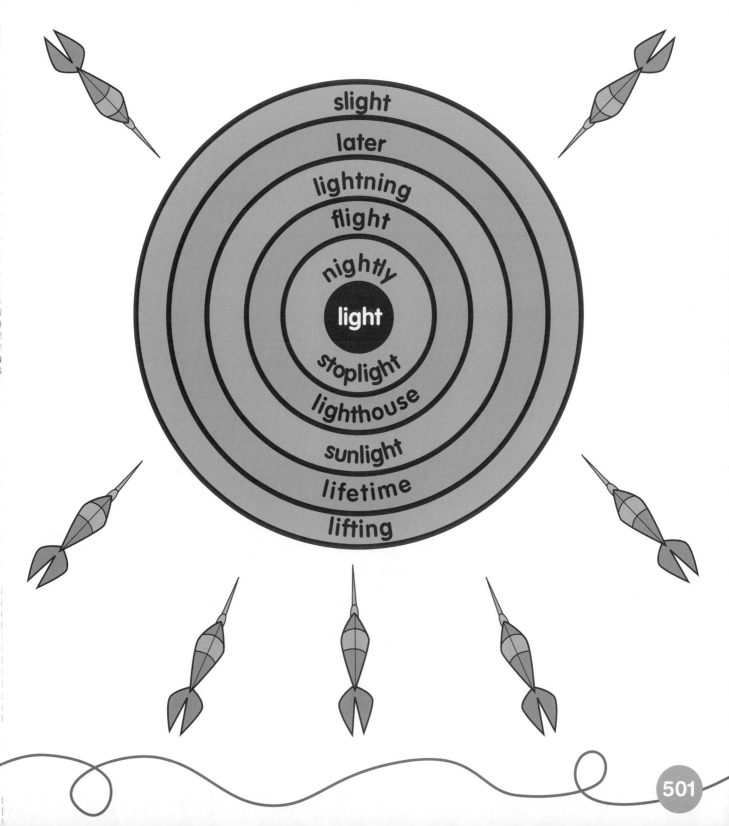

slight

later

lightning

flight

nightly

light

stoplight

lighthouse

sunlight

lifetime

lifting

Say the word if aloud as you trace it.

Now practice writing the word once on each line.

We'll go to the beach
_____ it's sunny.

Pen Pals

Circle the word **if** every time it appears in the letters. Count how many circled words are in each letter, and write the number in the box. Find out which pen pal used the word **if** more.

Dear Bonnie,

I wonder if we can see each other this summer. Do you know if you are taking a summer vacation? It would be fun to see you if you are in my area. I will ask my parents if you can stay with us. If you want, we can sleep in a tent in my backyard.

Sincerely,

Betty

Dear Betty,

I will ask my parents if I can come to visit you. I'm sure that if we are in your area, it will be okay. It would be fun to sleep in a tent if it's not too cold. I've always wanted to do that! If we talk to our parents about it, I bet they will say yes!

Sincerely,

Bonnie

Review: Crossword Puzzle!

Use the sentence clues below to solve the crossword puzzle.

hot   drink   their   light   if

Across

2. It's dark in here! Who turned off the _____ ?

4. We go swimming when it's _____ outside.

5. Ask your mom _____ you can play.

Down

1. I need to get a _____ of water.

3. My brothers have a bunk bed in _____ room.

Review: High Five

Look for the review words as you read the sentences inside each box. Put a check in the box that uses all five review words.

1. ☐ If I wake up before it's light outside, I make hot chocolate for my family. It's their favorite drink.

2. ☐ My brothers forgot to turn off their bedroom light. The lightbulb gets very hot if it's on all day long.

3. ☐ My parents like to drink hot tea every night. Then they turn out the light and go to sleep.

4. ☐ If I can't fall asleep, I turn on the light and get a drink of hot milk.

draw

say the word draw aloud as you trace it.

draw

Now practice writing the word once on each line.

I like to _____ pictures.

Search and Splash

Find the word **draw** three times in the word search.

d	r	w	w	d
r	d	a	d	r
a	r	d	r	a
d	a	r	a	a
w	w	a	w	w

Do the letters go together to make the word **draw**?
Circle Yes or No.

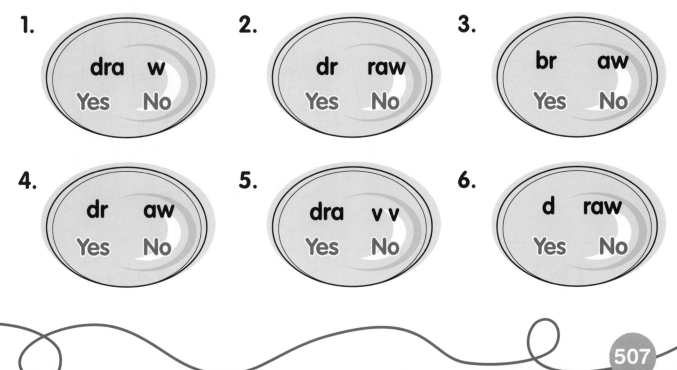

1. dra w Yes No

2. dr raw Yes No

3. br aw Yes No

4. dr aw Yes No

5. dra v v Yes No

6. d raw Yes No

seven

Say the word seven aloud as you trace it.

seven

Now practice writing the word once on each line.

There are _____ days in a week.

What's the Order?

If the letters can be unscrambled to make the word seven, write it on the line. If the letters don't make the word seven, leave the line blank.

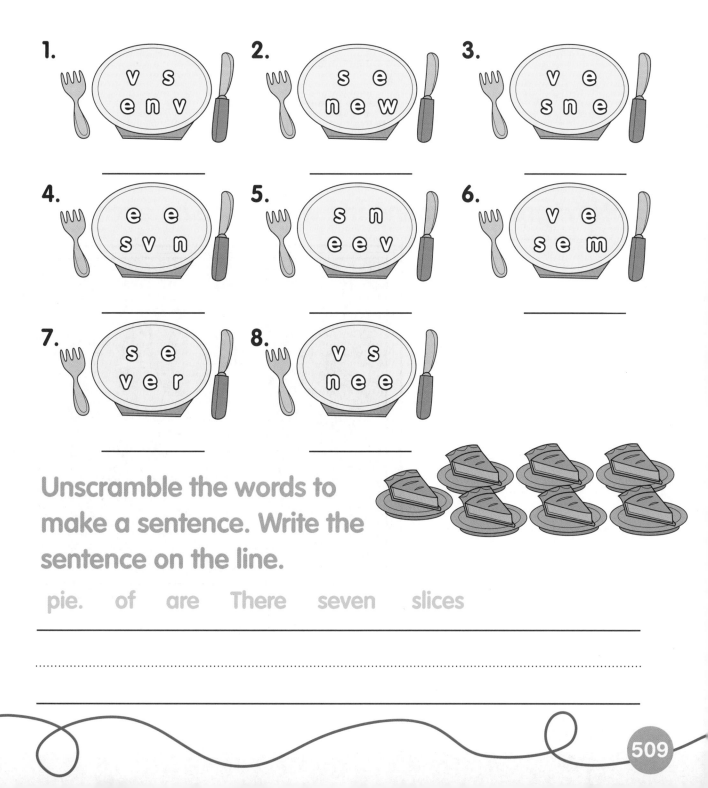

1. v s e n v

_____

2. s e n e w

_____

3. v e s n e

_____

4. e e s v n

_____

5. s n e e v

_____

6. v e s e m

_____

7. s e v e r

_____

8. v s n e e

_____

Unscramble the words to make a sentence. Write the sentence on the line.

pie.   of   are   There   seven   slices

_____

....

_____

 **write**

say the word write aloud as you trace it.

_____

write

Now practice writing the word once on each line.

I can _____ my name on the board.

Stop and Go

Draw a line to connect the letters and make the word **write**.

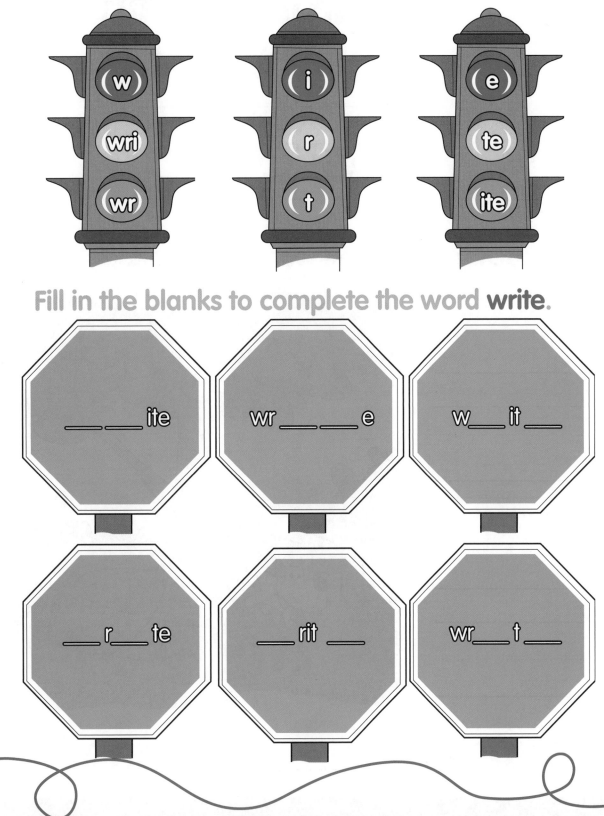

Fill in the blanks to complete the word **write**.

____ite

wr____e

w__it__

__r__te

__rit__

wr__t__

 **around**

Now practice writing the word once on each line.

The puppy runs _____ the tree.

Amazing Maze

Look for the word **around** in the maze. Connect all the words that spell **around** to find your way out of the maze.

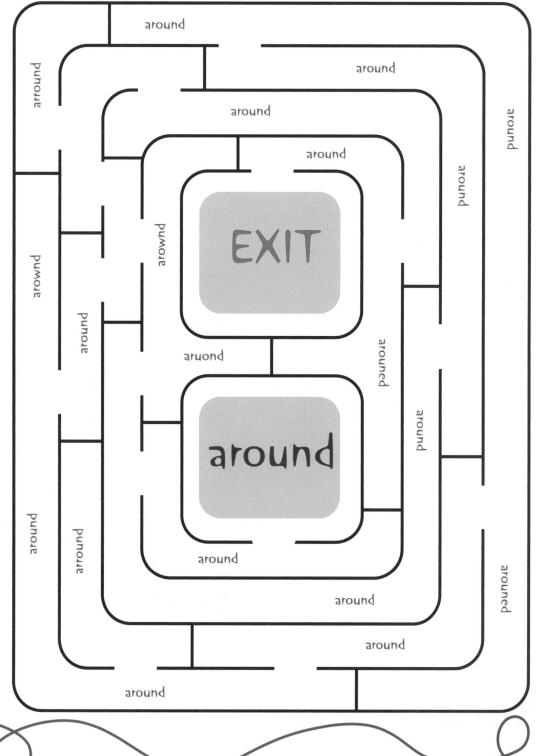

about

say the word **about** aloud as you trace it.

:::about:::

Now practice writing the word once on each line.

This book is all _____ bees.

Picture Puzzle

Find the word **about** in each sentence and circle it. Draw a line to connect the circled words in each sentence and see which letter your line passes through. Write the letters below to solve the picture puzzle.

1. Tell me all about yourself.

      l   c   d   r   s

2. I don't know what that movie is about.

      n   a   g   i   q

3. Talk about your summer plans.

      c   a   b   u   m

4. I need to write a report about robots.

      d   c   d   e   a

5. We learned about animals at the zoo.

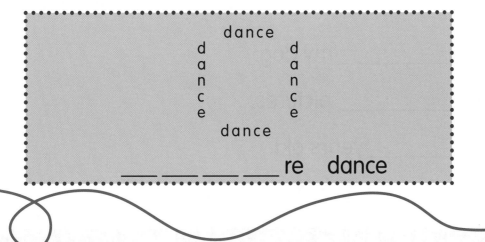

____ ____ ____ ____ re   dance

Review: Crossword Puzzle!

Use the sentence clues below to solve the crossword puzzle.

draw   seven   write   around   about

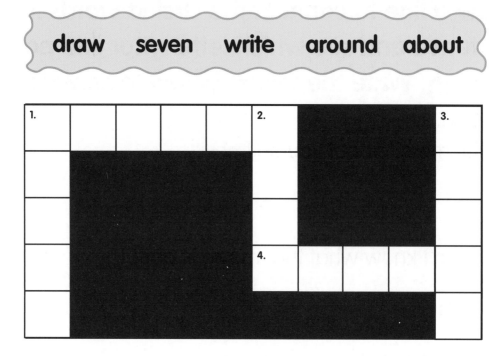

Across

1. Put a circle _____ the answer.

4. I like to _____ letters to my friends.

Down

1. I wrote a story _____ my dog.

2. In art class we _____ pictures.

3. My sister is _____ years old.

Review: Story Code

Crack the code by writing the correct review word in each blank. Write the word that goes with each symbol in the box below.

When I was _____ years old, we moved to a new
                    @

town. I was sad _____ moving. My friends gathered
                       #

_____ to say goodbye. We said we would _____
     *   &

letters.

     Our new house was so big, it had _____ bedrooms.
                                                  @

We had a big yard where our dog could run _____ . I didn't
                                                  *

forget to _____ my friends and tell them _____ our
              &   #

new house. They wrote back and asked me to _____ a
                                                          !

picture of my new house. It was fun to _____ pictures and
                                             !

_____ my friends letters.
     &

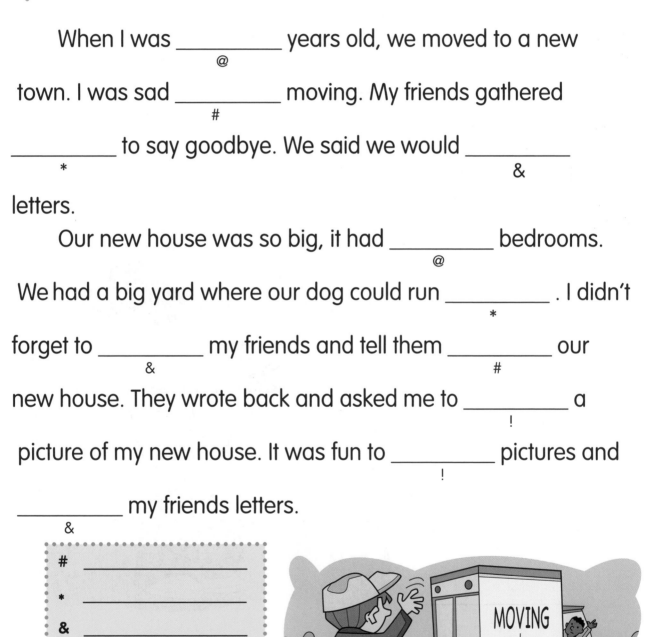

- # _____
- * _____
- & _____
- @ _____
- ! _____

 **got**

Say the word got aloud as you trace it.

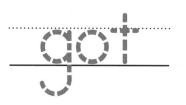

Now practice writing the word once on each line.

I _____ a puppy for my birthday.

Keep on Track

Look for the word **got** in each track. Circle it each time you see it. Then count the number of circled words in each track and write it in the sign.

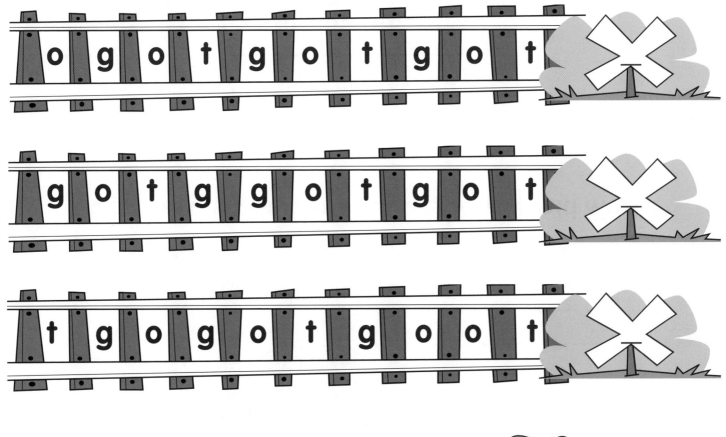

o g o t g o t g o t

g o t g g o t g o t

t g o g o t g o o t

get pot gof got goat got got got

keep

say the word keep aloud as you trace it.

keep

Now practice writing the word once on each line.

You can _____ your toys in the box.

520

Word Watch

Circle the birds that have the word **keep** inside.

 **say the word both aloud as you trace it.**

both

Now practice writing the word once on each line.

We _____ have the same hat.

Crack the Code

The word **both** is hidden once in each column. Find the word and circle the letters. Then use the code to complete the riddle below.

b	**1: a**	b	**1: A**	b	**1: d**
o	**2: g**	o	**2: j**	a	**2: o**
o	**3: i**	t	**3: e**	t	**3: n**
t	**4: f**	h	**4: l**	h	**4: v**
h	**5: W**	b	**5: p**	b	**5: l**
b	**6: a**	o	**6: r**	o	**6: y**
o	**7: y**	h	**7: i**	t	**7: b**
t	**8: l**	t	**8: t**	h	**8: u**
b	**9: t**	d	**9: y**	o	**9: T**
o	**10: t**	o	**10: e**	t	**10: h**
t	**11: o**	t	**11: d**	h	**11: i**
h	**12: n**	h	**12: s**	b	**12: r**

What's in the middle of a jellyfish?

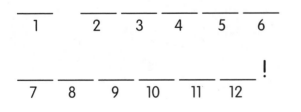

$$\overline{}_{1} \quad \overline{}_{2} \; \overline{}_{3} \; \overline{}_{4} \; \overline{}_{5} \; \overline{}_{6}$$

$$\overline{}_{7} \; \overline{}_{8} \; \overline{}_{9} \; \overline{}_{10} \; \overline{}_{11} \; \overline{}_{12} !$$

 **grow**

Say the word **grow** aloud as you trace it.

 grow

Now practice writing the word once on each line.

Plants need the sun to _____.

Target Words

Circle the words that have **grow** hidden inside.
Underline the letters **g-r-o-w** in each circled word.

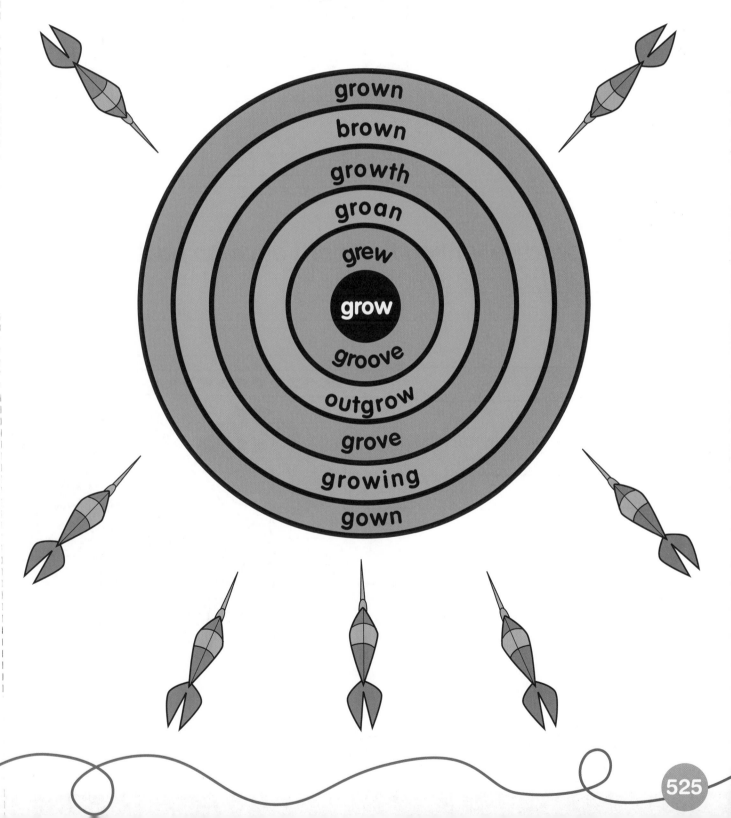

grown

brown

growth

groan

grew

grow

groove

outgrow

grove

growing

gown

together

say the word **together** *aloud* *as you trace it.*

together

Now practice writing the word once on each line.

SCHOOL

Let's walk home _____.

Pen Pals

Circle the word **together** every time it appears in the letters. Count how many circled words are in each letter, and write the number in the box. Find out which pen pal used the word **together** more.

Dear Jake,

I can't wait to get together this weekend. I've planned lots of fun things for us to do together. We can play in the backyard together. I like to gather up all the leaves and make a big pile. Together, we can make the biggest pile ever! See you soon!

Sincerely,

Steve

Dear Steve,

We always have fun when we're together. My dad and I will ride together on the train to get to your house. We will play games together to pass the time. I'll bring my basketball with me. Maybe we can get together a group to play basketball. I'm excited to spend time together.

Sincerely,

Jake

Review: Crossword Puzzle!

Use the sentence clues below to solve the crossword puzzle.

got   keep   both   grow   together

Across

3. Let's go to the party _____ .

5. The present is for _____ of us.

Down

1. I _____ some new shoes for school.

2. Please _____ this door open.

4. When I _____ up, I want to be a teacher.

Review: High Five

Look for the review words as you read the sentences inside each box. Put a check in the box that uses all five review words.

1. I keep both of my fish together in the same tank. I got some new fish food to help them grow.

2. My sister and I both like to grow flowers together. We keep all of our gardening tools in the yard.

3. My friend got two puppies this year. He takes both of them on walks together. They are starting to grow into big dogs.

4. Dad got a gift for both me and my brother. We opened it together. We plan to keep it forever.

 **pick**

say the word pick aloud as you trace it.

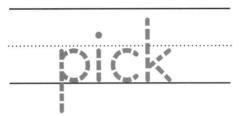

Now practice writing the word once on each line.

You can _____ a book to read.

Search and Splash

Find the word **pick** three times in the word search.

p i c p k
p p k i c
i p i c k
c i c k p
k c k p i

Do the letters go together to make the word pick?
Circle Yes or No.

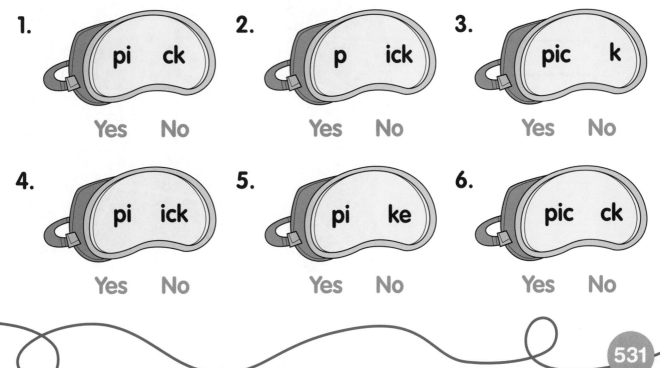

1. **pi ck**   Yes   No

2. **p ick**   Yes   No

3. **pic k**   Yes   No

4. **pi ick**   Yes   No

5. **pi ke**   Yes   No

6. **pic ck**   Yes   No

 **eight**

say the word
eight **aloud as
you trace it.**

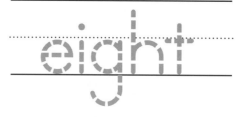

Now practice writing the word once on each line.

A spider has _____ legs.

What's the Order?

If the letters can be unscrambled to make the word **eight**, write it on the line. If the letters don't make the word **eight**, leave the line blank.

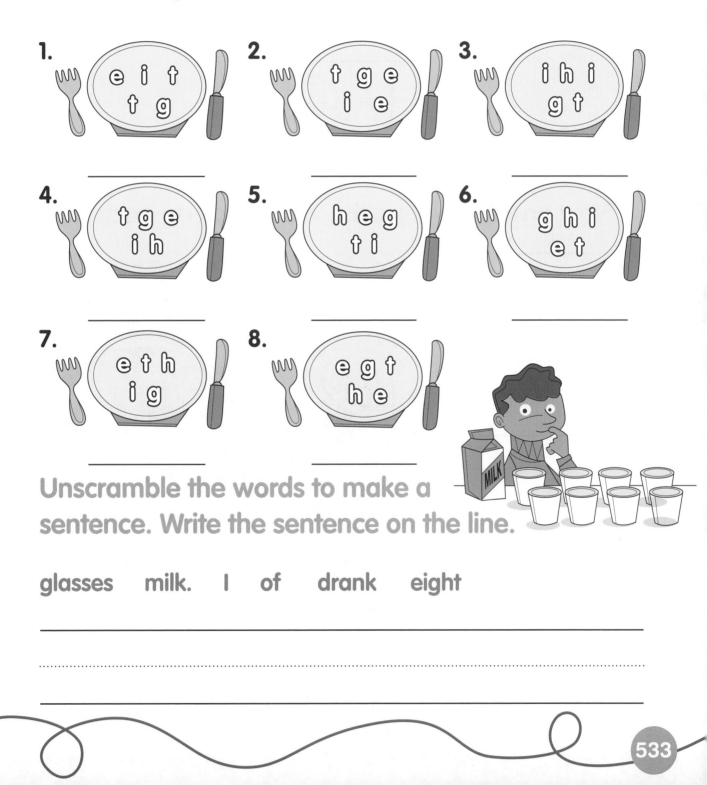

1. e i t t g

2. t g e i e

3. i h i g t

4. t g e i h

5. h e g t i

6. g h i e t

7. e t h i g

8. e g t h e

Unscramble the words to make a sentence. Write the sentence on the line.

glasses   milk.   I   of   drank   eight

today

say the word **today** aloud as you trace it.

today

Now practice writing the word once on each line.

We're going to the zoo _____.

Stop and Go

Draw a line to connect the letters and make the word **today**.

Fill in the blanks to complete the word **today**.

tod ___ ___

___ od ___ y

___ ___ day

t ___ da ___

___ oda ___

to ___ ___ y

 **work**

Say the word work aloud as you trace it.

work

Now practice writing the word once on each line.

My mom goes to _____ every day.

Amazing Maze

Look for the word work in the maze. Connect all the words that spell work to find your way out of the maze.

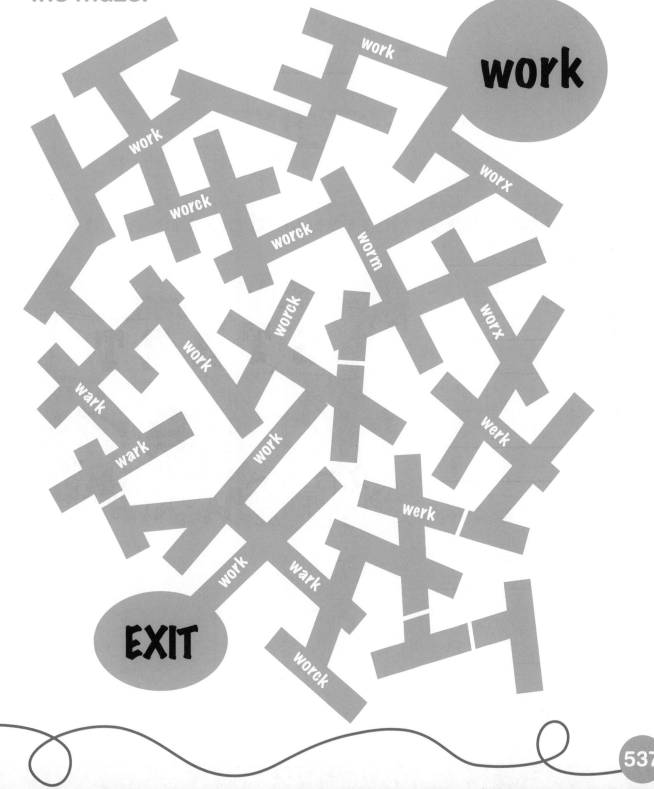

 **start**

Say the word start aloud as you trace it.

⋯⋯⋯start⋯⋯⋯

Now practice writing the word once on each line.

⋯⋯⋯⋯⋯⋯⋯⋯⋯⋯

⋯⋯⋯⋯⋯⋯⋯⋯⋯⋯

⋯⋯⋯⋯⋯⋯⋯⋯⋯⋯

It's time to _____ the race.

Picture Puzzle

Find the word **start** in each sentence and circle it. Draw a line to connect the circled words in each sentence and see which letter your line passes through. Write the letters below to solve the picture puzzle.

1. Don't start the game without me.

l   t   o   h   g

2. When does the movie start?

w   y   l   a   i

3. Wash your hands before you start.

c   r   w   g   c

4. Start the timer now, please.

p   h   r   s   n

5. You can start first, and I'll go next.

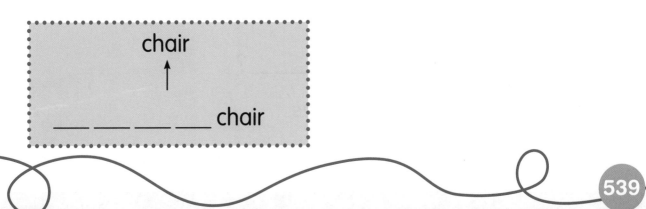

chair

↑

___ ___ ___ ___ chair

Review: Crossword Puzzle!

Use the sentence clues below to solve the crossword puzzle.

pick   eight   today   work   start

Across

2. What do you want to do _____ ?

4. The trip will take _____ hours.

5. After school I _____ at the ice cream shop.

Down

1. What time does school _____ ?

3. Let's _____ up all the toys.

Review: Story Code

Crack the code by writing the correct review word in each blank. Write the word that goes with each symbol in the box below.

We're going to the library _____. I need to get an early
&

_____. My friend will _____ me up at _____ o' clock.
 #   !   @

We need to _____ on a project for school.
          *

I will _____ out about _____ books for us to read.
       !   @

It's going to be a lot of _____. We won't finish the whole
                          *

project _____, but we will get a good _____!
        &   #

```
# _____
* _____
& _____
@ _____
! _____
```

 **call**

say the word **call** aloud as you trace it.

Now practice writing the word once on each line.

I like to _____ my friends on the phone.

Keep on Track

Look for the word **call** in each track. Circle it each time you see it. Then count the number of circled words in each track and write it in the sign.

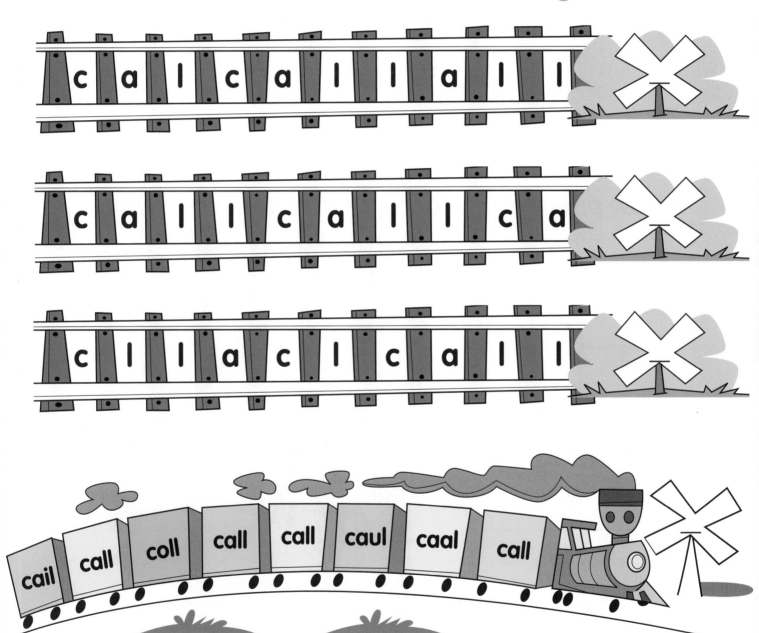

upon

Say the word upon aloud as you trace it.

_____

upon

Now practice writing the word once on each line.

Once _____ a time, there was an old king.

Word Watch

Circle the birds that have the word **upon** inside.

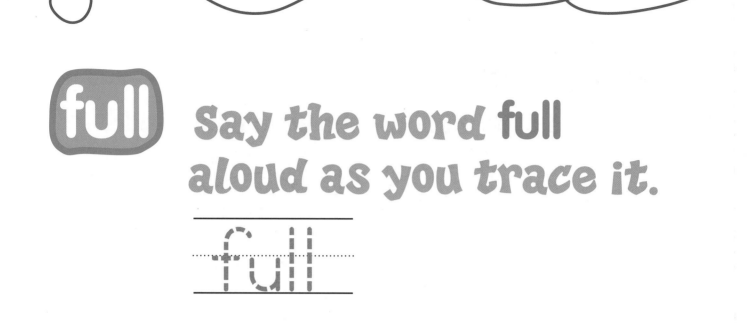

full say the word full
aloud as you trace it.

full

Now practice writing the word once on each line.

The glass is _____.

What's the Order?

If the letters can be unscrambled to make the word **full**, write it on the line. If the letters don't make the word **full**, leave the line blank.

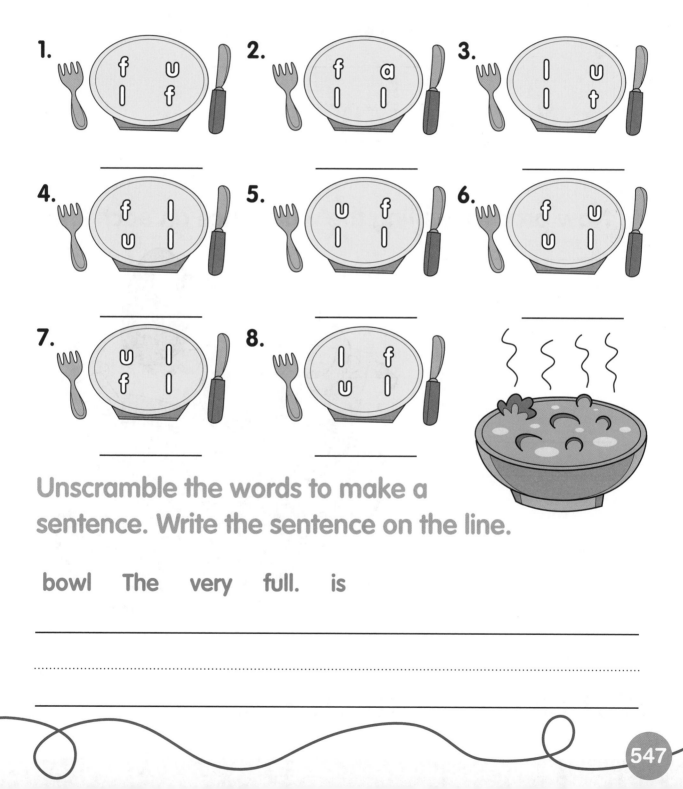

1.

2.

3.

4.

5.

6.

7.

8.

Unscramble the words to make a sentence. Write the sentence on the line.

bowl   The   very   full.   is

_____

....

_____

laugh say the word **laugh** aloud as you trace it.

laugh

Now practice writing the word once on each line.

The clown makes me _____.

Stop and Go

Draw a line to connect the letters and make the word **laugh**.

Fill in the blanks to complete the word **laugh**.

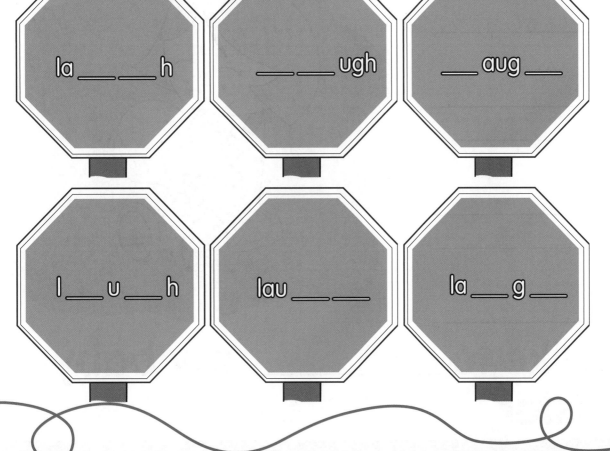

Say the word hold aloud as you trace it.

hold

Now practice writing the word once on each line.

I like to _____ my baby sister.

Amazing Maze

Look for the word hold in the maze. Connect all the words that spell hold to find your way out of the maze.

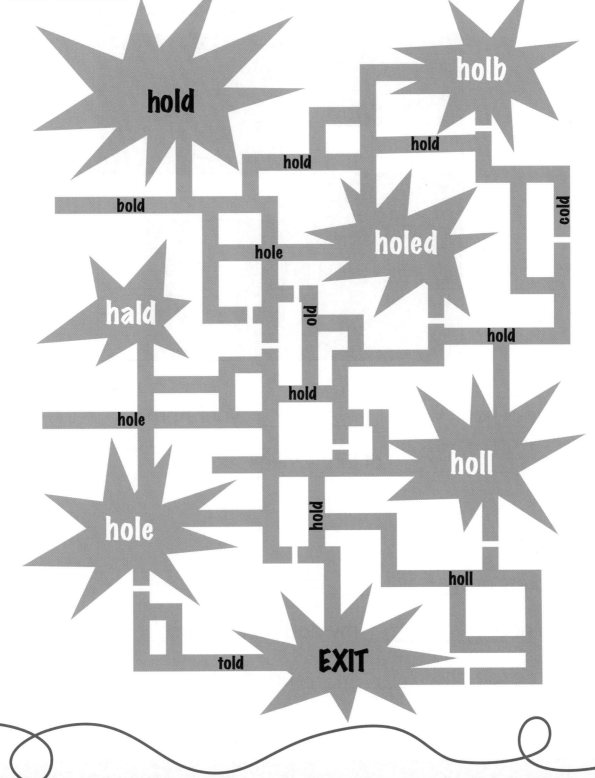

Review: Crossword Puzzle!

Use the sentence clues below to solve the crossword puzzle.

call   upon   full   laugh   hold

Across

2. Raise your hand when I _____ your name.

3. I always _____ at funny jokes.

Down

1. My pockets are _____ of coins.

4. I like to ride _____ my dad's shoulders.

5. Get in a circle and _____ hands.

Review: Story Code

Crack the code by writing the correct review word in each blank. Write the word that goes with each symbol in the box below.

Once _____ a time, there was a very funny boy. He liked
        #

to do tricks and make people _____ . People liked to
               @

_____ him "the Joker." His magic bag was _____ of all
                                                           !
  &

his tricks. He never let anyone else _____ his magic bag.
                                            *

He had so many tricks that his bag got too _____. It was
                                                !

too heavy for the boy to _____ . He put his bag _____ a
                      *   #

horse. He decided to _____ his horse "Trick Trot." Trick Trot
                            &

and the Joker were good at making people _____ .
                                        @

_____

* _____

& _____

@ _____

! _____

Review: ABC Gumballs

Write the review words in alphabetical order.

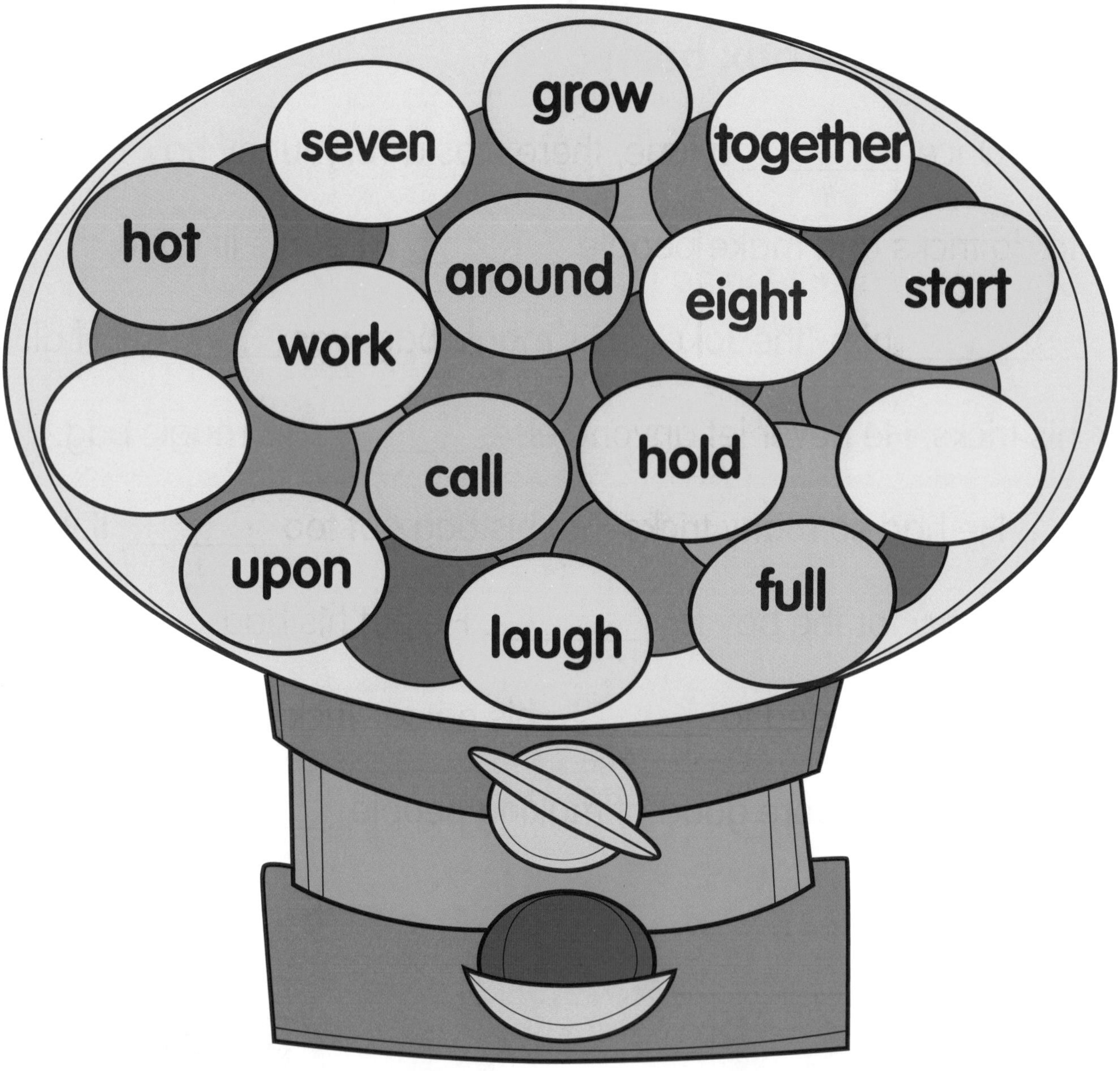

grow

seven

together

hot

around

eight

start

work

call

hold

upon

full

laugh

1. _____

2. _____

3. _____

4. _____

5. _____

6. _____

7. _____

8. _____

9. _____

10. _____

11. _____

12. _____

13. _____

Review: Sentence Squares

Read each group of sentences. Then find the group of words below that completes the sentences. Fill the missing words in the blanks.

1. _____ my parents are _____ thirsty, lemonade is _____ favorite thing to _____ .

2. I need to _____ my bedroom _____ on so I can _____ my report _____ tigers.

3. In art class _____ , I _____ to _____ my favorite color and _____ a picture.

| today | draw | | about | keep |
| got | pick | | light | write |

| drink | If |
| their | both |

Answers Level A

Page 7

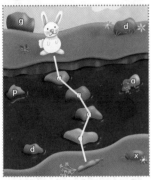

Page 9

Page 11

1. up
3. up
5. up

Page 13

Page 15

These words have **for** hidden inside:
<u>for</u>k
<u>for</u>m
<u>for</u>t
<u>for</u>get

Page 16

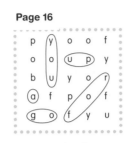

Box 2 is colored.

Page 17

1. 2
2. 3
3. 2
4. 4
5. 1

Worm 4 is the winner.
Sentences will vary.

Page 19

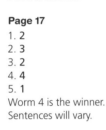

the	tbe	the
hte	teh	the
thh	the	the

Page 21

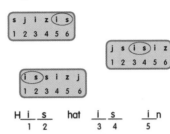

H <u>i</u> <u>s</u>   hat   <u>i</u> <u>s</u>   <u>i</u> n
  1 2   3 4   5

the <u>s</u> ink.
      6

Page 23

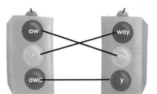

Page 25

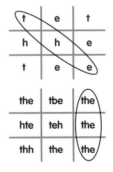

1. I like ice cream.
   a a c b n
2. Dad and I went to get ice cream.
   w e g a r
3. "It's a big scoop," I said.
   c a b q m
4. It was much more than I could eat.
   d a p s o
5. So I shared it with my dad.

What did the cone say to the ice cream?
Dessert is <u>o</u> <u>n</u> <u>m</u> e!

Page 27

These pictures should be circled:
<u>s</u>and
<u>st</u>and
<u>h</u>and
<u>l</u>and

Page 28

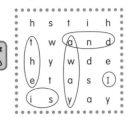

Box 4 is colored.

Page 29

My dog's name <u>is</u> Roofus.
I took him to <u>the</u> beach.
Roofus played <u>and</u> I swam.
Then, <u>I</u> couldn't find him!
Did he run <u>away</u>?

Where was Roofus?
Roofus was under the <u>sand</u>.

Page 31

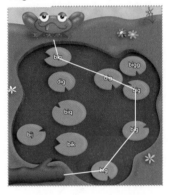

Page 33

557

Page 35

1. look
3. look
6. look

Page 37

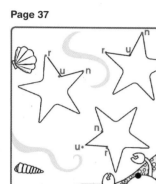

Page 39

These words have **see** hidden inside:
seed
seem
seek
seesaw

Page 40

Box 1 is colored.

Page 41

1. **3**
2. **1**
3. **2**
4. **3**
5. **4**
Worm 5 is the winner.
Sentences will vary.

Page 43

o	n	o
n	o	t
t	n	t

not	nat	not
not	nof	not
hot	not	not

Page 45

e	m	e	n	e	m
1	2	3	4	5	6

e	m	n	e	m	e
1	2	3	4	5	6

m	e	e	m	m	i
1	2	3	4	5	6

Sam's new medal is under
 1 2   3 4
the mess.
   5 6

Page 47

Page 49

1. I can help at home.

  m p r w a

2. Folding clothes is one thing I can do.

  o s d b a

3. I can get it done quickly.

  s n z k t

4. Can you help me at home too?

  d b p b c

5. I think I can!

I'm all __w__ __a__ __s__ __h__ ed up!

Page 51

These pictures should be circled:
chin
pin
win
fin

Page 52

h	r	e	h	c
n	e	t	e	a
m	i	n	r	h
e	a	o	e	c
c	n	t	i	t

Box 5 is colored.

Page 53

My brother plays hide and seek with <u>me</u>.
I can hide <u>in</u> the kitchen.
"Ready or <u>not</u>, here I come!" he says.
He'll never find me in <u>here</u>.
<u>Can</u> you find me?

Where is he?
He's hiding in the <u>ca</u><u>bin</u>et.

Page 55

Page 57

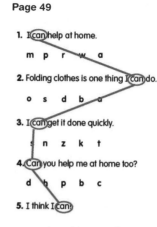

Page 59

2. said
4. said
5. said

Page 61

Page 63

These words have **ran** hidden inside:

<u>ran</u>ch

<u>ran</u>t

b<u>ran</u>

g<u>ran</u>d

Page 64

Box 3 is colored.

Page 65

1. 3
2. 4
3. 1
4. 2
5. 2

Worm 2 is the winner.
Sentences will vary.

Page 67

d	r	d
r	e	r
r	r	d

red	red	ned
wed	red	red
rde	red	rod

Page 69

Sam's <u>d o g</u> is <u>n</u> ear the <u>w i n d o w</u>.
1 2   4   3 8 5 6 7

Page 71

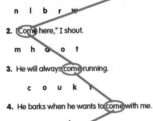

Page 73

1. Everywhere I go, my dog will come along.

   n l b r w

2. "Come here," I shout.

   m h a o t

3. He will always come running.

   c o u k r

4. He barks when he wants to come with me.

   u s v i e

5. He can't come with me to school!

A <u>w</u> <u>a</u> <u>t</u> <u>c</u> h dog!

Page 75

These pictures should be circled:

h<u>am</u>

c<u>l</u>am

<u>j</u>am

s<u>l</u>am

Page 76

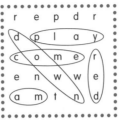

Box 4 is colored.

Page 77

I asked Beth to <u>come</u> over.
We decided to <u>play</u> in my tree house.
Beth said, "I <u>am</u> hungry."
We didn't want to get <u>down</u> from the tree house.
What did we eat that is <u>red</u> and juicy?

What did we eat?
We ate <u>an</u> <u>apple</u> from the tree.

Page 78

2. said
3. up
4. here
5. where
6. away
7. to
8. I
9. and
10. you
11. look
12. play
13. is
14. big
15. a

Page 79

A pair of slippers

Page 81

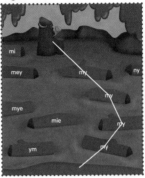

Page 83

Page 85

1. but
2. but
5. but

Page 87

Page 89

These words have **good** hidden inside:
goodnight
goodbye
goodness
goodly

Page 90

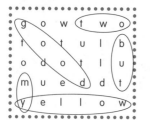

Box 1 is colored.

Page 91

There is a tree in my backyard.
The yellow lemons are ready to eat.
We had two yellow lemons today.
I went to pick them, but they were gone.
My mom used them to make something good!

What did she make?
A glass of lemonade.

Page 93

a	w	s
w	a	w
s	s	s

was	was	saw
mas	wsa	was
was	was	was

Page 95

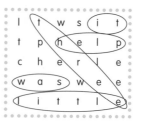

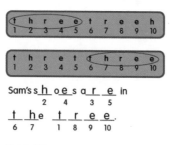

Page 97

Page 99

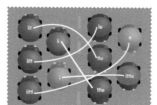

1. I always help my mom.

   d g n u t

2. Sometimes she asks me to help make dinner.

   v s i y n

3. I like to help her in the kitchen.

   t i q m

4. I can help my mom cook the food.

   u o h x a

5. When dinner is ready, I can help eat it all up!

To have a well- b a l a nced meal!

Page 101

These pictures should be circled:
sit
hit
lit
bit

Page 102

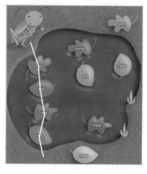

Box 5 is colored.

Page 103

1. **3**
2. **3**
3. **4**
4. **2**
5. **1**
Worm 3 is the winner.
Sentences will vary.

Page 105

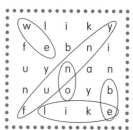

Page 107

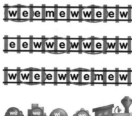

Page 109

1. like
2. like
6. like

Page 111

Page 113

These words have **be** hidden inside:
begin
become
believe
because

Page 114

Box 2 is colored.

Page 115

1. **4**
2. **3**
3. **2**
4. **2**
5. **2**
Worm 1 is the winner.
Sentences will vary.

Page 117

y	s	y
(y	e	s)
e	s	e

yes	yss	yes
yee	yes	yes
yes	yes	yec

Page 119

Sam's s_o_c_k_s are _o_n
     1 2 3   4

the s_t_o_v_e
    5 6

Page 121

Page 123

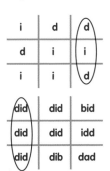

1. It was time to put on my coat.

   l g i n t

2. It wasn't hanging on the coat rack.

   p e s a o

3. I looked on my bed, but no coat.

   d b y r h

4. Oops! I didn't turn the lights on

   c i w v l

5. It was on the table all along.

   A _t_a_b_l_e!

Page 125

These pictures should be circled:
c<u>all</u>
f<u>all</u>
t<u>all</u>
b<u>all</u>
w<u>all</u>

Page 126

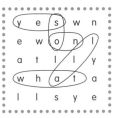

y	e	s	w	n
e	w	o	n	l
a	t	l	l	y
w	h	a	t	a
l	l	s	y	e

Box 4 is colored.

Page 127

It was <u>so</u> cold outside today.
The ground was <u>all</u> covered in snow.
Did we go outside? <u>Yes</u>, we did!
We put <u>on</u> our warm clothes.
<u>What</u> did we do?

What did we do outside?
We h<u>a</u>d a <u>snow</u>b<u>all</u> figh<u>t</u>!

Page 129

Page 131

1. make
3. make
6. make

Page 133

i	d	d
d	i	i
i	i	d

did	did	bid
did	did	idd
did	dib	dad

Page 135

Sam's b_a_s_e_b_a_l_l is
      1 4 5 2 6

_u_n_d_e_r the r_u_g.
 3   8   7

Page 137

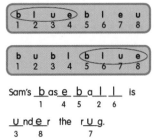

Page 138

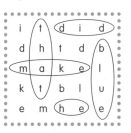

Box 5 is colored.

Page 139

1. 3
2. 2
3. 5
4. 3
5. 2
Worm 3 is the winner.

Page 140

2. no
3. my
4. that
5. funny
6. help
7. all
8. did
9. say
10. three
11. yes
12. like
13. yellow
14. blue
15. it

Page 141

An umbrella

Answers Level B

Page 145

Page 147

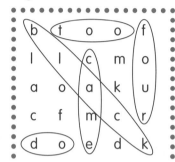

Page 149

3rd floor: four
5th floor: four

Page 151

(Do) we want to win?
Yes, we (do)!
We'll (do) all we can.
How about you?
Team A: 3

We'll (do) just great!
We'll (do) our best.
How (do) we (do) it?
We'll (do) better than the rest!
Team B: 5

Team B has the higher number.

Page 153

These words have **too** hidden inside:
tool
stoop
tooth
cartoon
stool
toot

Page 154

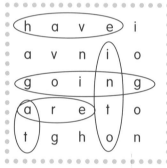

Row 3 is colored.

Page 155

1. too
2. came
3. black
4. do
5. four
Square B has all its boxes marked off first.

Page 157

Because it stays out all night long!

Page 159

Page 161

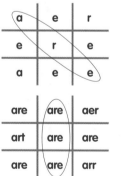

1. No
2. Yes
3. No
4. Yes

Page 163

(Have) you seen my hat? I (have) been looking for half the day. I need some help to find it. I usually hang it in the hall. I (have) a special hook for my hat. But it's not there! I (have) to find it soon. My head needs a hat. It's the only hat I (have)!

These hats are circled:
1. have
3. have
4. have

Page 165

These pictures are circled:
hat
rat
bat
mat
cat

Page 166

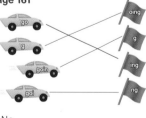

Row 3 is colored.

Page 167

I always have my birthday party at home. This year, I wanted to have it someplace new. ✓
    "We are going somewhere different," my family said. "You are going to have a great time."
    We all got into the car.
    "Where are we going?" I asked.
    "It's a surprise," they said. "You have to close your eyes."
    "Are we there yet?" I asked.
    "You have to be patient!" they said.
    After a long drive, the car stopped. ✓
    "We're at the beach!" I said.
    We all jumped into the water.

Page 169

Page 171

Page 173

3rd floor: soon
4th floor: soon
6th floor: soon

Page 175

When I (say) "go" you (say) "fight." Go! Go! Fight! Fight! When I (say) "win" you (say) "tonight." Win! Win! Tonight! Tonight!
Team A: 4

You (say) you're so great. You (say) you're the best. But we're here to (say) we're better than the rest.
Team B: 3

Team A has the higher number.

Page 177

These words have **under** hidden inside:
th<u>under</u>
<u>under</u>stand
<u>under</u>neath
<u>under</u>wear
<u>under</u>ground

Page 178

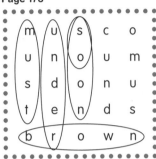

Row 4 is colored.

Page 179

1. so
2. soon
3. must
4. brown
5. under
Square B has all its boxes marked off first.

Page 181

She want<u>ed</u> to sav<u>e</u> <u>it</u> for a <u>r</u>ainy <u>d</u>ay.

Page 183

e	t	g
g	e	t
g	t	e

got	pet	get
get	get	gte
get	get	get

Page 185

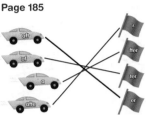

1. Yes
2. Yes
3. No
4. No

Page 187

I have twin brothers, Tim and Jim. They look exactly the same. They have brown hair and blue eyes. Today they have on matching clothes. Both of them are wearing white shirts and jeans. Hey, I can't tell them apart! I hope they tell me who is who. If not, then they will be in big trouble!

These shirts are circled:
2. they
3. they
4. they

Page 189

These words are circled:
<u>date</u>
<u>gate</u>
<u>late</u>
<u>plate</u>

Page 190

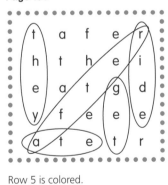

Row 5 is colored.

Page 191

Amy and Ella went to the fair. First they saw the animals. A pony ate a carrot out of Ella's hand. After that, Ella wanted to go on a ride.

"Let's ride the Ferris wheel," Ella said.

"We need to get some tickets first," Amy said.

After they got tickets, they went on the ride. Then they decided to get hot dogs.

After they ate, they went home. They decided to come to the fair every year!

Page 193

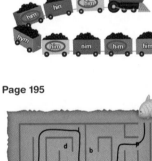

Page 195

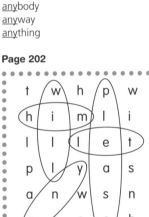

Page 197

2nd floor: let
3rd floor: let
4th floor: let
6th floor: let

Page 199

Who will clap their hands?
Who will give a cheer?
Who will shout "Go Team"?
So everyone will hear!
Team A: 4

Our team will play
Our team will score
And when they win
The crowd will roar
Team B: 3

Team A has the higher number.

Page 201

These words have **any** hidden inside:
m<u>any</u>
<u>any</u>one
<u>any</u>where
<u>any</u>body
<u>any</u>way
<u>any</u>thing

Page 202

Row 2 is colored.

Page 203

1. please
2. let
3. him
4. Will
5. any
Square A has all its boxes marked off first.

Page 205

There <u>was</u>n't <u>any</u>body for him to go <u>with</u>.

Page 207

n	w	n
w	n	e
e	e	w

new	mew	new
mew	new	new
new	new	now

Page 209

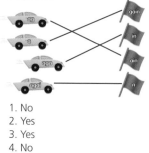

1. No
2. Yes
3. Yes
4. No

Page 211

Where did all the cookies go? This morning there were three cookies. They were right there in the jar. Now, there aren't any cookies! They're all gone! But I can still smell cookies. It's coming from over there by the oven. There is a new batch of cookies! I can't wait to eat them all up.

These cookie jars are circled:
1. there
2. there
6. there

Page 213

These words are circled:
heat
neat
seat
meat

Page 214

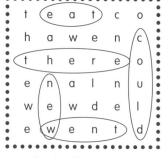

t	e	a	t	c	o
h	a	w	e	n	c
t	h	e	r	e	o
e	n	a	l	n	u
w	e	w	d	e	l
e	w	e	n	t	d

Row 4 is colored.

Page 215

Zack could not think of anything fun to do. He wanted to try something new. He decided to bake a pie that he could eat.

Then, his friend Josh came over with a new ball. The boys went outside to play with it. Zack forgot there was a pie baking in the oven.

"I'm so hungry, I could eat a pie," Josh said.

"There is a pie in the oven!" Zack said. The boys went inside. The pie was burned. There was nothing they could do.

"Let's bake a new pie," Josh said.

"And this time, let's make sure we get to eat it!" Zack said.

Page 216

Knock knock.
Who's there?
Anita.
Anita who?
Anita ride to school!

Page 217

2. do
3. any
4. get
5. too
6. four
7. into
8. at
9. they
10. went
11. could
12. going
13. brown
14. under
15. after

Page 219

Page 221

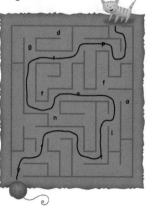

Page 223

1st floor: this
2nd floor: this
6th floor: this

Page 225

Give me a W!
Give me an I!
Give me an N!
What does it spell?
Win!
Team A: 3

Put your hands together.
Give your team a shout!
You can also give a cheer.
That's what it's all about!
Team B: 2

Team A has the higher number.

Page 227

These words have **every** hidden inside:
everybody
everywhere
everyone
everything

Page 228

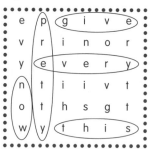

e	p	g	i	v	e
v	r	i	n	o	r
y	e	v	e	r	y
n	t	i	i	v	t
o	t	h	s	g	t
w	y	t	h	i	s

Row 4 is colored.

Page 229

1. give
2. every
3. this
4. pretty
5. now
Square A has all its boxes marked off first.

Page 231

So he would have sweet dreams.

Page 233

s	w	w
w	a	w
s	w	s

saw	saw	swa
saw	saw	saw
sow	sew	saw

Page 235

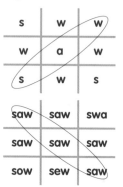

1. No
2. Yes
3. Yes
4. No

Page 237

I'm looking for my favorite ball. It's made of rubber bands. It can bounce off anything! I seem to lose it often. I looked in all of my toy boxes. I also looked on top of my dresser. It checked my dad's office too. Hey, there it is! It's at the bottom of my backpack. I hadn't thought of that!

These balls are circled:
1. of
3. of
4. of

Page 239

These words are circled:
sour
hour
scour
flour

Page 240

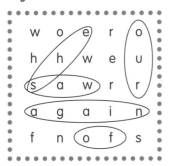

Row 2 is colored.

Page 241

This morning we saw a kitten in our backyard. She was playing with a ball of yarn.
   "None of our neighbors have a kitten," I said. "She must be lost."
   When we looked up again, the kitten was gone.
   Later that day, we saw her again. She was sleeping on top of our car.
   "I saw a sign about a lost kitten at our bus stop," my dad said.
   The sign had a picture of a kitten. It looked just like the kitten we saw!
   We called the owners of the kitten. They came to pick her up at our house.
   They were so happy to see their kitten again!

Page 243

Page 245

Page 247

1st floor: want
3rd floor: want
4th floor: want

Page 249

We know how to play.
We know how to win.
We'll show them how it's done.
Now let's begin!
Team A: 3

How will we beat the other team?
How will we win tonight?
We know how and starting now, we'll show them how to do it right!
Team B: 4

Team B has the higher number.

Page 251

These words have **some** hidden inside:
somewhere
somebody
someone
sometimes
handsome
something

Page 252

h	o	s	m	w
w	a	n	t	e
s	o	m	e	l
o	h	o	w	l
w	h	i	t	e

Row 2 is colored.

Page 253

1. well
2. white
3. How
4. want
5. some

Square A has all its boxes marked off first.

Page 255

Try to cheer him up!

Page 257

w	w	h
w	h	w
o	w	o

wno	who	who
who	hoo	wha
who	who	who

Page 259

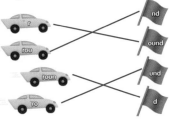

1. No
2. No
3. Yes
4. Yes

Page 261

Today I lost my hamster. She is very small. Her fur is white as snow. I looked all over the house, as did my mom. Just as I was about to give up, I heard a noise. It sounded as if my hamster was in the bathtub. I looked in the tub, and there she was! She was playing with the bath toys, happy as she could be.

These ducks are circled:
1. as
2. as
5. as

Page 263

These words are circled:
shout
pout
sprout
snout
spout

Page 264

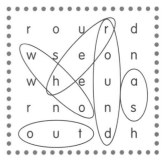

Row 1 is colored.

Page 265

On my sister's birthday, someone gave her a gift as a surprise. They left it out on our front steps. The box was big and round.

"Who is it from?" my sister asked.

"It doesn't say who it's from," I told her.

Just as we were about to open it, a puppy jumped out of the box! The puppy had big round eyes and fur white as snow. He licked her face and let out a bark. He was as cute as could be. We never found out who gave her the puppy. We loved it as one of the family.

Page 267

Page 269

2nd floor: with
5th floor: with
6th floor: with

Page 271

a	h	a
d	a	d
h	d	h

had	had	had
had	had	hand
dad	bad	hod

Page 273

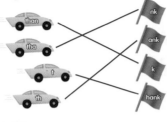

1. Yes
2. No
3. No
4. Yes

Page 275

I lost my book. It's written by my favorite author. I can read the whole book by myself. I like to read it before I go to bed. By the time I find it, it will be too late to read it. I have to go to bed by eight o'clock. Maybe tomorrow I can buy a new book. Wait! I found it! It was right by my bed all along.

These books are circled:
1. by
5. by
6. by

Page 276

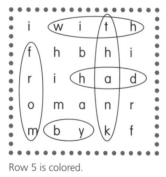

Row 5 is colored.

Page 277

1. by
2. from
3. with
4. had
5. thank

Square A has all its boxes marked off first.

Page 278

Knock, knock.
Who's there?
Justin.
Justin who?
Justin time for lunch!

Page 279

2. she
3. by
4. want
5. now
6. give
7. well
8. from
9. thank
10. again

Answers Level C

Page 283

Page 285

Page 287

top secret

Page 289

overdo
overhead
clover
leftover
oversee
overtime

Page 291

Q: Were Bill and Tim at school today?
A: Yes, they were both at school.

Q: Why were you cold?
A: I didn't wear my coat.

Q: What were you doing at the park?
A: We were having a picnic.

Q: Where were you today?
A: I was at work.

Q: 4
A: 2

Page 292

Page 293

1. fly
2. very
3. over
4. were
5. found
Square B has all of its boxes marked off first.

Page 295

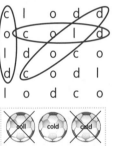

Page 297

1. warm
2. warm
5. warm
6. warm

Page 299

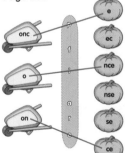

What did the pumpkin say after Thanksgiving?

Good-pie

Page 301

We've been playing hide and seek today. I hid under a chair. I had to bend down very low. Nobody has been able to find me. They have been looking for a long time. Everyone else has been found. Finally, somebody looked beneath the chair. I've been found too!

1. been
5. been
6. been

Page 303

These words rhyme with **old**:
gold
hold
fold
sold

Page 304

Page 305

Box 1 is checked.

Page 307

Page 309

Page 311

A pair of pants

Page 313

sleepwalk
asleep
sleeping
sleepy
sleepless
sleepily

Page 315

Q: What is your first name?
A: My first name is Kim.

Q: Who was first in line?
A: She was in line first.

Q: Is it time for us to eat lunch?
A: Yes, but first we need to wash our hands.

Q: Can I try the new toy first?
A: First your little brother gets a turn.

Q: 3
A: 4

Page 316

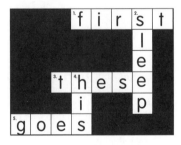

567

Page 317

1. sleep
2. first
3. goes
4. his
5. these

Square B has all of its boxes marked off first.

Page 319

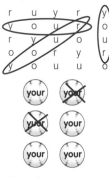

Page 321

2. open
3. open
5. open
7. open

Page 323

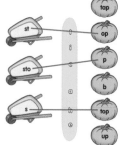

What did the pumpkin sew?
A pumpkin pa<u>tch</u>

Page 325

I lost a five dollar bill. I don't know where it is.

My mom asked, "Do you remember the last time you saw it?"

"No, I don't remember," I said.
"Why don't I help you look for it?" Mom asked.

Mom and I looked all over the house. When we were done, we still hadn't found it.

"Are you sure you don't have it in your pocket?" Mom asked.

I looked in my pocket, and there it was! I don't believe it!

2. don't
3. don't
4. don't

Page 327

These words rhyme with **own**:
gr<u>own</u>
kn<u>own</u>
bl<u>own</u>
sh<u>own</u>

Page 328

Page 329

Box 3 is checked.

Page 331

Page 333

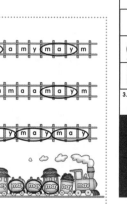

Page 335

One <u>in</u> <u>a</u> million

Page 337

f<u>right</u>
b<u>right</u>
down<u>right</u>
<u>right</u>ly
up<u>right</u>
<u>right</u>ful

Page 339

Q: Do you know how to swim?
A: I know how to swim very well.

Q: Have you met Chris before?
A: Yes, we already know each other.

Q: How do you know Susan?
A: I know her from my class.

Q: Which way is it to the park?
A: I don't know.

Q: 2
A: 4

Page 340

Page 341

1. may
2. right
3. read
4. think
5. know

Square A has all of its boxes marked off first.

Page 343

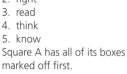

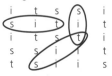

Page 345

3. walk
4. walk
5. walk
8. walk

Page 347

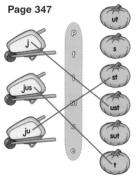

What do you call a chubby pumpkin?

A <u>plump</u>kin

Page 349

My family likes to camp more than anything. Last time we camped, I lost my flashlight. I looked in our tent, then I looked outside. It was so dark, I bumped into my dad! Then we both bumped into my mom.

"If we had a flashlight, then we could find our way!" I told them.

"We don't need a flashlight," Dad said. Then he lit a match to give us light.

We found our way back to the tent. Only then did we find the flashlight. It was inside my sleeping bag!

2. then
3. then
5. then
6. then

Page 351

These words rhyme with **an**:
m<u>an</u>
r<u>an</u>
pl<u>an</u>
v<u>an</u>
p<u>an</u>

Page 352

j u s t
i
t h e n
w a
l n
k

Page 353

Box 3 is checked.

Page 354

1. an
2. been
3. cold
4. does
5. don't
6. fly
7. goes
8. just
9. old
10. own
11. sleep
12. these
13. think
14. very
15. warm

Page 355

1. You <u>may</u> have the toy <u>first</u>, and <u>then</u> it's <u>his</u> turn.
2. I try to <u>sit</u> down and <u>read</u> a story <u>once</u> a day.
3. To get to the park, <u>walk</u> to the <u>stop</u> sign at the corner. Turn <u>right</u> and go <u>over</u> the bridge.
4. I <u>found</u> the keys that <u>open</u> the door. They <u>were</u> under <u>your</u> coat.

Page 357

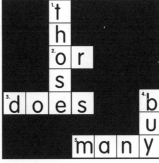

Page 359

Page 361

<u>sandbox</u>

Page 363

<u>form</u>
<u>for</u>
<u>order</u>
<u>orange</u>
<u>storm</u>
<u>born</u>

Page 365

Q: Where does Mom keep the cookies?
A: She keeps them in the jar.

Q: Does Emily know how to swim?
A: Yes, she does.

Q: How does your dad wash the car?
A: He does it with a hose.

Q: When does the mall open?
A: It opens at 10:00 AM.

Q: 4
A: 2

Page 366

t
h o r
o
s
d o e s b
u
m a n y

Page 367

1. does
2. buy
3. or
4. many
5. those
Square B has all of its boxes marked off first.

Page 369

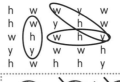

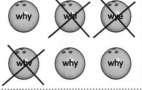

Page 371

1. off
3. off
4. off
7. off

Page 373

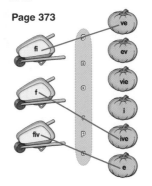

What do you call a pumpkin that's in a bad mood?

A <u>grumpkin</u>

Page 375

I can't find my rain boots. It's raining outside, so I need to wear (them) They are usually in my closet. I looked in the closet, but they weren't there. Then I looked under my bed. I can't find (them) anywhere. The last time I wore (them) was yesterday. I took (them) off when I put down my umbrella. I know where they are now! I put (them) under my umbrella.

3. them
5. them
6. them

Page 377

These words rhyme with **its**:
<u>sits</u>
<u>fits</u>
<u>hits</u>
<u>bits</u>

Page 378

w
t h e m
y
o
f
f i v e
t
s

Page 379

Box 2 is checked.

Page 381

Page 383

Page 385
<u>downtown</u>

Page 387
mouth<u>wash</u>
a<u>wash</u>
<u>wash</u>er
<u>wash</u>ed
<u>wash</u>ing
<u>wash</u>out

Page 389
Q: May I (tell) you a secret?
A: Sure, you may (tell) me a secret.

Q: Will you (tell) me where the cookies are?
A: I can't (tell) you until after lunch!

Q: Should we (tell) Dad about this?
A: Of course we should (tell) him.

Q: Would you (tell) Mom I'm ready?
A: I already told her!

Q: 4
A: 3

Page 390

Page 391
1. has
2. tell
3. pull
4. green
5. wash
Square B has all of its boxes marked off first.

Page 393

b	e	t	b	t
b	s	e	s	b
e	b	e	s	t
s	b	b	e	e
t	b	e	t	s

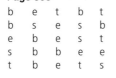

Page 395
2. put
6. put
7. put
8. put

Page 397

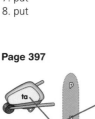

What does a pumpkin say when you ask "How are you"?

I'm <u>vine</u>.

Page 399
I don't know where my lunchbox is. When all the kids are eating, I'll have no lunch! I went to the lost and found. It wasn't there. When was the last time I had my lunch box? I know I had it when I got to school. I was on the playground before school. Maybe I left it by the swings when I was playing there. When I went and looked by the swings, my lunchbox was there! I can hardly wait to eat lunch!

2. when
3. when
4. when

Page 401
These words rhyme with **ask**:
t<u>ask</u>
b<u>ask</u>
fl<u>ask</u>
m<u>ask</u>

Page 402

Page 403
Box 3 is checked.

Page 405

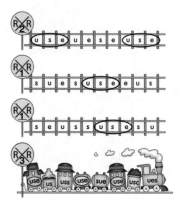

Page 407
Q: Who (gave) you that hat?
A: My brother (gave) it to me.

Q: How did you get home so fast?
A: My friend (gave) me a ride home.

Q: Who (gave) you gifts for your birthday?
A: My family and friends (gave) me gifts.

Q: Where did all the cookies go?
A: I (gave) them to my friends.

Q: 2
A: 4

Page 409
1. jump
3. jump
5. jump
7. jump

Page 411

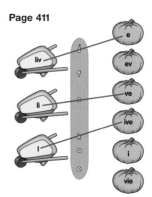

What do you call a pumpkin that likes to tell jokes?

A <u>joke</u> o'lantern

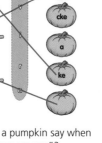

Page 413

I lost my best scarf! I (made) this scarf myself. It was the first one I have ever (made) I was mad that I had lost it. I (made) my brother help me look. We (made) a list of all the places the scarf could be. Then we asked the maid if she had seen it. She thought maybe she saw our dog with the scarf. We found the dog in the middle of the living room, wearing my scarf! It (made) me laugh.

2. made
4. made
6. made

Page 414

Page 415

1. live
2. gave
3. made
4. use
5. jump
Square B has all of its boxes marked off first.

Page 416

1. ask
2. does
3. its
4. jump
5. live
6. made
7. off
8. or
9. pull
10. take
11. those
12. why

Page 417

1. How <u>many</u> toys did you <u>buy</u>? Make sure to <u>put</u> them all away.
2. My neighbor <u>has</u> a long hose. Maybe we can <u>use</u> it to <u>wash</u> the car.
3. I saw <u>five</u> ducks <u>when</u> we were at the pond. I watched <u>them</u> walk across the <u>green</u> grass.
4. My dad <u>gave</u> me the <u>best</u> birthday gift! I want to <u>tell</u> all my friends about it.

Answers Level D

Page 421

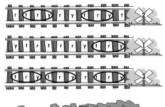

Page 423

Page 425

n	1: h	s	1: c	s	1: d
n	2: c	n	2: l	n	2: o
g	3: l	g	3: e	n	3: i
s	4: a	i	4: a	g	4: f
s	5: n	n	5: b	i	5: h
i	6: g	g	6: p	s	6: u
n	7: e	i	7: f	i	7: r
g	8: t	n	8: i	n	8: g
i	9: t	g	9: o	g	9: a
s	10: e	n	10: v	s	10: w
n	11: t	g	11: r	i	11: a
g	12: h	s	12: y	n/g	12: y

Why did the burglar take a shower?
He wanted to make a <u>clean getaway</u>!

Page 427

<u>tent</u>
<u>tenth</u>
<u>tennis</u>
<u>tense</u>
<u>tend</u>
<u>pretend</u>

Page 429

Dear Alex,
I hope you can visit me this summer. There are so many things for (us) to do. My dad will make (us) pancakes every day. Our tree house is big enough for (us) to sleep in. You can stay with (us) as long as you want!
Sincerely,
Justin
Inside box: 4

Dear Justin,
You've planned a lot of fun things for (us) My parents want you to come camping with (us) They will take (us) to the mountains. There is a tent just for (us) Call (us) and let (us) know if you can come.
Sincerely,
Alex
Inside box: 6

Page 430

				1.u	s
					i
		3.t	e	n	
4.b	e	t	t	e	r
				y	

Page 431

Box 3 is checked.

Page 433

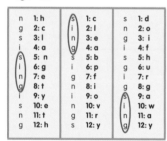

1. yes
2. no
3. no
4. yes
5. yes
6. no

Page 435

These letters can be unscrambled to make the word **fast:**
1. fast
5. fast
6. fast
You ate your meal fast.

Page 437

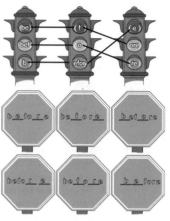

Page 439

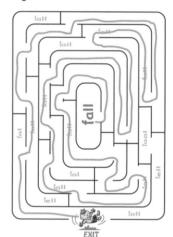

Page 441

1. I have (never) been to New York.
2. I told my mom I would (never) do it again.
3. I (never) wake up on time.
4. The snow is something I have (never) seen.
5. I would (never) tell a lie.
<u>grow</u>ing old

Page 442

					1.n
	2.b	e	3.f	o	r	e
			a		v
	4.w		l		e
	i		l		r
5.f	a	s	t		
	h				

Page 443

My birthday <u>wish</u> was to go to the lake. I had <u>never</u> been there <u>before.</u> My <u>wish</u> came true. <u>Before</u> we left, my brother said, "Be careful not to <u>fall</u> in the lake!"

We got to the lake, and <u>before</u> anyone could stop me, I ran to the water very <u>fast</u>. I was running so <u>fast</u>, I fell into the water.

"I knew you would <u>fall</u> in!" said my brother.

I <u>wish</u> I had <u>never</u> gone to the lake!
wish
★ never
& before
@ fall
! fast

Page 445

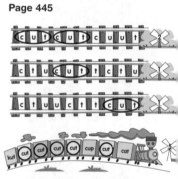

Page 447

Page 449

r	1: c	u	1: y	h	1: H
h	2: k	r	2: e	u	2: e
t	3: l	t	3: s	r	3: f
u	4: a	h	4: l	t	4: e
h	5: r	u	5: l		5: a
u	6: e	r	6: t	g	6: t
n	7: n	t	7: c	i	7: h
t	8: o	u	8: r	g	8: e
u	9: u	h	9: w	s	9: s
r	10: m	u	10: a	i	10: r
t	11: m	r	11: s	n	11: e
	12: y	d	12: n	g	12: t

Why did the cookie go to the doctor?
<u>He felt crummy</u>!

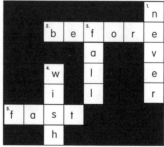

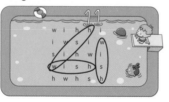

Page 451

<u>far</u>m
<u>far</u>ther
a<u>far</u>
<u>far</u>mer

Page 453

Dear Emily,
I can't go to the beach today (because) it's raining. Rainy days are nice (because) I can stay inside and write letters. I am excited (because) I can use my new pen. My dad gave it to me (because) I did well on my spelling test. I hope to become the best speller in my class! I study every night (because) I want to be in the spelling bee!
Sincerely,
Anna
Inside box: 5

Dear Anna,
I like getting your letters (because) they are always fun to read. I like rainy days too, but not (because) I can write letters. I like rainy days (because) I can read by the fire. Sometimes on rainy days I read old letters from my pen pals. I never throw away a letter (because) I might want to read it again. I keep all my letters in a box right beside my bed.
Sincerely,
Emily
Inside box: 4

Page 454

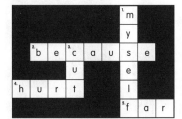

Page 455

Box 4 is checked.

Page 457

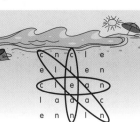

1. yes
2. no
3. no
4. no
5. yes
6. yes

Page 459

These letters can be unscrambled to make the word **much**:
3. much
4. much
5. much
7. much
How much do you want?

Page 461

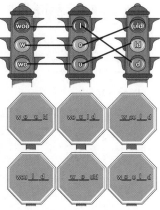

Page 463

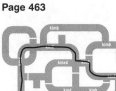

Page 465

1. Please (carry) your plate to the sink.
2. My bag is too heavy to (carry).
3. I like to (carry) my brother on my back.
4. There are too many books to (carry).
5. I can't (carry) this to the car!
<u>tall</u> tale

Page 466

Page 467

I have a very <u>kind</u> neighbor. She always helps us <u>carry</u> the groceries in from the car. My family likes her very <u>much</u>.
One day, she asked if I <u>would</u> help her. She needed to <u>clean</u> out her garage. There was too <u>much</u> stuff for her to <u>carry</u>. I told her I <u>would</u> help her.
When we were done, her garage was so <u>clean</u>! It felt good to do something <u>kind</u> for her.
\# kind
* would
& clean
@ much
! carry

Page 469

Page 471

Page 473

done			
d	1: F	d	1: c	o	1: V
o	2: i	o	2: o	d	2: e
n	3: r	n	3: d	o	3: r
e	4: e	e	4: e	n	4: y
o	5: a	d	5: g	e	5: c
o	6: t	o	6: A	d	6: r
e	7: h	n	7: t	o	7: a
n	8: i	e	8: h	n	8: c
e	9: t		9: k	e	9: l
d	10: r	d	10: e	n	10: a
o	11: u	o	11: r	d	11: r
n	12: n	n	12: s	e	12: b

What do firemen put in their soup?
<u>Fire crackers!</u>

Page 475

<u>long</u>ing
<u>long</u>er
life<u>long</u>
a<u>long</u>
be<u>long</u>
<u>long</u>est

Page 477

Dear Noah,
Whenever I go on a trip, I (always) bring a pen and paper along. It's (always) fun to send you a letter about my trip. My family (always) camps at the same place every year. This year, the place we (always) go to is full. So we drove around until we found a new place to camp. I like the new place even better!
Sincerely,
Gabe
Inside box: 4

Dear Gabe,
I (always) like reading your letters. You (always) have a fun story to tell. My family (always) camps at the same place too. Whenever we camp, we (always) go on a hike. I wanted to go on the hike alone, but my parents wouldn't allow it. They said you should (always) hike with a buddy.
Sincerely,
Noah
Inside box: 5

Page 478

Page 479

Box 3 is checked.

Page 481

1. no
2. no
3. no
4. yes
5. yes
6. yes

Page 483

These letters can be unscrambled to make the word **which**:
1. which
2. which
5. which
6. which
Which one do you want?

Page 485

Page 487

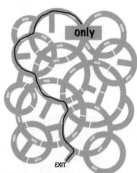

Page 489

1. This shirt is too small.
2. A small bug was on the ground.
3. I would like to order a small drink.
4. I'm too small to go on that ride.
5. These shoes are too small.
falling star

Page 490

Page 491

What shall we do when Grandpa comes to visit? He will only be here for a few days. I told him to bring his favorite game. I wonder which game he will bring.

Which room will Grandpa sleep in? My room is very small, and I only have one pillow. Grandpa says that my room is not too small for him. He will bring his own pillow. So, we shall be roommates!

shall
* bring
& which
@ only
! small

Page 492

1. before
2. cut
3. fall
4. far
5. fast
6. never
7. only
8. shall
9. sing
10. six
11. small
12. ten
13. which
14. wish
15. would

Page 493

1. When Grandma comes to visit us, she likes to bring gifts. She has done this for a long time, and we like it very much.

2. My sister always does kind things. When I hurt my foot, she helped carry me home. I will try to be kind to her, too.

3. I needed to clean my room because I made a mess. My room looked so much better, so I wanted to show it to my family. I was very proud of myself.

Page 495

Page 497

Page 499

t	1: F		t	1: g			1: W
h	2: o		h	2: r		h	2: i
e	3: r		e	3: l		e	3: t
r	4: t		r	4: b		i	4: h
e	5: h		e	5: n		r	5: t
	6: o		t	6: t		h	6: h
h	7: m		h	7: k		t	7: r
e	8: a		r	8: o		e	8: s
i	9: t		e	9: a		i	9: l
t	10: o			10: d			10:a
h	11: a			11: p		t	11: r
e	12: n		h	12: a		h	12: b
i	13: d		e	13:s		e	13: r
e	14: g		i	14: t		i	14: a
r	15: a		r	15: d		r	15: d

How do you repair a broken tomato?
With tomato paste!

Page 501

slight
lightning
flight
stoplight
lighthouse
sunlight

Page 503

Dear Bonnie,
I wonder if we can see each other this summer. Do you know if you are taking a summer vacation? It would be fun to see you if you are in my area. I will ask my parents if you can stay with us. If you want, we can sleep in a tent in my backyard.
Sincerely,
Betty
Inside box: 5

Dear Betty,
I will ask my parents if I can come to visit you. I'm sure that if we are in your area, it will be okay. It would be fun to sleep in a tent if it's not too cold. I've always wanted to do that! If we talk to our parents about it, I bet they will say yes!
Sincerely,
Bonnie
Inside box: 4

Page 504

Page 505

Box 1 is checked.

Page 507

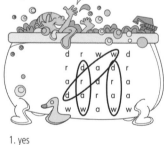

1. yes
2. no
3. no
4. yes
5. no
6. yes

Page 509

These letters can be unscrambled to make the word **seven**:

3. seven
4. seven
5. seven
8. seven

There are seven slices of pie.

Page 511

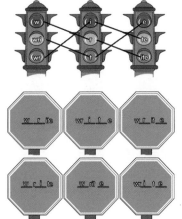

Page 513

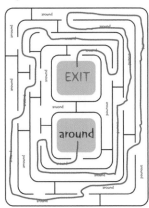

Page 515

1. Tell me all about yourself.
2. I don't know what that movie is about.
3. Talk about your summer plans.
4. I need to write a report about robots.
5. We learned about animals at the zoo.

square dance

Page 516

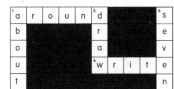

Page 517

When I was <u>seven</u> years old, we moved to a new town. I was sad <u>about</u> moving. My friends gathered <u>around</u> to say goodbye. We said we would <u>write</u> letters.

Our new house was so big, it had <u>seven</u> bedrooms. We had a big yard where our dog could run <u>around</u>. I didn't forget to <u>write</u> my friends and tell them <u>about</u> our new house. They wrote back and asked me to <u>draw</u> a picture of my new house. It was fun to <u>draw</u> pictures and <u>write</u> my friends letters.

\# about
* around
& write
@ seven
! draw

Page 519

Page 521

Page 523

What's in the middle of a jellyfish?
<u>A jelly button!</u>

Page 525

<u>grow</u>n
<u>grow</u>th
out<u>grow</u>
<u>grow</u>ing

Page 527

Dear Jake,
I can't wait to get together this weekend. I've planned lots of fun things for us to do together. We can play in the backyard together. I like to gather up all the leaves and make a big pile. Together we can make the biggest pile ever! See you soon!
Sincerely,
Steve
Inside box: 4

Dear Steve,
We always have fun when we're together. My dad and I will ride together on the train to get to your house. We will play games together to pass the time. I'll bring my basketball with me. Maybe we can get together a group to play basketball. I'm excited to spend time together.
Sincerely,
Jake
Inside box: 5

Page 528

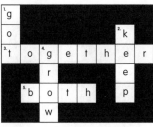

Page 529

Box 1 is checked.

Page 531

1. yes
2. yes
3. yes
4. no
5. no
6. no

Page 533

These letters can be unscrambled to make the word **eight**:

4. eight
5. eight
6. eight
7. eight

I drank eight glasses of milk.

Page 535

Page 537

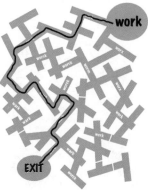

Page 539

1. Don't (start) the game without me.
2. When does the movie (start)?
3. Wash your hands before you (start).
4. (Start) the timer now, please.
5. You can (start) first, and I'll go next.

highchair

Page 540

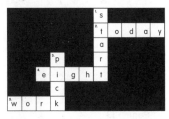

Page 541

We're going to the library <u>today</u>. I need to get an early <u>start</u>. My friend will <u>pick</u> me up at <u>eight</u> o' clock. We need to <u>work</u> on a project for school.

I will <u>pick</u> out about <u>eight</u> books for us to read. It's going to be a lot of <u>work</u>. We won't finish the whole project <u>today</u>, but we will get a good <u>start</u>!

\# start
* work
& today
@ eight
! pick

Page 543

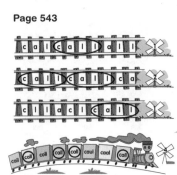

Page 545

Page 547

These letters can be unscrambled to make the word **full**:

4. full
5. full
7. full
8. full

The bowl is very full.

Page 549

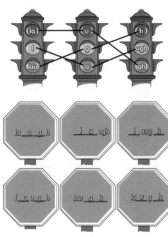

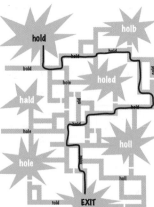

Page 551

Page 552

Page 553

Once <u>upon</u> a time, there was a very funny boy. He liked to do tricks and make people <u>laugh</u>. People liked to <u>call</u> him "the Joker." His magic bag was <u>full</u> of all his tricks. He never let anyone else <u>hold</u> his magic bag.

He had so many tricks that his bag got too <u>full</u>. It was too heavy for the boy to <u>hold</u>. He put his bag <u>upon</u> a horse. He decided to <u>call</u> his horse "Trick Trot." Trick Trot and the Joker were good at making people <u>laugh</u>.

\# upon
* hold
& call
@ laugh
! full

Page 554

1. around
2. call
3. eight
4. full
5. grow
6. hold
7. hot
8. laugh
9. seven
10. start
11. together
12. upon
13. work

Page 555

1. <u>If</u> my parents are <u>both</u> thirsty, lemonade is <u>their</u> favorite thing to <u>drink</u>.

2. I need to <u>keep</u> my bedroom <u>light</u> on so I can <u>write</u> my report <u>about</u> tigers.

3. In art class <u>today</u>, I <u>got</u> to <u>pick</u> my favorite color and <u>draw</u> a picture.